图书馆名言集

塔季扬娜·埃斯克特兰德 选编

李恺 译　严向东 审校

國家圖書館出版社

图书在版编目(CIP)数据

图书馆名言集/塔季扬娜·埃斯克特兰德选编;李恺译;严向东审校.—北京:国家图书馆出版社,2013.1

ISBN 978-7-5013-4672-1

Ⅰ.①图… Ⅱ.①塔… ②李… Ⅲ.①图书馆工作—格言—汇编—世界 Ⅳ.①G25

中国版本图书馆 CIP 数据核字(2011)第 193098 号

责任编辑:王涛

书名 图书馆名言集

著者 塔季扬娜·埃斯克特兰德选编 李恺译 严向东审校

出版 国家图书馆出版社(原北京图书馆出版社)

(100034 北京市西城区文津街7号)

发行 010-66139745 66151313 66175620 66126153

66174391(传真) 66126156(门市部)

E-mail cbs@nlc.gov.cn(投稿) btsfxb@nlc.gov.cn(邮购)

Website www.nlcpress.com→投稿中心

经销 新华书店

印刷 北京科信印刷有限公司

开本 880×1230(毫米) 1/32

印张 5.25

版次 2013年1月第1版 2013年1月第1次印刷

字数 150千字

书号 ISBN 978-7-5013-4672-1

定价 24.00元

序

图书馆是社会文明进步的标志，为传承历史、延续文明、开拓未来提供着信息与知识保障；是社会教育的重要阵地，公民学习的终身课堂，承担着提高公民学习与创新能力、滋养公民文明素质的重要责任；是通向知识之门，为启迪民智、传播文化提供着资源与智力支撑；是公共文化服务体系的重要组成部分，在为社会公众提供普遍均等的公共文化服务、保障大众基本文化权益、满足公众日益增长的精神文化需求等方面发挥着重要作用。

经过数千年的发展与变革，今天，图书馆已经成为共享知识、激荡思维的文化交流空间，“不分年龄、种族、性别、宗教信仰、国籍、语言或社会地位，向所有的人提供服务”。平等自由、包容开放的图书馆精神已经深入人心，图书馆作为“知识的圣殿”，正在逐渐成为社会公众身边须臾不可缺少的精神家园。

千百年来，人们对图书馆给予了最崇高的赞誉，也对她的守护者们不断表达着最诚恳的感激。他们说，“天堂应该是图书馆的模样”，“一座好的图书馆是一座皇宫，所有国家和世代的高尚灵魂在这里相遇”，“没有了图书馆，我们还有什么呢？我们既没有过去，也没有未来”；在人们心目中，“断定一个人是名图书馆员”，只因为他有着“优雅的口音、轻柔的嗓音和显而易见的无所不知”。这些满怀着深情挚意的言语，穿越历史，跨越时空，至今读来仍然倍感亲切。对于每一位投身这项高尚事业的图书馆员来说，都是极大的鞭策与鼓舞；对于众多徜徉于图书馆知识海洋中的好学之士而言，更是一场心灵共鸣的盛宴。

本书由美国资深编目员塔季扬娜·埃斯克特兰德编纂，汇集了许多关于图书馆及图书馆员的见解和言论，其中既有约翰·昆西·亚当斯、弗朗西斯·培根等知名人士对图书馆的高度评价，也有作家、研究人员、商人等普通读者对图书馆的渴望，还有图书馆员对自己所从事工作的热爱，而正是这些构成了人们眼中图书馆的绚丽画卷。这本书不仅仅是送给“图书馆员的最佳礼物”，更是帮助社会公众了解和亲近图书馆的一座桥梁，对于图书馆精神的传承和弘扬意义深远。

中国图书馆学会、国家图书馆出版社为本书的面世做了大量细致的工作，值得赞许。希望本书的出版能够吸引越来越多的人们认识图书馆、走进图书馆、利用图书馆，让图书馆丰富我们的人生，启迪我们的智慧。

周和平

中国国家图书馆馆长

中国图书馆学会名誉理事长

2012 年冬于北京

导　言

我从第一天开始就能品尝到图书馆的甜蜜。图书馆里有着有趣而让人激动的书，这份宝藏直接唤起了我对学习和探索新世界的热爱。在我四年级的时候，学校的图书馆员问我是否有兴趣在我们学校的小图书馆里帮忙。就像是在糖果商店里的孩子一样，我立刻就同意了，不久之后我就开始用业余时间整架、填写借书卡片、坐在图书馆流通台的后面。当这个神奇的地方的管理员让我无比激动。我的图书馆员职业生涯从此开始了。

接下来的职业道路——不管是当图书馆的学生助理还是专业图书馆员——不仅满足了我一直以来对研究和组织信息的渴望，它还向我展示了图书馆在社会教育中所扮演的重要角色。通过向所有人免费提供信息，图书馆有助于保存民主价值，这让我对图书馆员的身份非常自豪。

尽管我从事图书馆工作已经这么多年了，但是我最近对这个职业不再着迷。预算紧缩、规模减小、糟糕的工资以及不断发展的技术迫使我自问：为什么我成为一名图书馆员？为了寻求内心的宁静，也是为了回答这个难题，我寻找用真正的、本来的方式描述图书馆和图书馆员的词句。很高兴，我发现的是名言和逸闻的宝藏，它们重新点燃了我对这个职业的热爱。

这本《图书馆名言集》选取了将近两百则名言，其中绝大多数对我来说都是称赞图书馆事业的。正如你即将读到的，这些睿智的言论的作者，既有声名显赫的大人物也有默默无闻的小人物，既有图书馆的读者也有图书馆员，既有当代之人也有早就辞世的前辈。满怀着真诚和幽默，图书馆和图书馆员们在这本书中得到了来自不同方面的称颂：民主的支持者、对抗审查的战士、知识的守护者、信息世界的导航员，以及欢迎所有人的社区中心和人类灵魂避难所的提供者。

这些话可能会鼓励我们所有投身于这个高贵职业的人，即便没有，它们也能为我们提供一餐职业的“美味”，正如图书馆员和藏书家 R · 李 · 哈登所说：“图书馆员：从野生的图书馆林中摘取图书馆莓，做成图书馆派的人。”

献给我的母亲，
艺术家
以及我的父亲，
哲学家
感谢你们培养了
我对美
和意义的欣赏。
我爱你们！

在我的图书中随意挑选，
可以消遣忘忧。

莎士比亚：《泰特斯·安庄尼克斯》
（译文摘自梁实秋译本）

Come take choice of all my library,
And so beguilethy sorrow.

William Shakespeare,
Titus Andronicus

图书馆里的第一样东西便是书架，文献常常装饰其上，但是书架才是最主要的东西。

芬利·彼得·邓恩：
《杜力先生》

Th' first thing to have in a libry is a shelf. Fr'm time to time this can be decorated with lithrachure. But th' shelf is th' main thing.

Finley Peter Dunne,
Mr. Dooley Says

在图书馆四墙之内，是学生的罗马城，和他的整个闪耀光辉的意大利；在书中，是他的古代世界的遗迹，和新世界的荣耀。

亨利·华兹华斯·朗费罗：

《许珀里翁：罗曼斯》

The student has his Rome, his whole glowing Italy,within the four walls of his library. He has in his books the ruins of an antique world and the glories of a modern one.

Henry Wadsworth Longfellow,

Hyperion: A Romance

美国的图书馆是伟大民主制的产物。它们之所以能够存在，是因为我们相信，记忆和真相是重要的；因为我们还相信，信息和知识并不只属于特定类型或特定阶级的人，它们属于所有想要学习的人。民主社会重视图书馆这样的机构。

罗伯特·S·马丁

在众议院教育听证会上

America's libraries are the fruits of a great democracy. They exist because we believe that memory and truth are important. They exist because we believe that information and knowledge are not the exclusive domain of a certain type or class of person but rather the province of all who seek to learn. A democratic society holds these institutions in high regard.

Robert S. Martin At A House Subcommittee

Hearing On Education

图书馆乃庙堂圣地，古圣贤之遗迹陈列于兹，

保存于兹，满布真德，绝无虚饰。

弗朗西斯·培根：《论学习的熟练和进步二书》

Libraries are as the shrines where all the relics of the ancient saints, full of true virtue, and that without delusion or imposture, are preserved and reposed.

Francis Bacon, *The Two Bookes Of Francis Bacon: Of The Proficience And Aduancement Of Learning, Diuine And Humane*

今天的图书馆员——未来的图书馆员更是如此——并非是书和读者之间脾气暴躁的火龙。他们是有益的公仆，出于公众的利益管理图书馆……许多人仍然觉得,伟大的读者,或者书的作者能成为出色的图书馆员。这种观点实则谬之千里。

威廉·奥斯勒爵士:《图书馆协会记录 17》(1917)

The librarian of today, and it will be true still more of the librarians of tomorrow, are not fery dragons interposed between the people and the books. They are useful public servants, who manage libraries in the interest of the public . . . Many still think that a great reader, or a writer of books, will make an excellent librarian. This is pure fallacy.

Sir William Osler,

Library Association Record 17 **(1917)**

真正伟大的图书馆，它包含的有些东西会冒犯所有人。

乔·古德温

A truly great library contains something in it to offend everyone.

Jo Godwin

图书馆员具有让人难以理解的力量。只要手腕一翻，他们就能让你的论文藏在一堆古老的《田野与溪流》杂志的后面。他们能够给你的学期论文找到数据，你甚至都不知道这些数据的存在。他们还能告诉你新的、适当的主题词。一个人知道的太多了，所以他成为图书馆员。他们的知识超越各种范畴。学科没办法束缚住他们。图书馆员无所不知，无所不见。他们给混乱带来了秩序。他们给民众带来了智慧和文化。它们保存所有的人类知识。图书馆员管理着……

艾瑞卡·奥尔森：

Librarianavengers.Org

Librarians wield unfathomable power. With a fip of the wrist they can hide your dissertation behind piles of old Field and Stream magazines. They can fnd data for your term paper that you never knew existed. They may even point you toward new and appropriate subject headings. People become librarians because they know too much. Their knowledge extends beyond mere categories. They cannot be confned to disciplines. Librarians are all-knowing and all-seeing. They bring order to chaos.

They bring wisdom and culture to the masses.

They preserve every aspect of human knowledge. Librarians rule . . .

Erica Olsen, LibrarianAvengers.org

如果说图书馆事业连接了人和思想——我相信这正是对我们工作最正确的定义——那么重要的是要记得，我们必须不仅仅保存并提供好的、高贵的思想，我们还应该保存并提供坏的思想、愚蠢的思想，而且甚至是危险和邪恶的思想。

格拉桑·A·德卡迪多：

《我们讲述自己的故事，在技术的营火周围》

If librarianship is the connecting of people to ideas—and I believe that is the truest defnition of what we do—it is crucial to remember that we must keep and make available, not just good ideas and noble ideas, but bad ideas, silly ideas, and yes, even dangerous and wicked ideas.

Graceanne A. Decandido,

"Technology Is The Campfire Around Which We Tell Our Stories"

不要加入焚书者的队伍。不要以为你可以隐藏错误曾经存在的证据，这样它们就仿佛不曾存在过。不要害怕走进图书馆，阅读每一本书。

德怀特 · D · 艾森豪威尔：

毕业演说，达特摩斯大学，1953

Don't join the book burners. Don't think you're going to conceal faults by concealing evidence that they never existed. Don't be afraid to go in your library and read every book.

Dwight D. Eisenhower,

Commencement Address, Dartmouth College, 1953

我一生中最喜欢的两个东西是图书馆和自行车。它们都能让人们前进而不用浪费任何东西。完美的一天就是：骑着自行车去图书馆。

彼得 · 高尔金：引用于 wordsmith.org

My two favorite things in life are libraries and bicycles. They both move people forward without wasting anything. The perfect day: riding a bike to the library.

Peter Golkin, as quoted at Wordsmith.Org

一座好的图书馆是一座皇宫，所有国家和世代的高尚灵魂在这里相遇。

萨缪尔·尼格尔：《黄色字体》

A good library is a place, a palace where the lofty spirits of all nations and generations meet.

Samuel Niger, ***Geklibene Shriftn***

如果这个国家要变得既明智又强大，如果我们想要完成我们的使命，那么我们需要更多的新思想，要更多的聪明人在更多的公共图书馆里阅读更多的好书。这些图书馆应该向所有人开放——除了审查官之外。我们必须知道所有的事实，了解所有的选择，并且倾听所有的批评。让我们欢迎引起争论的书和作者吧，因为《人权法案》是我们安全和自由的保卫者。

约翰·F·肯尼迪：《星期六评论》，1960.10.29

If this nation is to be wise as well as strong, if we are to achieve our destiny, then we need more new ideas for more wise men reading more good books in more public libraries. These libraries should be open to all—except the censor. We must know all the facts and hear all the alternatives and listen to all the criticisms. Let us welcome controversial books and controversial authors. For the Bill of Rights is the guardian of our security as well as our liberty.

John F. Kennedy, *Saturday Review*, 29 October 1960

你们必须狂热地生活在图书馆中。大学对你毫无帮助，除非你每天在图书馆里生活、长大。

雷·布拉德伯里：《作家文摘》，1976 年 2 月

You must live feverishly in a library. Colleges are not going to do you any good unless you are raised and live in a library every day of your life.

Ray Bradbury, *Writer's Digest*, February 1976

精神的食粮。

柏林皇家图书馆的铭文

Nutrimentum spiritus. (Food for the soul.)

Inscription On The Berlin Royal Library

书是脆弱的，它经受时间的冲刷，它害怕蠹虫、水火和笨拙的手……所以图书馆员不仅要让书远离人类的破坏，他还要让书免受自然的侵蚀，并且终其一生投入到和遗忘力量的斗争中。

昂伯托·艾柯：《玫瑰之名》

A book is a fragile creature, it suffers the wear of time, it fears rodents, the elements and clumsy hands . . . so the librarian protects the books not only against mankind but also against nature and devotes his life to this war with the forces of oblivion.

Umberto Eco, ***The Name Of The Rose***

图书馆把我们和洞见、知识连接在一起。这些洞见和知识从自然中痛苦地获得，它们是由最伟大的心灵在最好的老师的教导下，从我们整个星球和我们的全部历史中得到。它们不断地教导我们，激励我们为人类的集体知识贡献我们自己的力量。我认为，我们的文明是否健康，我们巩固文化的意识有多深，以及我们有多少对未来的关注，都可以从我们支持图书馆的程度看出来。

卡尔·萨根：《宇宙》

The library connects us with the insight and knowledge, painfully extracted from Nature, of the greatest minds that ever were, with the best teachers, drawn from the entire planet and from all our history, to instruct us without tiring, and to inspire us to make our own contribution to the collective knowledge of the human species. I think the health of our civilization, the depth of our awareness about the underpinnings of our culture and our concern for the future can all be tested by how well we support our libraries.

Carl Sagan, ***Cosmos***

图书馆是学习的殿堂，通过学习获得解放的人比历史上的所有战争加起来解放的人还要多。

卡尔 · 罗文，引用于

《美国图书馆》，1995 年 2 月

The library is the temple of learning, and learning has liberated more people than all the wars in history.

Carl Rowan, As Quoted In

***American Libraries*,February 1995**

图书馆不是崇拜书的圣地。图书馆不是一座神庙，在这里，人们不必焚香祈祷，或者用仪式来表达对书的虔诚。图书馆，如果借用苏格拉底那个有名的隐喻来说，应当是孕育观念的产房——在这里，历史进入生活。

诺曼 · 卡森斯：《美国图书馆协会简报》,1954 年 10 月

The library is not a shrine for the worship of books. It is not a temple where literary incense must be burned or where one's devotion to the bound book is expressed in ritual. A library, to modify the famous metaphor of Socrates, should be the delivery room for the birth of ideas—a place where history comes to life.

Norman Cousins, *ALA Bulletin*,

October 1954

世界上最富有的人——实际上世界上所有富人加在一起——都不能给你这样取之不尽、令人难以置信的财富，然而你当地的图书馆却能够给你。你可以通过一个文明、一个国家或者一个人为保存所有现在、过去和未来的记录所作的努力，来判断他们的见识、心胸和智慧。

马尔科姆·福布斯：《福布斯》杂志，

1981.2.16

The richest person in the world—in fact, all the riches in the world—couldn't provide you with anything like the endless, incredible loot available at your local library. You can measure the awareness, the breadth and the wisdom of a civilization, a nation, a people by the priority given to preserving these repositories of all that we are, all that we were, or will be.

Malcolm Forbes, *Forbes*,

16 February 1981

对偷书者的诅咒： 从这座图书馆里偷书的人，偷窃的书变成他手上的毒蛇，撕裂他。让他染上瘫痪，四肢震颤。让他在痛苦中受到煎熬，大声哭着祈求宽恕，但这大痛苦不会结束，直到他神灭形消。让书蠹啃噬他的内脏，而这虫永不死亡。当他面对最后的审判，让地狱之火永远永远地摧毁他。

圣佩德罗·巴塞罗那主教

Curse Against Book Stealers

For him that stealeth a Book from this Library, let it change into a serpent in his hand and rend him. Let him be struck with Palsy, and all his Members blasted. Let him languish in Pain cry-ing aloud for Mercy and let there be no surcease to his Agony till he sink in Dissolution. Let Bookworms gnaw his entrails in token of the Worm that dieth not, and when at last he goeth to his fnal Punishment, let the fames of Hell consume him for ever and aye.

Monastery of san Pedro, Barcelona

一座图书馆——对于热爱文字的人来说——永远不仅仅是保存或存放图书的地方，它是一个活的存在，有自己的个性甚或是心情，我们应当去理解并且学习和它共同生活。

弗朗西斯科·马尔奎斯·维兰纽瓦

A library is never—for lovers of the written word—simply a place for conserving or storing books but rather a sort of living creature with a personality and even moods which we should understand and learn to live with.

Francisco Márquez Villanueva

过去，图书馆很像博物馆，而图书馆员就是在发霉的图书间不断搜寻的人。现在，图书馆是一座学校，图书馆员在其最高的意义上就是老师。

梅尔维尔·杜威：

《美国图书馆杂志》，1876 年 9 月

The time was when a library was very like a museum and the librarian a mouser in musty books. The time is when the library is a school and the librarian in the highest sense a teacher.

Melvil Dewey,

***American Library Journa*l, September 1876**

你要小心你的图书馆。你是否预先知道你要在里面做什么？这很难确定。但真正的问题是，它会对你做什么？你要来到这里，拿到书，这些书会打开你的眼睛，打开你的耳朵，打开你的好奇心，让你焕然一新。

拉尔夫·沃尔多·爱默生：

《杂志中的爱默生》

Be a little careful of your Library. Do you foresee what you will do with it? Very little to be sure. But the real question is, What it will do with you? You will come here & get books that will open your eyes, & your ears, & your curiosity, & turn you inside out or outside in.

Ralph Waldo Emerson,

Emerson In His Journals

真正的礼物

生命中最好的东西都是真正免费的

爱、幽默、高贵的心灵……

以及我的本地图书馆。

贝弗利·托娜：《布法罗新闻》，2000.9.20

Real Gifts

The best things in life are really free

Love, honor, a noble mind . . .

And my local library.

Beverly Tona,

***Buffalo News*, 20 September 2000**

世界上没有一座大学是伟大的，除非它有一座同样伟大的图书馆……如果事情不再是这样，那么我们的文明也将走到尽头。

劳伦斯·克拉克·鲍威尔：《问题的核心》

No university in the world has ever risen to greatness without a correspondingly great library . . . When this is no longer true, then will our civilization have come to an end.

Lawrence Clark Powell,

At The Heart Of The Matter

就算是最不合群的孩子
当他看到图书馆的宝藏，
便坐在了全世界的天才中间
转动打开整个世界的钥匙。

泰德·休斯：《再次听到》

Even the most misftting child
Who's chanced upon the library's worth,
Sits with the genius of the Earth
And turns the key to the whole world.

Ted hughes, "*Hear It Again*"

我们保存了书，书保护了我们。

大卫·本－古里安，

引自约瑟夫·L·巴郎《犹太名言集》

We have preserved the Book, and the Book has preserved us.

David Ben-Gurion, as quoted in

Joseph L. Barron's

A Treasury Of Jewish Quotations

这并不令人惊讶：设计一座完备的学校，一个很好的起点就是设计一座图书馆，让它荫蔽学校的其余部分。

西奥多·赛泽

Not surprisingly, one good way to start designing an essential school is to plan a library and let its shadow shape the rest.

Theodore sizer

[图书馆是] 一种共产主义，我们当中最不革命的人也会自豪的拥护它。

约瑟夫 · 张伯伦，引于约翰 · J · 奥格《免费的图书馆》

[Libraries are] a kind of communism which the least revolutionary among us may be proud to advocate.

Joseph Chamberlain, as quoted in John J. Ogle's "*The Free Library*"

陈列在我们周围书架上的
是已经朽去的作者。

贝亚德 · 泰勒：《诗人杂志》

Shelved around us lie
The mummied authors.

Bayard Taylor, ***The Poet's Journal***

图书馆伴你度过没钱的时光，好过金钱伴你度过没有图书馆的时光。

安·赫伯特：《下一部全球目录》

Libraries will get you through times of no money better than money will get you through times of no libraries.

Anne Herbert, ***The Next Whole Earth Catalog***

图书馆不是奢侈品，而是生活的必需品。

亨利·沃德·比切

A library is not a luxury but one of the necessities of life.

Henry Ward Beecher

在这个世界上，要让一样东西永远消失，没有比在一座大图书馆里把它放错位置更好的方法了。

诺曼·麦克林：《年轻人与火》

There is no better way in this world to lose something forever than to misfle it in a big library.

Norman Maclean, ***Young Men And Fire***

这是一座图书馆，欢迎孩子们和探险者，其他人请勿入内。

迪恩·孔茨：《寒焰》

This is a library. Kids and adventurers welcome. All others stay out.

Dean Koontz, ***Cold Fire***

图书馆员……非常文雅。他们常常被问到地球上最愚蠢的问题，可是这些图书馆员能容忍各种古怪和愚蠢的人。

盖瑞森·凯勒：《草原家庭指南》

1997.12.13

Librarians . . . possess a vast store of politeness. These are people who get asked regularly the dumbest questions on God's green earth. These people tolerate every kind of crank and eccentric and mouth-breather there is.

Garrison Keillor, ***A Prairie Home Companion,***

13 December 1997

我已经醉了差不多一个礼拜了，我认为坐在图书馆里能让我清醒过来。

F · 司各特 · 菲茨杰拉德：《伟大的盖茨比》

I've been drunk for about a week now, and I thought it might sober me up to sit in a library.

F. Scott Fitzgerald, *The Great Gatsby*

在全球信息永不停歇的海啸中，图书馆员送给我们浮板，教会我们如何游泳。

林顿 · 维克斯：《华盛顿邮报》，2001.1.13

In the nonstop tsunami of global information, librarians provide us with foaties and teach us how to swim.

Linton Weeks, *Washington Post*, 13 January 2001

我在公共图书馆的经验是：我查的书的第一卷被借走了，如果我正好想要它的第二卷，那么第二卷也已经没有了。

老奥利弗 · 温代尔 · 福尔摩斯：《早餐桌上的诗人》

My experience with public libraries is that the first volume of the book I inquire for is out, unless I happen to want the second, then that is out.

Oliver Wendell Holmes Sr.,

The Poet At The Breakfast Table

图书馆……是……一个安静的储藏所，它保存了人类的记忆。在这里，桌上书页发出轻轻的摩擦声，思维静谧的激荡着。

约翰·查第：《星期六评论》，1961.8.26

A library . . . is . . . a quiet storage place, and what it stores is the memory of the human race. It is a place for the soft rustle of pages and the quiet stir of thoughts over the reading tables.

John Ciardi, *Saturday Review*, 26 August 1961

谢拉的两个编目法则：

法则 1：没有编目员会认可其他任何编目员的工作。

法则 2：没有编目员会认可他 / 她自己在六个月以前的工作。

杰西 · 谢拉

Shera's two laws of cataloguing

Law #1: no cataloger will accept the work of any other cataloger.

Law #2: no cataloger will accept his/her own work six months after the cataloging.

Jesse shera

图书馆员就是图书馆员：他们不是看护者、养育者、社会工作者、代理家长、福利代理人或者治疗师。归根结底，图书馆员的角色很简单：他们收集东西，给这些东西加上些许秩序，然后让它们能够被公众获得。

布莱斯 · 克洛宁：《图书馆杂志》，2002.5.15

Librarians are librarians: they are not caregivers, nurturers, social workers, surrogate parents, welfare agents, or therapists. When all is said and done, their role is straightforward: they gather stuff, impose some order on said stuff, and make the stuff available to the public.

Blaise Cronin, *Library Journal*, 15 May 2002

我们的图书馆不是精英的修道院。他们是为了民众建立的。如果没人使用图书馆，那么这个错误应该归咎于那些没有利用自己财富的人。

路易斯·拉莫尔：《浪人的教育》

Our libraries are not cloisters for an elite. They are for the people, and if they are not used, the fault belongs to those who do not take advantage of their wealth.

Louis L'amour,

Education Of A Wandering Man

当我们劝说一个孩子，任何一个孩子，去穿越门槛，那道神奇的门槛——进入图书馆，我们就永远的改变了他们的生活，让他们的生活变得更好。

巴拉克·奥巴马：基本政策演说，

美国图书馆协会年会，2005

At the moment that we persuade a child, any child, to cross that threshold, that magic threshold into a library, we change their lives forever, for the better.

Barack Obama, Keynote Address, ALA

Annual Conference, 2005

每座公共图书馆里都有太多的书，却没有足够的人拭去书上的尘土。

艾文 · 艾沙：《妙语名言 20000 句》

There are too many books in every public library, and not enough people to dust them.

Evan Esar, 20,000 Quips And Quotes

只有两种人相信自己不用查一大堆资料就能看得懂 MARC 数据：少数顶尖的编目员或是迷幻于毒品的人。

罗伊 · 特南特：《图书馆杂志》，2002.10.15

There are only two kinds of people who believe themselves able to read a MARC record without referring to a stack of manuals: a handful of our top catalogers, and those on serious drugs.

Roy Tennant, *Library Journal*,

15 October 2002

我们图书馆员也会告诉你现在是几点或者厕所在哪，但是这并不意味着我们不能帮你解决一些重要问题，帮助你了解绝大多数的事情。最好的参考咨询活动应该是：读者找到了他们想要的，甚至没有意识到图书馆员全程提供了服务。

杰萨敏·韦斯特：

《图书馆计算机》杂志，2003.10

The fact that we as librarians will also tell you what time it is or where the bathroom is does not mean that we're not doing some serious question alchemy to help you find most things. The best reference interactions are ones in which the patrons find what they want and are not even aware that the librarians have been giving them reference interviews the entire time.

Jessamyn West,

***Computers In Libraries*, October 2003**

图书馆是你不应当在里面偷东西的那个美国机构。

芭芭拉·金索佛：《动物之梦》

Libraries are the one american institution you shouldn't rip off.

Barbara Kingsolver, ***Animal Dreams***

所以我过去所爱的美国依旧存在，但它并不存在于
白宫、最高法院、参议院、众议院或者是媒体中。
我所爱的美国存在于我们公共图书馆的服务台上。

库尔特·冯内果：《在这个时代》杂志，2004.8.6

So the America I loved still exists, if not in the White House or the Supreme Court or the Senate or the House of Representatives or the media. The America I love still exists at the front desks of our public libraries.

Kurt Vonnegut Jr.,

***In These Times*, 6 August 2004**

眉批垂直排列是文摘，眉批水平排列是教科书，教科书按照字顺排列就是百科全书。每过几年，一些研究者就会把其中一些著作拆散，然后从最近的研究中增加一些眉批，将这些搅拌均匀，然后就为这个主题带来一本最新的书。法律图书馆因此而成长。

小泽查瑞尔·查菲：

《哈佛法律评论》，

1917年30卷3期

Headnotes arranged vertically make a digest. Headnotes arranged horizontally make a textbook. Textbooks arranged alphabetically make an encyclopedia. Every few years some investigator has to disintegrate one of these works into its constituent atoms, add some more headnotes from recent decisions, stir well, and give us the latest book on the subject. And so law libraries grow.

Zechariah Chafee Jr.,

Harvard Law Review **30, No. 3 (1917)**

当我还是孩子的时候
在我能说话之前
我会按照字母顺序
连起我的所有字母积木
如今这是我的职业
带着我的激情，去分配
一个个十进制号码的书架
给一本本分好类的图书

我是名图书馆员，我是名图书馆员
我喜欢它的安静
书页都能被听到

我是名图书馆员，我是名图书馆员
因为热爱文字，让我来干这一行。

乔纳森·伦德曼：

《图书馆员》，来自公共图书馆论坛，2004

when i was just a baby,
before i could speak
i would line up all my letter
blocks alphabetically
and now it's my vocation
and my passion to assign
every decimal-numbered shelf
to every decimal-numbered spine

i'm a librarian, i'm a librarian
and i like it quiet
so the pages can be heard

i'm a librarian, i'm a librarian
and i do it for the love of the word

JonaThan rundman, "*Librarian*",

From The Album Public Library, 2004

人在图书馆面前会感到既兴奋又害怕，因为图书馆提醒了他，他的过去、现在，以及未来绝大多数的可能性。

比尔·默亚思：《思想的世界》

One gets thrilled and frightened at the same time in the presence of a library because it reminds one about one's past, present, and, most, of the possibilities of the future.

Bill Moyers, ***World Of Ideas***

我们不可能有好的图书馆，除非我们有好的图书馆员——他们要接受过适当的教育，专业合格，并且得到过公正的奖励。

赫伯特·S·怀特：

《图书馆杂志》，1999.10.15

We cannot have good libraries until we frst have good librarians—properly educated, professionally recognized, and fairly rewarded.

Herbert S. White,

Library Journal, **15 November 1999**

所以，我认为这就是图书馆的新使命，它的重要性是之前的使命无法比拟的。直到现在，图书馆员对于书，主要还把它看做一种事物，一种物理对象。但从现在开始，图书馆员必须注意书的活着的功能。他必须成为警察，成为动力强大的书的主人。

何塞·奥特嘉·伊·加塞特，演讲，书目编撰者和图书馆员国际大会，1934

Here, then, is the point at which I see the new mission of the librarian rise up incomparably higher than all those preceding. Up until the present, the librarian has been principally occupied with the book as a thing, as a material object. From now on he must give his attention to the book as a living function. He must become a policeman, master of the raging book.

José Ortega Y Gasset, Address, International Congress Of Bibliographers And Librarians, 1934

你们绝大多数人都没有意识到帮助人们分享图书是一种颠覆性的行为……事实是，你们选择了一个变得激进的职业。

诺欧米·克莱恩：

《为什么作图书馆员是一个激进的选择》

Most of you didn't think that helping people share books would be a subversive act . . . Yet the fact is you have chosen a profession that has become radical.

Naomi Klein,

"*Why being a librarian is a Radical Choice*"

读者用于阅读的范畴，以及阅读本身所属的范畴——也就是说，人们习得的社会和政治范畴，以及图书馆被划分进的物理范畴—— 一直以来都在相互影响，这种变化的方式看起来或多或少是随意的，而且或多或少源自于人们的想象……不管选择了怎样的范畴，每一座图书馆都对阅读行为施加暴政，强迫读者——好奇的读者、警觉的读者——把书从它被判决的范畴中拯救出来。

阿尔维托·曼古埃尔：

《阅读史》

The categories that a reader brings to a reading, and the categories in which that reading itself is placed—the learned social and political categories, and the physical categories into which a library is divided—constantly modify one another in ways that appear, over the years, more or less arbitrary or more or less imaginative . . . Whatever categories have been chosen, every library tyrannizes the act of reading and forces the reader—the curious reader, the alert reader—to rescue the book from the category to which it has been condemned.

Alberto Manguel,

A History Of Reading

公共图书馆是所剩不多人们可以保持隐私的地方。

劳伦斯·克拉克·鲍威尔

The public library is one of the few places left where one can be private.

Lawrence Clark Powell

图书馆的存在并非是为了劝善或者传布福音，它存在是因为知识。好的图书馆并非取决于，其作为机构，分享、传播的是你的还是我的核心价值,还是司法部长的核心价值，或者是萨达姆·侯赛因的核心价值。图书馆一直都是帮助人们进行选择的工具，而且只是你的选择，而不是你的领导人的选择。

罗伯特·休斯：《美国图书馆》，2002年8月

The point of a library's existence is not persuasion or evangelism, but knowledge. It is irrelevant to the good library whether, as an institution, it shares or promotes your core values or mine, or the Attorney General's or Saddam Hussein's. The library is always an instrument of choice, and the choice is always yours, not your elected or designated leaders.

Robert Hughes, *American Libraries*, August 2002

让书成为你的同伴。

让书箱和书架成为你的

快乐的庭院和花园。

犹大·伊本·提朋：《伦理的意志》

Make thy books thy companions.

Let thy cases and shelves be thy

pleasure grounds and gardens.

Judah Ibn Tibbon,"Ethical Will"

图书馆——任何一座图书馆——的一个强大功能就在于，它能让我们远离我们熟悉、并且感觉安逸的世界，让我们进入既无法预测也无法控制的世界。它引导我们走在新的道路上，这里的轮廓和风景给我们提供了新的视野。

理查·F·托马斯：《哈佛杂志》，1997年5–6月

One of the powerful functions of a library—any library—lies in its ability to take us away from worlds that are familiar and comfortable and into ones which we can neither predict nor control, to lead us down new roads whose contours and vistas provide us with new perspectives.

Richard F. Thomas,

***Harvard Magazine*, May-June 1997**

图书馆和博物馆是我们文化的 DNA。

瓦坦·格雷戈里恩

：基本政策演说，白宫学校图书馆会议

Libraries and museums are the DNA of our culture.

Vartan Gregorian,

Keynote Address,White House Conference

On School Libraries

自由的图书馆是市民的起居室，是研究者的宝藏，知识自由的图书馆是独裁者的恐怖屋。

邦特·赫尔姆奎维斯特，引于

新希望免费图书馆，www.nhslibrary.org

The free library is a living room to an ordinary citizen, a treasury to a researcher, and a chamber of horrors to a dictator.

Bengt Hjelmqvist, as quoted in

Free Library Of New Hope, www.nhslibrary.org

图书馆不仅包含“小房间中的无尽财富”，而且还能让我们坐在家里却又同时出现在地球上的所有角落。

约翰·鲁波克：《生活的愉悦》

Not only does a library contain “infnite riches in a little room,” but we may sit at home and yet be in all quarters of the earth.

John Lubbock, ***The Pleasures Of Life***

免费获取信息不是一种特权，而是任何自由社会中的一项必需品。

爱德华·阿斯纳

The free access to information is not a privilege,
but a necessity for any free society.

Edward Asner

给我一个较真的电脑专家，我会给你一个图书馆员。

帕特里西亚·威尔逊·伯格：

《芝加哥论坛报》，1990.6.29

Show me a computer expert that gives a damn,
and I'll show you a librarian.

Patricia Wilson Berger, ***Chicago Tribune*****, 29 June 1990**

如果真理即是美，为什么没人在图书馆里美发呢？

珍妮·瓦格纳：莉莉引文，www.lilytomlin.com

If truth is beauty, how come no one has their hair done in a library?

Jane Wagner, Lily Quotes, www.lilytomlin.com

图书馆员：比 Google 搜索引擎更强大，比 AskJeeves 搜索网站更友好，也是市面上最好的自然语言处理器。

艾瑞卡·奥尔森：librarianavengers.org

Librarians: more powerful than a Google search, friendlier than AskJeeves, and the best natural language processor on the market.

Erica Olsen, librarianavengers.org

书籍的守护者

我曾经不止一次造访这个世界，

邂逅了名人、圣人和罪人，

诗人和艺术家，国王和女皇，

老去的明星和冉冉升起的新星，

我曾去过无人曾经到达的地方，

从作家和厨师那里了解秘密，

而这只需要一张图书馆的门票，

你就可以到达奇妙的书的世界

来源未知

A Keeper Of Books

I I've traveled the world twice over,

Met the famous; saints and sinners,

Poets and artists, kings and queens,

old stars and hopeful beginners,

I've been where no-one's been before,

Learned secrets from writers and cooks

All with one library ticket

To the wonderful world of books.

Source Unknown

图书馆员：从野生的图书馆林中摘取图书馆莓，做成图书馆派的人。

R·李·哈登，

引于“图书馆果汁”（Library Juice）博客，

2000.4.12

Liberrian: One who picks liberries from wild liberry bushes and makes a liberry pie.

R. Lee Hadden,

as quoted in Library Juice,

12 april 2000

图书馆

人们在这里，

常能看到，

压低声音

高举心灵。

理查德·亚摩：《轻装甲》

LIBRARY

Here is where people,

One frequently finds,

Lower their voices

And raise their minds.

Richard Armour, Light Armour

分类，就其宽泛的定义来说，是将无序的知识宇宙序化的活动。人们把它看作是人类心智最基本的活动。

麦麟屏：《编目和分类：导论》

Classifcation, broadly defned, is the act of organizing the universe of knowledge into some systematic order. It has been considered the most fundamental activity of the human mind.

Lois Mai Chan, ***Cataloging And Classification: An Introduction***

在正确的地点用正确的方式获取信息需要我们日积月累的实践。这是的一种特殊的技巧，在家使用电脑的人很少能练出像职业图书馆员那样的速度和精度。

西奥多·罗斯扎克：《信息崇拜》

It takes daily hands-on skill to go hunting for information in just the right way in just the right places. It is a special skill that few home computer users will ever be able to develop to a professional librarian's level of speed and precision.

Theodore Roszak, ***The Cult Of Information***

对于图书馆来说，其存在的事实本身就是一份声明——就像是马丁·路德钉在门上的那份倡议一样。

阿奇巴尔德·麦克莱什：《意义的前提》

For the existence of a library, the fact of its existence, is, in itself and of itself, an assertion—a proposition nailed like Luther's to the door of time.

Archibald Macleish, "The Premise Of Meaning"

图书馆购买我们买不起的，保藏我们珍视并且崇拜的，它修复陈旧，忽略流行，摒弃偏见。

威廉·H·加斯，引于美国国家科学数字
图书馆白板报，2003 年 11 月

Libraries acquire what we cannot afford, retain
what we prize and would adore, restore the worn,
ignore fashion, and repulse prejudice.

William H. Gass, as quoted in
***NSDL Whiteboard Report*, November 2003**

他们［图书馆员］是颠覆性的。你以为他们只是坐在桌子后面，一言不发，无所事事。他们像是在谋划革命，老兄，换了我就不会去打扰他们。你知道，他们的经费被削减了，工资没有了，书被撕成了两半。他们好像总是最倒霉的，不是么？

迈克尔 · 摩尔：Buzzflash 网站，2002.3.13

They [librarians] are subversive. You think they're just sitting there at the desk, all quiet, and everything. They're like plotting the revolution, man. I wouldn't mess with them. You know, they've had their budgets cut. They're paid nothing. Books are falling apart. The libraries are just like the ass end of everything, right?

Michael Moore, Buzzflash, 13 March 2002

伟大的公共图书馆的目录以及书在书架上的位置，
构成了一座文学的纪念碑。

罗伯特 · 梅兰肯：
《当代世界文学》，1982 年春季

A great public library, in its catalogue and its physical disposition of its books on shelves, is the monument of literary genres.

Robert Mélan.on,
World Literature Today, **Spring 1982**

如果你的图书馆是够“安全”的，那它或许是没有尽职吧。

约翰 · N · 贝里三世，《图书馆杂志》，1999.10.1

If your library is not “unsafe” , it probably isn't doing its job.

John N. Berry III,
*Library Journa*l, **1 October 1999**

图书馆员几乎总是乐于助人，而且经常是博学到近乎荒谬。他们的技能可能被严重低估了，而且在很大程度上没有得到利用。

查理斯·梅达沃：《社会审计消费者手册》

Librarians are almost always very helpful and often almost absurdly knowledgeable. Their skills are probably very underestimated and largely underemployed.

Charles Medawar, ***The Social Audit Consumer's Handbook***

我还是个孩子的时候，我最好的朋友是我小学里的图书馆员。我当时相信图书馆里所有的书都是她的。

艾玛·邦贝克

As a child, my number-one best friend was the librarian in my grade school. I actually believed that all of those books belonged to her.

Erma Bombeck

拥有一座图书馆和一座花园，人生别无所求。

西塞罗

Anyone who has a library and a garden wants for nothing.

Marcus Tullius Cicero

不管我们的图书馆花费有多大，相比起改变一个无知的民族，这个代价都是值得的。

沃尔特·克朗凯特

Whatever the cost of our libraries, the price is cheap compared to that of an ignorant nation.

Walter Cronkite

图书馆是我们的知识屋，是我们超凡的宇宙，但只有一个例外：没有人从图书馆里毕业。没有也不应当有人能从图书馆里毕业。

瓦坦·格雷戈里恩

The library is our house of intellect, our transcendental university, with one exception: no one graduates from a library. No one possibly can, and no one should.

Vartan Gregorian

图书馆是灵魂的墓地。图书馆是死荫之地。

亨利·沃德·比切：《星书》

A library is but the soul's burial-ground. It is the land of shadows.

Henry Ward Beecher, ***Star Papers***

在你长大的过程中，有两个机构影响你最多：一个是教堂，它属于上帝；一个是公共图书馆，它属于你。公共图书馆是一个伟大的平衡器。

凯斯·理查兹

When you are growing up, there are two institutional places that affect you most powerfully—the church, whichbelongs to God, and the public library, which belongs to you. The public library is a great equalizer.

Keith Richards

很少有人会考虑图书馆员们所扮演的高尚角色。我们收集、组织并且保存我们前人的声音和洞察，这对于我们作为种族的延续至关重要。

约书亚·阿伦：《通过软件的更好的生活》，2003.1.4

Few people think about the noble role that librarians play. Our ability to collect, organize, and preserve the voices and observations of those who came before us is critical to our continued survival as a species.

Joshua Allen,

***Better Living through Software*, 4 January 2003**

一般来讲，图书馆员是社交中的开心果，通常幽默和上进，而且自然的，还非常广博。

比尔·霍尔：《美国图书馆》，2002 年 1 月

As a general rule, librarians are a kick in the pants socially, often full of good humor, progressive, and,naturally, well read.

Bill Hall, *American Libraries*, January 2002

在历史上，公共图书馆一直是美国民主和机会的重要工具……通过在公共图书馆中阅读获得了机会和成就的人极大地影响了我们的历史。

小亚瑟·梅耶尔·施莱辛格：

《图书馆新闻》，1982 年冬季号

The public library has been historically a vital instrument of democracy and opportunity in the United States . . . Our history has been greatly shaped by people who read their way to opportunity and achievements in public libraries.

Arthur Meier Schlesinger Jr.,

***Library News*, Winter 1982**

我以为我会成为一名图书馆员，直到我遇到了一些疯狂的人。

爱德华·戈里：《波士顿环球报》，1998.12.17

I thought I'd be a librarian until I met some crazy ones.

Edward Gorey,

***Boston Globe*, 17 December 1998**

获得快乐并不难

只要你拥有一张图书馆证

马克·布朗：《亚瑟的图书馆歌曲》

Having fun isn't hard

When you've got a library card.

Marc Brown, "*Arthur's Library Song*"

图书馆可以成为提升国家智力水平以及促进领导者成长的一个重要因素。对于因为全球重大问题而感到挫折的人，图书馆还能在很大程度上支持他们的信念。世界越复杂，传播书本中的知识和智慧就越有必要。

艾迪斯·帕特森·迈耶尔：《和未来相遇》

The library can become a big factor in raising the level of intelligence in the country and in developing leaders. It can also play a large part in bolstering the faith of individuals who feel frustrated and upset by the tremendous problems that face the world. The more complex the world grows, the more necessary it is to spread the knowledge and wisdom to be found in books.

Edith Patterson Meyer, ***Meet The Future***

我在书架迷宫中找了半天徒劳无功，只为了搜寻一名图书馆员几分钟就可以帮我找到的信息，我这么笨，真该有人踢我的屁股。

迈克尔·佩里：《自由写作手册》

I deserve a swift kick in the shorts for all the times I've stubbornly wound my way through the library stacks, my mule head leading the way, searching fruitlessly for information a librarian could put in my hands in a matter of minutes.

Michael Perry , *Handbook For Freelance Writing*

读者把图书馆从一座陵墓变成许多剧场。

梅森·库里：《城市警句》

Readers transform a library from amausoleum into many theaters.

Mason Cooley, *City Aphorisms*

成为图书馆员最大的乐趣之一就在于，图书馆是博学多才之人的最后避难所——你曾经读到的、知道的或者意识到的东西都可能在你手边出现。

格拉桑·A·德卡迪多：《新图书馆员的十个优雅之处》

One of the great joys of being a librarian is that it is the last refuge of the renaissance person—everything you have ever read or learned or picked up is likely to come in handy.

Graceanne A. Decandido,
"*Ten Graces for New Librarians*"

图书馆死亡的观点把图书馆的功能限制为信息库。如果图书馆的功能仅此而已，那么认为它最终会被更方便的电子存储所取代是非常合乎情理的观点。但是图书馆还是一个聚集的场所，就像是老镇的广场或者街角的杂货店一样。人们去图书馆可能主要是为了查找信息，但是他们在这里也能遇到其他的人。

罗伯特·D·普特南：《更好的共存：美国社区的恢复》

Death-of-the-library scenarios define libraries as information repositories. If they were no more than that, then their eventual displacement by more convenient electronic repositories would make perfect sense. But the library is a gathering place, too,like an old town square or the corner grocer. People may go to the library looking mainly for information, but they find each other there.

Robert D. Putnam,

Better Together: Restoring the American Community

对于用耳去倾听的人来说，图书馆是非常喧闹的地方。在书架上，我们听到了被捕捉进书里的好多世纪前的对话，这些对话构成了我们或者其他任何一个文明。

蒂莫西 · S · 希利：《图书馆和学习》

To those with ears to hear, libraries are really very noisy places. On their shelves we hear the captured voices of the centuries-old conversation that makes up our civilization, or any civilization.

Timothy S. Healy, "*Libraries and Learning*"

在早先，我努力不给图书馆员制造任何麻烦，制造麻烦是我最主要的错误。但是图书馆员喜欢有人制造麻烦：他们因麻烦而存在，而且他们做好了准备应付麻烦。对于放错了位置的一卷书，没有编目的资料，出色的图书馆员有着如猎犬一样灵敏的鼻子，让她闻到一丝气味，她就挣脱皮带，眼睛闪着战斗的光芒。

凯撒琳·敦肯·包恩：《一名书目家的探险》

In early days, I tried not to give librarians any trouble,which was where I made my primary mistake. Librarians like to be given trouble; they exist for it, they are geared to it. For the location of a mislaid volume, an uncatalogued item, your good librarian has a ferret's nose. Give her a scent and she jumps the leash, her eye bright with battle.

Catherine Drinker Bowen,

Adventures of a Biographer

我的图书馆是一块足够大的公爵领地。

威廉·莎士比亚：《暴风雨》

My library was dukedom large enough.

William Shakespeare, *The Tempest*

互联网的作用不可思议。但是现在有人宣称互联网让图书馆变成老古董，这个说法就和说鞋让脚变的不必要一样愚蠢。

马克·赫尔林：《美国图书馆》，2001年4月

The Internet is marvelous, but to claim, as some now do, that it's making libraries obsolete is as silly as saying shoes have made feet unnecessary.

Mark Y. Herring, *American Libraries*, April 2001

保护你的本地图书馆，因为你的自由有赖于它。

约翰・杰克斯

Defend your local library as if your freedom depended on it.

John Jakes

如果文学院和科学院是大学的心脏，那么图书馆就是大学的灵魂。

查理斯・E・杨，引于
《布鲁因日报》，1998.12.7

If the College of Letters and Science is the heart of the University, the Library is its soul.

Charles E. Young,
as quoted in *Daily Bruin*, 7 December 1998

图书馆意在满足好奇者的好奇心，为孤独者提供场所，让他们能够享受词语的陪伴和温暖。[图书馆] 为手艺人提供手册，为失眠者提供小说，为学者提供研究资料，它还提供了文学作品，让人们难以忘怀。

威廉 · H · 加斯：《为书所做的辩护》

The library is meant to satisfy the curiosity of the curious,provide a place for the lonely where they may enjoy the companionship and warmth of the word. [The library]supplies handbooks for the handy, novels for insomniacs,scholarship for the scholarly, and makes available works of literature to those people they will eventually haunt so successfully.

William H. Gass, "*In Defense Of The Book*"

说到底，如果图书馆真的渴求秩序，那么在每个主题下只会有一本书……但图书馆恰恰没有这样做。相反，它们赞颂意义的多样性：图书馆寻求异端，把不同的观点放在一起，并且邀请读者从中发现他们自己的意义。

芭芭拉·费斯特：《图书馆和知识的范畴》

After all, if the library truly wanted order it would have one ultimate book on each topic . . . But that is precisely what libraries don't do. Instead, they celebrate the multiplicities of meaning by seeking out dissention and putting it together, inviting the explorer to make their own meaning of it.

Barbara Fister,

"*Libraries and the Cartography of Knowledge*"

图书馆或许是郊区购物中心潜在影响的最好的解毒药。作为一个负责任的市民，我们需要给年轻人一个选择的机会，让他们选择是游戏厅还是阅读室。我们要给他们机会在思想的市场中浏览，而非货物和服务的市场。

索尼·雅普

The library is perhaps the best antidote to the insidious influence of the suburban shopping mall. As responsible citizens, we need to give the young a chance to choose between a video arcade and a reading place, a chance to browse in a marketplace of ideas instead of a marketplace of goods and services.

Sonny Yap

图书馆是保证信息富人和信息穷人之间的差距尽可能小的关键。

利恩·艾利逊：Incite 杂志，1998 年 10 月

Libraries are the key to ensuring that the divide between information rich and poor is kept as narrow as possible.

Lyn Allison, *Incite*, October 1998

每一座图书馆都应该尽可能的穷尽某些主题，即便仅仅是大头针的历史这样的主题。

老奥利弗·温代尔·福尔摩斯：《早餐桌上的诗人》

Every library should try to be complete on something, if it were only the history of pinheads.

Oliver Wendell Holmes Sr.,

The Poet at the Breakfast Table

我洗劫了公共图书馆，发现到处都是沉没的宝藏。

维吉尼亚·伍尔夫，引于 H·李：《维吉尼亚·伍尔夫》

I ransack public libraries, and find them
full of sunk treasure.

Virginia Woolf, as quoted in H. Lee's

Virginia Woolf

获取信息和拥有解释信息的智慧是不同的。

克利福德·斯托尔：《高技术的异端》

There is a difference between having access to information and having the savvy it takes to interpret it.

Clifford Stoll, *High Tech Heretic*

图书馆呈现出其收集者的思想，他的想象和缺点，他的长处和弱点，他的偏见和喜好。尤其重要的是，它是否在收藏者的性格之外增加了（或者试图增加）学生的品德，这些学生想要了解书以及这些书的作者的生平。他们生活中的友谊，他们的成长阶段，他们思想中的异想天开，所有这些也都会在图书馆中呈现出来。

威廉·奥斯勒爵士：《奥斯勒书目》

A library represents the mind of its collector, his fancies and foibles, his strength and weakness, his prejudices and preferences. Particularly is this the case if to the character of a collector he adds—or tries to add—the qualities of a student who wishes to know the books and the lives of the men who wrote them. The friendships of his life, the phases of his growth, the vagaries of his mind, all are represented.

Sir William Osler, Bibliotheca Osleriana

公众在哪里还能游荡十个小时而不会被盘问呢？

巴里·鲍维斯：《在书架之间》

Where else could a member of the public linger for over ten hours without being questioned?

Barry Bowes, "*Between the Stacks*"

图书馆就像音乐厅，这里有来自所有时间和所有地点的最美妙的声音。

让·保尔·立克特：《长庚星》

Libraries are the concert hallsof the finest voices gathered from all times and places.

Jean Paul Richter, *Hesperus*

当我还是个坐在参考咨询台后面的学生助理，观察着那些可爱的图书馆员工作的时候，我就知道有一天我会成为大学图书馆员。“我觉得图书馆没有这本书”，读者这样开始，然后图书馆员会把书递给他，就是那本他认为不存在的书。不浪漫？这可是一个参考咨询馆员的幻想曲。

伊丽莎白·迈克克拉肯：《巨人的房子：罗曼司》

I knew I would be a librarian in college as a student assistant at a reference desk, watching those lovely people at work. “I don't think there is such a book,” a patron would begin, and then the librarian would hand it to them, that very book. Unromantic? This is a reference librarian's fantasy.

Elizabeth Mccracken, ***The Giant's House: A Romance***

图书馆应该是一双张开的手臂。

罗杰·罗森布拉特

A library should be like a pair of open arms.

Roger Rosenblatt

获得知识是真正伟大的文明的卓越的最高法令。在所有意图实现这个目标的机构之中，知识自由的图书馆几乎是傲然独立的完成这个使命。

托尼 · 莫里斯，于纽约公共图书馆，1999

Access to knowledge is the superb, the supreme act of truly great civilizations. Of all the institutions that purport to do this, free libraries stand virtually alone in accomplishing this mission.

Toni Morrison, at the New York Public Library, 1997

除非我们买书花的钱比买口香糖花的钱多，否则这就不是一个文明的国家。

阿尔伯特 · 哈伯德：《无知者》杂志，1907 年 6 月

This will never be a civilized country untilwe expend more money for books than we do for chewing gum.

Elbert Hubbard, *The Philistine*, June 1907

美国的图书馆现在是，而且必须永远是自由而好奇的心灵的家。对于图书馆来说，我们的市民——不管他的种族、年龄，也不管他的宗教和政治信仰——必须能够满怀信心的来到图书馆，相信他们能够在这里自由的找到全部的真理，这些真理没有被涂抹上时尚，也没有受到权宜之计的玷污。

德怀特·D·艾森豪威尔：
《给美国图书馆协会年会的信》

The libraries of America are and must ever remain the home of free, inquiring minds. To them, our citizens—of all ages and races, of all creeds and persuasions—must be able to turn with clear confidence that there they can freely seek the whole truth, unvarnished by fashion and uncompromised by expediency.

Dwight D. Eisenhower, "*Letter to the American Library Association's Annual Conference*"

图书馆的味道几乎都是一样的——旧布料的霉味掺杂着没有洗澡的人难闻的体臭，这就是图书馆馆长称之为“社会汤的蒸汽”的东西。

彼得·阿克罗伊德：《查特顿》

And the smell of the library was always the same—the musty odour of old clothes mixed with the keener scent of unwashed bodies, creating what the chief librarian had once described as “the steam of the social soup.”

Peter Ackroyd, *Chatterton*

图书馆是“世界的索引”。

约翰·科顿·达那

Libraries are the “Index to the World.”

John Cotton Dana

学者们很容易就忘掉了，他们被迫和维持他们思想的生命形式共同进化。问题尤其在于，学者们通常忽略了作为其自身生存重要方面的图书馆的进化……在这个朝向集体协商的运动中，图书馆员应当起到领导的作用……图书馆员……更容易看到整个教育社区即将发生的转变会造成的影响……我们协同进化的命运就掌握在你们的手中。

蒂莫西·C·维斯科尔：

《大学和研究型图书馆》，1986 年 11 月

Scholars easily forget that they are locked in coevolution with the life-forms that sustain their thought. In particular, they often neglect the evolution of libraries as a vital aspect of their own survival . . .in this movement toward collective deliberation, librarians will have to take the lead . . . Librarians . . .are more likely to see the implications of the coming transformations for the entire educational community . . . our coevolutionary fate is in your hands.

Timothy C. Weiskel,

***College and Research Libraries*, November 1986**

当生活看起来没有价值的时候，在图书馆里待上十分钟就会证明这是错的。

米弗·夏夫

When life seems not worth living, ten minutes in the library proves otherwise.

Miv Schaaf

图书馆是一个值得尊敬的地方，人们在这里保存了他们的经验，他们试探性的试验，他们的发现以及他们的计划的各种历史……在书中，我们会发现日常生活的诀窍——对头脑和心灵的处方。

乔治·杜阿美尔：《为文学辩护》

A library is that venerable place where men preserve the history of their experience, their tentative experiments, their discoveries, and their plans. . . . In books may be found the recipes for daily living—the prescriptions for the mind and the heart.

Georges Duhamel, *In Defence of Letters*

我的家庭没有多少书，也没有多少钱让一个小孩去买书，所以当我知道只要我是本地市民，我就能从市中心那座朴素的建筑里获得任何我想要的书，我觉得这简直就是太好了……同样让人满意的还有集体所有的观念，资产为了公众的利益而共有。我需要小心对待我借到的书，原样的把它们按时还回去，这是因为它们不只是我的，它们属于每一个人。这个观念对我的启蒙，就和我在书中读到的任何观念对我的启蒙一样多。

菲利普·罗斯：《纽约时报》，1969.3.1

Since my family did not own many books, or have the money for a child to buy them, it was good to know that solely by virtue of my municipal citizenship I had access to any book I wanted from that grandly austere building downtown . . . No less satisfying was the idea of communal ownership, property held in common for the common good. Why I had to care for the books I borrowed, return them unscarred and on time, was because they weren't mine alone, they were everybody's. That idea had as much to do with civilizing me as any I was ever to come upon in the books themselves.

Philip Roth, *New York Times*, 1 March 1969

我的笔是我的竖琴和七弦琴，我的图书馆是我的花园和果园。

犹大·哈列维，引于罗纳德·H·伊萨克的《伟大犹太建议的生活小书》

My pen is my harp and my lyre; my library is my garden and my orchard.

Judah Ha-Levi, as quoted in Ronald H. Isaacs's ***Life's Little Book Of Big Jewish Advice***

所以你哪里去找一个研究者，他又博学，又有想象力，能够熟练的使用电脑，投身于对真理的探求，精通数学、技术、历史和文学，而且还能干脏活又不求回报呢？吃完午饭，我开车去了城里的图书馆……

詹姆斯·李·伯克：《去艾利笙广场的最后一辆车》

So where do you go to find a researcher who is intelligent, imaginative, skilled in the use of computers, devoted to discovering the truth, and knowledgeable about science, technology, history, and literature, and who usually works for dirt and gets credit for nothing? After lunch I drove to the city library . . .

James Lee Burke, ***Last Car to Elysian Fields***

绝不要把书借给别人——没人会还书，我自己图书馆的唯一一本书正是从别人那里借的。

阿纳托尔·法朗士

Never lend books—nobody ever returns them, the only books that I have in my library are those which other folks have lent me.

Anatole France

注：原文中即 books 而非 book，非笔误。

有些人推测编目员是来自遥远星系的外星人，他们来到地球是为了让东西变整齐一点。

威尔·曼利：《美国图书馆》，1994 年（6/8）期

Some speculate that [catalogers] are aliens from a faraway galaxy who have come to earth to tidy things up a bit.

Will Manley, American Libraries, July/August 1994

没有一个地方比公共图书馆能够更清楚的证明人类希望之渺小了。

塞缪尔·约翰逊：《漫游者》杂志，1751.3.23

No place affords a more striking conviction of the vanity of human hopes than a public library.

Samuel Johnson, *The Rambler*, 23 March 1751

我总是告诉别人，我成为作家并不是因为我上过学，而是因为我妈妈带我去了图书馆。我想成为作家，是因为我想看到我的名字出现在卡片目录上。

桑德拉·希斯内罗丝

I always tell people that I became a writer not because I went to school but because my mother took me to the library. I wanted to become a writer so I could see my name in the card catalog.

Sandra Cisneros

图书馆暗含了一种信仰的行为。

维克多·雨果：《六月》，发表于《凶年集》

A library implies an act of faith.

Victor Hugo, "*Juin*" from L'Annee Terrible

所谓“电子图书馆”在高等教育中的发展会产生对大学图书馆员更大的需求，因为传播媒介越不清楚，中介就越重要。

阿伦·B·维纳：

《大学和研究型图书馆》，1985年5月

The development of the so-called electronic library in higher education will impose even greater demands on academic librarians for, the less visible the medium, the greater the need for the intermediary.

Allen B. Veaner,

***College and Research Libraries*, May 1985**

网络的确很酷，但是图书馆是神奇的。还有哪个地方，一代一代作家的精神能够激动你的灵魂呢？许多作家都谈到图书馆奠定了他们神奇的道路，这样的例子简直太多了。但是我们知道这是真的。在书架间漫步，你能感受到那些梦，以及充斥在每一卷书中的那些独特的世界。图书馆的魔法潜移默化的进入了你的身体。在网上，你或许能感受到智慧和幸运，而且身不由己的下载——但是你很少能够去梦想和写作。

亚瑟·普罗特尼克：《作家杂志》，2003 年 11 月

The Web is cool, but the library is magic. Where else can the spirit of generations of writers stir your soul? So many writers talk about libraries setting them on their magical paths, it's almost a groaner. But we know it's true. Wander through the stacks and you can feel the dreams, the unique worlds bubbling within each volume. The magic enters you as if by osmosis. On the Web, you may feel clever, lucky and driven to download—but rarely inspired to dream and to write.

Arthur Plotnik, *The Writer Magazine*, November 2003

图书馆专业是……渊博的，能够给人启发的专业，它被强烈而美丽的爱书的精神所点亮。这份爱如此宏大，因而它影响了一个又一个社区，让我们的时代变得与众不同、卓尔不群、充满创造力和真正的精神。

弗朗西斯·克拉克·萨耶斯：《被书召唤》

The library profession is . . . a profession that is informed, illuminated, radiated by a fierce and beautiful love of books. A love so overwhelming that it engulfs community after community and makes the culture of our time distinctive, individual, creative and truly of the spirit.

Frances Clark Sayers, ***Summoned by Books***

借书者——是为珍藏本的破坏者，书本排列的捣乱者，零星残书的创造者。

查尔斯·兰姆：《伊利亚随笔选》

Borrowers of books—those mutilators of collections, spoilers of the symmetof shelves, and creators of odd volumes.

Charles Lamb, ***Essays of Elia***

每当我告诉所有人说我是个图书馆员，他们看着我就好像我是夏天里的最后一朵玫瑰……我并不总是愿意介绍我自己，除非我觉得这时候应该有人站出来说，图书馆员也是人。我们不会在头发上戴着小圆发髻，我们中的一些人甚至不戴眼镜……我想说的是，我们中有结婚的图书馆员，订婚的图书馆员，当母亲的图书馆员，甚至是漂亮的图书馆员。

小哈瑞耶特·弗朗克：《带光晕的女孩》

The minute I tell anybody that I'm a librarian, they look at me as if I were the last rose of summer . . . I wouldn't ordinarily get so personal about myself, except that I think it's high time somebody made it clear that librarians are people. We do not wear our hair in little buns. Some of us don't even need glasses . . . What I am trying to say is there are married librarians, engaged librarians, librarians who are mothers, even beautiful librarians.

Harriet Frank Jr., ***The Girl with the Glow***

我们的图书馆里有已经发明出的最有效率的搜索引擎——图书馆员。

威廉·R·布罗迪：

《约翰·霍普金斯大学校刊》，2004.12.6

Our library has the most effective search engines yet invented—librarians.

William R. Brody, *JHU Gazette*, 6 December 2004

图书馆是自由的军械库。

来源未知

A library is an arsenal of liberty.

Source Unknown

我受到最好的教育来自于公共图书馆……我的学费就是坐巴士的交通费，外加借书超期交的五分钱。你不需要知道很多才能开始，你只需要知道怎么去公共图书馆就够了。

莱斯利·康格

The best of my education has come from the public library . . . my tuition fee is a bus fare and once in a while, five cents for an overdue book. You don't need to know very much to start with, if you know the way to the public library.

Lesley Conger

也许在任何社区里都没有像城镇图书馆这样完全民主的地方了。你进入图书馆的唯一要求就是兴趣。

伯德·约翰逊女士

Perhaps no place in any community is so totally democratic as the town library. The only entrance requirement is interest.

Lady Bird Johnson

[图书馆的]真正美德是,它既保存了错误,也保存了真理;它既保存了无意义,也保存了意义。

哈利·戈尔登

[The library's] real virtue is . . . it preserves error as well as truth and nonsense as well as sense.

Harry Golden

你没有真的离开图书馆，如果你做了它要你做的事情，那么你其实是把图书馆带在了身边。

埃利·维瑟尔，引于“图书馆果汁”（Library Juice）博客，2000.8.23

[Y]ou do not really leave a library; if you do what
it wants you to do, then you are taking it with you.

Elie Wiesel, as quoted in Library Juice, 23 August 2000

大学只是围绕图书馆的一组建筑，
图书馆才是真正的大学。

谢尔比·福特：《南北战争》

A university is just a group of
buildings gathered around a library.
The library is the university.

Shelby Foote, The Civil War: A Narrative

图书馆就像是美国灵魂的一杯结霜的牛奶——美味又健康，而且是妈妈认可的饮料，更重要的，它是健康的智力生活的一个必不可少的组成部分。

社论，《乔治城之声》，2005.4.7

Libraries are like a frosty glass of milk for the American soul—tasty, wholesome, mother-approved and more importantly, a necessary part of a healthy intellectual life.

Editorial, *Georgetown Voice*, 7 April 2005

如果过去的历史全都是一场游戏，那么最富有的人会是图书馆员。

沃伦·巴菲特，引于《华盛顿邮报》，1988.4.17

If past history was all there was to the game,
the richest people would be librarians.

Warren Buffett,

as quoted in the *Washington Post*, 17 April 1988

一座好的图书馆既不会太整洁，也不会有太多尘土。因为总会有人在里面，从书架上取走书，读到很晚。

雷蒙尼·斯内奇：《凶险假电梯》

A good library will never be too neat, or too dusty, because somebody will always be in it, taking books off the shelves and staying up late reading them.

Lemony Snicket, *The Ersatz Elevator*

伟大图书馆的功用是储存不为人知的书。

尼克尔森·贝克：《纽约客》，1994.4.4

The function of a great library is to store obscure books.

Nicholson Baker, *New Yorker*, 4 April 1994

图书馆员的角色是让信息世界变得有意义。如果这不是超级英雄的行为，那么什么才是?

南希·珀尔，引于《西雅图时报》，2003.7.10

The role of a librarian is to make sense of the world of information. If that's not a qualification for superherodom, what is?

Nancy Pearl, as quoted in *Seattle Times*, 10 July 2003

现在，我不断的读到图书馆的预算被缩减再缩减的新闻。这让我想到了，大门正在关上，美国社会又找到了一条毁灭自己的道路。

艾萨克·阿西莫夫：《我，阿西莫夫》

Now, when I read constantly about the way in which library funds are being cut and cut, I can only think that the door is closing and that American society has found one more way to destroy itself.

Isaac Asimov, ***I, Asimov***

我的奶奶总是说，上帝创造了图书馆，这样人们就没有任何借口让自己变得愚蠢了。

琼·包尔：《路的规则》

My grandma always said that God made libraries so that people didn't have any excuse to be stupid.

Joan Bauer, ***Rules of the Road***

任何图书馆最重要的资产每天晚上都要回家——那就是图书馆员。

蒂莫西 · S · 希利，引于《图书馆杂志》，2003.4.1

The most important asset of any library goes home at night—the library staff.

Timothy S. Healy, as quoted in

***Library Journal*, 1 April 2003**

图书馆是通向多种生活的大门。

莎朗 · 克里奇：

《纽约图书馆协会简讯》，2001 年 (10/11) 期

A library is the door to many lives.

Sharon Creech,

***NYLA Bulletin*, October/November 2001**

图书馆是一项必不可少的服务，它肩负了贫穷和无知的重负。

弗朗西斯 · 凯普尔，演讲，

美国图书馆学会年会，1964

Libraries can be an indispensable service in lifting the dead weight of poverty and ignorance.

Francis Keppel, address, ALA

Annual Conference, 1964

如果认为图书馆是安静而端庄的地方，在这里我们被满身尘土、正襟危坐、戴眼镜的女人提醒安静，这种看法很滑稽。实际上，图书馆是言论自由、交流和争论的俱乐部。图书馆员已经勇敢地反对了《爱国者法案》，他们和吵闹的小孩同坐，并且到不识字的成人那里去。图书馆绝不会提醒你保持安静。

葆拉·庞德斯通，引于美国图书馆之友，www.folusa.org

It's funny that we think of libraries as quiet demure places where we are shushed by dusty, bun-balancing, bespectacled women. The truth is libraries are raucous clubhouses for free speech, controversy and community. Librarians have stood up to the Patriot Act, sat down with noisy toddlers and reached out to illiterate adults. Libraries can never be shushed.

Paula Poundstone, as quoted in

***Friends of Libraries* U.S.A., www.folusa.org**

图书馆是充满了无价珍宝的寺庙。

图书馆员是借出宝石的君王。

他们欢迎年老年幼的收割者来到王国

成为富人的君王，守卫着拱顶石。

潘·慕诺兹·里安，

美国学校图书馆员协会会议，2003

A library is a temple unabridged
with priceless treasure.
Librarians are the majesties who
loan the jewels of measure.
They welcome to the kingdom the
young and old of reapers
and reign among the riches as the
wondrous keystone keepers.

Pam Mu.oz Ryan,

AASL Conference, 2003

我们全部的美国生活方式是一场伟大的观念战争，图书馆员是向双方贩卖武器的军火商。

詹姆斯·奎因，

Westpac/NOCALL 联席会议，1990

Our whole American way of life is a great war of ideas, and librarians are the arms dealers selling weapons to both sides.

James Quinn,

1990 WESTPA C/NOCALL Joint Meeting

从他优雅的口音、轻柔的嗓音和显而易见的
无所不知来看，我断定他是名图书馆员。

乔治·奥威尔：《通往威根码头之路》

From his refined accent, quiet voice and apparenomniscience, I took him for a librarian.

George Orwell,

The Road to Wigan Pier Diary

没有了图书馆，我们还有什么呢？

我们既没有过去也没有未来。

雷·布拉德伯里

Without libraries what have we?

We have no past and no future.

Ray Bradbury

参考咨询馆员是图书馆的眼睛和耳朵。

小查理斯·W·拜利：

《参考咨询馆员在机构仓储中的作用》

Reference librarians are a library's eyes and ears.

Charles W. Bailey Jr.,

"The Role of Reference Librarians

in Institutional Repositories"

我们知道，没有图书馆，没有教育（它在很大程度上依赖于图书馆），我们就不可能有受教育的人民继续成功的实践我们的政体。

埃莉诺·罗斯福：《图书馆对国家意味着什么》

We know that without libraries, without education, which is based largely on libraries, we cannot have an educated people who will carry on successfully our form of government.

Eleanor Roosevelt,

"*What Libraries Mean to the Nation*"

一名好的图书馆员知道，给一本书分类的最好的方式就是理解读者会如何给它分类。

罗杰·华纳：《图书馆员是新的拿破仑》

A good librarian knows that the best way to file a book isto understand how a reader would classify it themselves.

Roger Warner, "*Librarians Are the New Napoleons*"

信仰者和实干者是我们所需要的——他是有信念的图书馆员，对书的存在保持谦卑……在图书馆是所有体验中最纯洁的一种。对图书馆的独一无二，甚至是神圣的本质的认识，应当被灌输给我们的下一代。

劳伦斯·克拉克·鲍威尔：《对书的激情》

Believers and doers are what we need—faithful librarians who are humble in the presence of books . . .To be in a library is one of the purest of all experiences. This awareness of a library's unique, even sacred nature, is what should be instilled in our neophytes.

Lawrence Clark Powell, ***A Passion for Books***

我认为，我们需要图书馆恰如我们需要荒野。二者都是国王的避难所，是多样性的储藏室。

安娜·柯克帕特里克：《完成夏天》

I think we need public libraries in the same way we need wilderness. Both are sanctuaries of a king. Both are storehouses of diversity.

Anna Kirkpatrick, "*Rounding Out the Summer*"

爱书之人会理解我，而且他们也会知道，图书馆的愉悦恰在于其存在本身。

珍·莫里斯

Book lovers will understand me, and they will know too, that part of the pleasure of a library lies in its very existence.

Jan Morris

着迷于经过精选的图书馆的人有数不清的菜肴，每一道都美味可口。

威廉·戈德温：

《探寻者》

He that revels in a well-chosen library has innumerable dishes, all of admirable flavour.

William Godwin,

The Enquirer

如果我们没有图书馆，许多渴望知识的人会脱水而死。

梅根·乔·泰特里克

If we didn't have libraries, many people thirsty for knowledge would dehydrate.

Megan Jo Tetrick

现存的图书馆，就其本身而言，质疑了当权者的权威。

阿尔贝托 · 曼古埃尔：

《审查制度索引》，1999 年 3 月

Existing libraries, in their very being, seem to question the authority of those in power.

Alberto Manguel,

Index on Censorship, **March 1999**

图书馆是文学的衣柜，受过得体教育的人能够在这里创造出一些装饰品，一些是为了好奇，更多的是为了使用。

乔治 · 戴尔：

《剑桥大学和学院史》

Libraries are the wardrobes of literature; whence men properly informed may bring forth something for ornament, much for curiosity, and more for use.

George Dyer,

History of the University and Colleges of Cambridge

不敬之人声称，在图书馆中，没有意义是正常的，而合理（甚或是谦卑以及纯粹的连贯）才是奇特的例外。

豪尔赫 · 路易斯 · 博尔赫斯：《巴别塔的图书馆》

The impious maintain that nonsense is normal in the Library and that reasonable (or even humble and pure coherence) is a miraculous exception.

Jorge Luis Borges, *The Library of Babel*

这座图书馆建好之后，慈祥的母亲问："我的孩子今天晚上去哪了？"回答会是："他在图书馆里。"然后她就会感谢上帝，因为这个地方让他不会受到任何伤害。

D · C · 斯万 · 温特史密斯

Were this library built and the fond mother would say, "Where is my boy tonight?" and the response should be, "He is at the Library," she could thank God that he is where no harm would come him.

D. C. Swan Wintersmith

对我来讲，伟大的图书馆员必须有一个清楚的头脑，一双强壮的手，而且最重要的是，一个伟大的心灵……我倾向于认为，绝大多数取得如此伟大成就的人都是女性。

梅尔维尔·杜威：《图书馆杂志》1899 年 1 月

To my thinking, a great librarian must have a clear head, a strong hand, and above all, a great heart . . . and I am inclined to think that most of the men who achieve this greatness will be women.

Melvil Dewey,

Library Journal, **January 1899**

图书馆事业旨在维持个人生活中自由思考。

A·布罗德菲尔德：《图书馆事业的哲学》

Librarianship has for its purpose the maintenance of the part of the life of the individual which is the activity of thinking freely.

A. Broadfield,

A Philosophy of Librarianship

对于那些没钱的人，通向梦想中黄金屋的道路开始于公共图书馆。

彼得·哈米尔：《纽约每日新闻》，2002.2.25

For those without money, the road to the treasure house of the imagination begins at the public library.

Pete Hamill, *New York Daily News*, 25 February 2002

……完美的平静生活只能在退休、忠诚的朋友以及好的图书馆那里找到。

埃弗拉·伯恩：《幸运的错误》

. . . that perfect tranquility of life, which is nowhere to be found but in retreat, a faithful friend, and a good library.

Aphra Behn, *The Lucky Mistake*

当我走进这座图书馆，我无法理解为什么我还会走出来。

玛丽·德·塞维尼：《塞维尼夫人写给她的女儿及其朋友的信》

When I step into this library, I cannot understand why I ever step out of it.

Marie de Sévigné,*Letters of Madame de Sévigné to her daughter and her friends*

世界上没有像免费的公共图书馆这样的民主发源地了，在这个文学的共和国里，人们一点都不会在乎地位、职位和财富。

安德鲁·卡内基

There is not such a cradle of democracy upon the earth as the Free Public Library, this republic of letters, where neither rank, office, nor wealth receives the slightest consideration.

Andrew Carnegie

公共图书馆是最持久的记忆，是对曾经出现的事件、人物或者感情的最真实的纪念碑。因为它，而且只有它，会被战争和革命所尊敬，而图书馆也让战争和革命永存。

马克·吐温：《写给米利森特图书馆的信》，1894.2.22

A public library is the most enduring of memorials, the trustiest monument for the presentation of an event or a name or an affection; for it, and it only, is respected by wars and revolutions, and survives them.

Mark Twain,

"*Letter to the Millicent Library*"22 February 1894

对学习的爱，

隐蔽的隐居所，

书的所有的甜蜜安宁。

亨利·沃兹沃斯·朗费罗：《将死之人向您致敬》

The love of learning,

the sequestered nooks,

and all the sweet serenity of books.

Henry Wadsworth Longfellow, "*Morituri Salutamus*"

我必须得说，我发现电视是非常有教育意义的。只要有人打开了电视，我就会去图书馆读书。

格罗克·马克思

I must say that I find television very educational. The minute somebody turns it on, I go to the library and read a book.

Groucho Marx

就所有的专业而言，图书馆专业可能是最缺乏原创性和最综合的一个了，它也最依赖更加正式的学科来建立自己的理论结构和实践体系。在过去，图书馆员倾向于把这个特点看作是这个专业本质上的不足，因而产生了强烈的专业自卑。但是，这个特点实际上让图书馆专业居于一个独特的战略位置，可以领导人类知识的整合，而且这个特点还能让图书馆专业成为一个伟大的统一力量，不止是在学术领域，而是贯穿全部的人类生活。

杰西·谢拉：《图书馆专业教育的基础》

Of all the professions, librarianship is probably the most derivative and synthetic, and is the most dependent upon the more formal disciplines for its own theoretical structure and its corpus of practice. In the past librarians have been disposed to view this characteristic as a fundamental weakness, and it has therefore generated a considerable feeling of professional inferiority. Yet this very quality has given librarianship a uniquely strategic position of leadership in the integration of human knowledge,and it could make of librarianship a great unifying force, not only in the world of scholarship, but also throughout all human life.

Jesse Shera, ***The Foundations for Education in Librarianship***

图书馆员把自己视作《第一修正案》的守护者。在墙那里，你有一千家《琼斯母亲》杂志！我热爱图书馆员，我感谢他们！

迈克尔·摩尔：《沙龙》，2002.1.7

Librarians see themselves as the guardians of the First Amendment. You got a thousand Mother Joneses at the barricades! I love the librarians, and I am grateful for them!

MICHAEL MOORE, *SALON*, 7 JANUARY 2002

我不喜欢说教，但是更多的人需要在图书馆里待上
和在篮球场上一样多的时间。

卡里姆·阿布杜尔－贾巴尔

I'm not comfortable being preachy, but more people need to start spending as much time in the library as they do on the basketball court.

Kareem Abdul-Jabbar

当我们的图书馆消失的时候，
黑暗时代将重新来临。

米奇·海格，引于 G·爱德华·尼克尔斯《诺曼·威廉斯公共图书馆》

When the lights go out in our libraries,
the Dark Ages are coming again!

Mitch Hager, as quoted in G. Edward Nichols's
The Norman Williams Public Library

有一个地方能让我发现我是谁，以及我会变成什么——那就是公共图书馆。

杰捷·考辛斯，
给纽约公共图书馆的推荐信

There was one place where I could find out who I was and what I was going to become. And that was the Public Library.

Jerzy Kosinski,
Testimonial for the New York Public Library

图书馆好玩，有教育意义，而且还是地球上最大的特惠品。

马德琳·奥尔布赖特，基本政策演说，美国图书馆年会，2006

Libraries are fun, educational, and the biggest bargain on the face of the earth.

Madeline Albright,

Keynote Address, ALA Annual Conference, 2006

我从没遇到过一名公共图书馆馆员会支持审查制度，或者不在某种程度上抵制它。

莱昂·卡尔诺夫斯基：《图书馆季刊》，1950（20）

I have never met a public librarian who approved of censorship or one who failed to practice it in some measure.

Leon Carnovsky, *Library Quarterly* 20 (1950)

提供获取知识的方式，是人类能够获得的最伟大的利益。它延长了生命本身，扩大了存在的领域。

约翰·昆西·亚当斯：《国闻报》，1836.2.17

To furnish the means of acquiring knowledge is the greatest benefit that can be conferred upon mankind. It prolongs life itself and enlarges the sphere of existence.

John Quincy Adams,*National Intelligencer*, 17 February 1836

对我来说，没有什么事比给小孩子书更重要的了。当他们十五岁的时候，给他们书比给他们药物治疗要更好。是否有人遇到过这样的情况：如果你在公共学校里建成了一座精美的图书馆，你就再也不需要把孩子抓到监狱里去了？

弗兰·勒波维茨，引于《纽约时报》，1994.8.10

To me, nothing can be more important than giving children books. It's better to be giving books to children than drug treatment to them when they're 15 years old. Did it ever occur to anyone that if you put nice libraries in public schools you wouldn't have to put them in prisons?

Fran Lebowitz,as quoted in the *New York Times*, 10 August 1994

我哀叹传统卡片目录的死亡，并不是我守旧，而是说过去的橡木抽屉让研究者可以在相邻的卡片中获得意外的利用和幸运的发现。这种偶然的信息有别于计算机严格的网状秩序。

安妮·普鲁：《通向散文之路》

I mourn the loss of the old card catalogs, not because I'm a luddite, but because the oaken trays of yesteryear offered the researcher an element of random utility and felicitous surprise through encounters with adjacent cards, information by chance that is different in kind from the computer's ramified but rigid order.

Annie Proulx, "*On the Road to Prose*"

我祈求我的孩子不会进入图书馆这样的地方。它们实际上是最危险的地方，孩子们如果被引诱到这个充满愉悦、激励、事实、激情和快乐的鬼地方，那可真是不幸呀！

威利·拉塞尔

I pray that no child of mine would ever descend into such a place as a library. They are indeed most dangerous places and unfortunate is she or he who is lured into such a hellhole of enjoyment, stimulus, facts, passion and fun.

Willy Russell

自由社会给我们的三份最重要的文件是：出生证明、护照和图书馆证。

E·L·多克托罗：《纽约时报》，1994.3.27

The three most important documents a free society gives are a birth certificate, a passport, and a library card.

E. L. Doctorow, *New York Times*, 27 March 1994

钻在古老的图书馆里，真是其所得哉！那些往昔的作家把自己的劳动成果传给了波德莱图书馆的这些职员，他们的精魂也就在这里安息，仿佛躺在什么寝室里，一排排，整整齐齐。我不去摸弄那些朽坏的书页，那是他们的尸衣，我不愿亵渎他们。我怕一摸，就有一个幽灵从书里走出来。我在这书林之中漫步，呼吸着学术的空气，那些带着虫蛀霉味的古书封套，散发出在无忧无虑的学艺园地里那些知识之果鲜花初放时的阵阵幽香。

查尔斯·兰姆：《伊利亚随笔选》

（译文摘自刘炳善译本，三联书店，1997 年出版）

What a place to be in is an old library! It seems as though all the souls of all the writers that have bequeathed their labours to these Bodleians were reposing here as in some dormitory, or middle state. I do not want to handle, to profane the leaves, their winding-sheets. I could as soon dislodge a shade. I seem to inhale learning, walking amid their foliage; and the odor of their old moth-scented coverings is fragrant as the first bloom of the sciential apples which grew amid the happy orchard.

Charles Lamb, ***Essays of Elia***

图书馆让学生和教员与过去的伟大心灵签订了契约，
这份契约居于所有学习的核心。

约翰·P·雷诺尔

Libraries give students and faculties a contact with the great minds of the past, a contact that is at the heart of all learning.

John P. Raynor

就在这里，那座奇妙的图书馆的气味，我怎能忘掉呢？图书馆的感觉——它们的样子、气味和声音——就像猛烈的初恋记忆一样徘徊不去。

苏珊·艾伦·托特：《阅览室》

There it is: that wonderful library smell. How could I have forgotten it? The feel of libraries—the way they look, smell, sound—lingers intensely as the memories of a fierce first love.

Susan Allen Toth, *Reading Rooms*

图书馆员没有很高的地位，也没挣很多钱，比诗人多点，但并没多多少，比如说，就没有成功的乞丐挣得多。所以理想对我们是非常重要的——对书的热爱、对知识的热爱、对真理和信息自由的热爱以及让人们自己探索万物的目标……

拉里·贝恩哈特：《图书馆员》

Librarians don't have a lot of status, and we don't make a lot of money, more than poets, but not so much, say, as your more successful panhandlers, so our ideals are important to us and the love of books and the love of knowledge and the love of truth and free information and letting people discover things for themselves . . .

Larry Beinhart, ***The Librarian***

地球的地层按照顺序的保存了过去的生物，图

书馆的书架也按照顺序保存了过去的错误以及它们

的期望，这些正如古时的生物一样栩栩如生，在它

们的时代产生了巨大的骚动，但是现在成为化石僵

硬的躺在那里，只有文学古生物学家才关注它们。

亚瑟·叔本华：《散文和格言》

As the strata of the earth preserve in succession the living creatures of past epochs, so the shelves of libraries preserve in succession the errors of the past and their expectations, which like the former were very lively and made a great commotion in their own age but now stand petrified and stiff in place where only the literary paleontologist regards them.

Arthur Schopenhauer, *Essays and Aphorisms*

他很聪明，知道知识之源——它们在哪里被写下，
在哪里能找到。

A · A · 霍奇

He is wise who knows the sources of knowledge—where it is written and where it is to be found.

A. A. Hodge

指责图书馆传播色情就像：你的孩子一个人跑到湖边，掉下去淹死了，你却指责这个湖。

大卫 · 索亚：

《发言人评论报》，2000.12.18

Blaming the library for exposure to pornography
is likeblaming the lake if your child walks up to it
alone, falls inand then drowns.

David Sawyer, ***Spokesman-Review,***

18 December 2000

图书馆不仅仅是一个社会所有、社会管理的机构，它是一个真正的为民众服务的信息机构——它的员工高度尊重知识的价值。他们是传统图书的保护者，所以图书馆员对数据、思想，以及事实和知识的等级关系有着合理的看法。

西奥多·罗斯扎克：《信息崇拜》

The library is not only there as a socially owned and governed institution, a true people's information service; it is staffed by men and women who maintain high respect for intellectual values. Because they are also the traditional keepers of the books, the librarians have a healthy sense of the hierarchical relationship between data and ideas, facts and knowledge.

Theodore Roszak, ***The Cult of Information***

图书馆员来自金星，技术人员来自火星。

道格·约翰逊：《技术连接》杂志，1998 年 4–5 月

Librarians are from Venus; Technologists are from Mars.

Doug Johnson, ***Technology Connection*****,**
May-June 1998

图书馆不需要窗户，

图书馆本身就是一扇窗户。

斯图尔特·布兰德：《如何建构学习》

A library doesn't need windows.

A library is a window.

Stewart Brand, How Buildings Learn

你将永生。

在这里，你的艺术非常安全

每一本书都是你的墓志铭。

亨利·沃恩：

《托马斯·博德利爵士的图书馆》

Thou can'st not die.

Here thou art more than safe

where every book is thy epitaph.

Henry Vaughan,

"*On Sir Thomas Bodley's Library*"

我们距离有序的宇宙最近的地方就是图书馆。

阿什莱·布睿良特：《唱唱反调》

The closest we will ever come to an orderly universe is a good library.

Ashleigh Brilliant, *Pot-Shots*

信息是一项基本的人权，也是形成民主制度的最基本的基础。

纳尔逊·曼德拉

Information is a basic human right and the fundamental foundation for the formation of democratic institutions.

Nelson Mandela

我儿时的图书馆小到不会让人觉得害怕。但是我觉得全部的世界都装在了那两间屋子里。我可以走在任何一个过道里，闻着智慧的味道。

丽塔·达夫

My childhood library was small enough not to be intimidating. And yet I felt the whole world was contained in those two rooms. I could walk any aisle and smell wisdom.

Rita Dove

关闭任何一座图书馆，都意味着社区失却了
它的灵魂。

库尔特·冯内古特：

《哈特福德新闻报》，1995.1.31

The death of a library, any library, suggests that
the community has lost its soul.

Kurt Vonnegut Jr.,

Hartford Courant, **31 January 1995**

在我看来，归根结底，图书馆坚持着启蒙和理性的观念，即人类通过获取知识和信息取得进步，而且这条路不应该设置任何障碍。

迈克尔·戈曼：《图书馆的价值》

It seems to me that libraries stand, above all, for the enlightened and rational notion that human beings are improved by the acquisition of knowledge and information and that no bar should be placed in their way.

Michael Gorman,

"*The Value and Values of Libraries*"

图书馆储存着点燃想象力的能量。它们打开了通向世界的窗口，鼓励我们探索并取得成功，它还致力于改善我们的生活质量。图书馆让生活变得更美好。

西德尼·谢尔顿

Libraries store the energy that fuels the imagination. They open up windows to the world and inspire us to explore and achieve, and contribute to improving our quality of life. Libraries change lives for the better.

Sidney Sheldon

伟大的图书馆藏有整个人类的记忆。

乔治·默瑟·道森，演讲，

伯明翰免费图书馆开馆式，1866.10.26

A great library contains the diary of the human race.

George Mercer Dawson, address,

opening of the Birmingham Free Library,

26 October 1866

图书馆员不仅仅是知识的守护者，他们是美洲印第安人对部落保存口头传说的特殊智者的称呼：守梦人。

詹姆斯·H·贝灵顿，演讲，

美国图书馆协会年会，1999

Librarians are not just gatekeepers to knowledge, they are what the American Indians used to call their special sages who preserved the oral legends of a tribe: dreamkeepers.

James H. Billington,

Address, ALA Annual Conference, 1999

我心里一直在暗暗设想，天堂应该是图书馆的模样。

豪尔赫·路易斯·博尔赫斯：《关于天赐的诗》

I have always imagined that Paradise will be some kind of library.

Jorge Luis Borges, "*Poem of the Gifts*"

传记辞典

卡里姆·阿布杜尔-贾巴尔 (Ab dul-Jabb ar, Kareem, 1947－) 美国职业篮球运动员

彼得·阿克罗伊德 (Ackroyd, Peter, 1949－) 英国作家

约翰·昆西·亚当斯 (Adams, John Quincy, 1767－1848) 第六任美国总统

马德琳·奥尔布赖特 (Albright, Madeline, 1937－) 美国大学教授和国务卿

约书亚·阿伦 (Allen, Joshua) 美国程序管理员和软件博客作者

利恩·艾利逊 (Allison, Lyn, 1946－) 澳大利亚政治人物和参议员

理查德·亚摩 (Armour, Richard, 1906－1989) 美国诗

人和作家

艾萨克·阿西莫夫 (Asimov, Isaac, 1920 – 1992) 美籍俄裔作家和大学教授

爱德华·阿斯纳 (Asner, Edward, 1929 –) 美国演员

弗朗西斯·培根 (Bacon , Francis, 1561 – 1626) 英国哲学家、政治家和作家

小查理斯·W·拜利 (Bailey, Charles W., Jr., 1950 –) 美国图书馆员和作家

尼克尔森·贝克 (Baker, Nicholson, 1957 –) 美国作家

琼·包尔 (Bauer, Joan, 1951 –) 美国少年文学作家

亨利·沃德·比切 (Beecher, Henry Ward, 1813 – 1887) 美国废奴主义者、社会改革者、以及公理会神职人员

埃弗拉·伯恩 (Behn, Aphra, 1640 – 1689) 英国作家和剧作家

拉里 · 贝恩哈特 (Beinhart, Larry) 美国作家

大卫 · 本 - 古里安 (Ben-Gurion, David, 1886 – 1973) 以色列第一任总理

帕特里西亚 · 威尔逊 · 伯格 (Berger, Patricia Wilson) 美国图书馆员，1989-90 年间任美国图书馆协会主席

约翰 · N · 贝里三世 (Berry, John N., II, 1933 –) 美国人，《图书馆杂志》的编者

詹姆斯 · H · 贝灵顿 (Billington, James H., 1929 –) 美国作家、大学教授、以及国会图书馆的图书馆员

艾玛 · 邦贝克 (Bombeck, Erma, 1927 – 1996) 美国幽默作家及专栏作家

豪尔赫 · 路易斯 · 博尔赫斯 (Borges, Jorge Luis, 1899 – 1986) 阿根廷作家

凯撒琳 · 敦肯 · 包恩 (Bowen, Catherine Drinker, 1897 – 1973) 美国传记作家

巴里 · 鲍维斯 (Bowes, Barry) 英国作家

雷 · 布拉德伯里 (Bradbury, Ray, 1920 –) 美国科幻小说作家

斯图尔特 · 布兰德 (Brand, Stewart, 1938 –) 美国作家、编辑、以及《全球目录》的作者

阿什莱 · 布睿良特 (Brilliant, Ashleigh, 1933 –) 英国出生的作家和卡通画家

A · 布罗德菲尔德 (Broadfield, A.) 英国图书馆员和作家

威廉 · R · 布罗迪 (Brody, William R., 1944 –) 美国放射学和工程学教授，霍普金斯大学校长

马克 · 布朗 (Brown, Marc, 1946 –) 美国儿童图书作家

沃伦 · 巴菲特 (Buffett, Warren, 1930 –) 美国投资家、商人、慈善家

詹姆斯·李·伯克 (Burke, James Lee, 1936 –) 美国悬疑小说作家

安德鲁·卡内基 (Carnegie, Andrew, 1835 – 1919) 苏格兰出生的企业家、商人、慈善家

莱昂·卡尔诺夫斯基 (Carnovsky, Leon, 1903 – 1975) 美国图书馆员、编辑和大学教授

约瑟夫·张伯伦 (Chamberlain, Joseph, 1836 – 1914) 英国政治家、商人

小泽查瑞尔·查菲 (Chafee, Zechariah, Jr., 1885 – 1957) 美国法律学者、哲学家、公民自由论者

麦麟屏 (Chan, Lois Mai, 1934 –) 美国作家、图书馆学教授

约翰·查第 (Ciardi, John, 1916 – 1986) 美国诗人、翻译家、词源学者

西塞罗 (Cicero, Marcus Tullius, 106 BC – 43 BC) 古罗马政治家、律师和哲学家

桑德拉·希斯内罗丝 (Cisneros, Sandra, 1954 –) 美国小说家、诗人以及短篇故事作家

梅森·库里 (Cooley, Mason, 1927 – 2002) 美国警句家、英语教授

莱斯利·康格 (Conger, Lesley) 美国作家

诺曼·卡森斯 (Cousins, Norman, 1915 – 1990) 美国政治记者、大学教授，以及世界和平的倡导者

莎朗·克里奇 (Creech, Sharon, 1945 –) 美国儿童图书作家

布莱斯·克洛宁 (Cronin, Blaise, 1949 –) 爱尔兰作家、编辑以及信息科学教授

沃尔特·克朗凯特 (Cronkite, Walter, 1916 –) 美国广播记者

约翰·科顿·达那 (Dana, John Cotton, 1856 – 1929) 美国图书馆员和博物馆馆长

乔治·默瑟·道森 (Dawson, George Mercer, 1849 – 1901) 加拿大科学家和勘测员

格拉桑·A·德卡迪多 (DeCandido, GraceAnne A.)

美国作家、教师和图书馆员

梅尔维尔·杜威 (Dewey, Melvil, 1851 – 1931) 美国图书馆员、杜威十进制分类法的发明者

E·L·多克托罗 (Doctorow, E. L., 1931 –) 美国作家

丽塔·达夫 (Dove, Rita, 1952 –) 美国诗人和作家，普利策得主

乔治·杜阿美尔 (Duhamel, Georges, 1884 – 1966) 法国作家

芬利·彼得·邓恩 (Dunne, Finley Peter, 1867 – 1936) 美国记者、幽默作家

乔治·戴尔 (Dyer, George, 1755 – 1841) 英国古典学家、作家

昂伯托 · 艾柯 (Eco, Umberto, 1932 –) 意大利中世纪研究者、小说家、哲学家

德怀特 · D · 艾森豪威尔 (Eisenhower, Dwight D., 1890 – 1969) 美国陆军将军、美国第三十四任总统

拉尔夫 · 沃尔多 · 爱默生 (Emerson, Ralph Waldo, 1803 – 1882) 美国散文家、哲学家、诗人，超验主义运动的领导者

艾文 · 艾沙 (Esar, Evan, 1899 – 1995) 美国幽默作家

芭芭拉 · 费斯特 (Fister, Barbara) 美国图书馆员、作家

F · 司各特 · 菲茨杰拉德 (Fitzgerald, F. Scott, 1896 – 1940) 美国小说家、短篇故事作家

谢尔比 · 福特 (Foote, Shelby, 1916 – 2005) 美国小说家、美国内战研究者

马尔科姆 · 福布斯 (Forbes, Malcolm, 1919 – 1990) 《福布斯》杂志的出版者

阿纳托尔·法朗士 (France, Anatole,1844 – 1924) 法国诗人、记者和小说家，诺贝尔奖得主

小哈瑞耶特·弗朗克 (Frank, Harriet, Jr., 1917 –) 美国编剧、制片人

威廉·H·加斯 (Gass, William H., 1924 –) 美国小说家、短篇故事作家、文学批评家以及哲学教授

威廉·戈德温 (Godwin, William, 1756 – 1836) 英国记者、政治哲学家以及小说家

哈利·戈尔登 (Golden, Harry, 1902 – 1981) 美国犹太作家、新闻出版者

彼得·高尔金 (Golkin, Peter, 1966 –) 美国博物馆发言人

爱德华·戈里 (Gorey, Edward, 1925 – 2000) 美国作家、艺术家

迈克尔·戈曼 (Gorman, Michael, 1941 –) 美籍英裔图书馆员、作家

瓦坦·格雷戈里恩 (Gregorian, Vartan, 1934－) 美国学者，纽约卡内基基金会主席

R·李·哈登 (Hadden, R. Lee, 1951－) 美国图书馆员

比尔·霍尔 (Hall, Bill, 1937－) 美国幽默作家、编辑、作家

彼得·哈米尔 (Hamill, Pete, 1935－) 美国记者、散文家、小说家

蒂莫西·S·希利 (Healy, Timothy S., 1923－1992) 耶稣会神父、乔治城大学校长、纽约公共图书馆馆长

安·赫伯特 (Herbert, Anne, 1952－) 美国作家、《协同进化季刊》副主编

马克·赫尔林 (Herring, Mark Y., 1952－) 美国图书馆员

邦特·赫尔姆奎维斯特 (Hj elmqvist, Bengt, 1903－) 瑞典图书馆员、作家以及盎格鲁 - 斯堪的纳维亚公

共图书馆会议的规划者

A · A · 霍奇 (Hodge, A. A., 1823 – 1886) 美国基督教长老会领导者

老奥利弗 · 温代尔 · 福尔摩斯 (Holmes, Oliver Wendell, Sr., 1809 – 1894) 美国医师、诗人、散文家

阿尔伯特 · 哈伯德 (Hubbard, Elbert, 1856 – 1915) 美国作家、出版商、艺术家以及哲学家

罗伯特 · 休斯 (Hughes, Robert, 1938 –) 澳大利亚出生的作家、艺术批评家

泰德 · 休斯 (Hughes, Ted, 1930 – 1998) 英国诗人、儿童图书作者

维克多 · 雨果 (Hugo, Victor, 1802 – 1885) 法国诗人、小说家、政治家

犹大 · 伊本 · 提朋 (Ibn Tibb on, Judah, ca. 1150 – 1230) 犹太哲学家、医生

约翰 · 杰克斯 (Jakes, John, 1932 –) 美国小说作家

道格 · 约翰逊 (Johnson, Doug, 1952 –) 美国作家、演讲人以及技术 / 图书馆顾问

伯德 · 约翰逊女士 (Johnson, Lady Bird, 1912 – 2007) 美国企业家，总统夫人

塞缪尔 · 约翰逊 (Johnson, Samuel, 1709 – 1784) 英国作家

犹大 · 哈列维 (Judah ha-Levi, ca. 1075 – 1141) 西班牙籍犹太哲学家、诗人

盖瑞森 · 凯勒 (Keillor, Garrison, 1942 –) 美国广播播音员、讲故事的人、幽默作家

约翰 · F · 肯尼迪 (Kennedy, John F., 1917 – 1963) 美国第三十五任总统

弗朗西斯 · 凯普尔 (Keppel, Francis, 1916 – 1990) 美国教育家，教育部长

芭芭拉 · 金索佛 (Kingsolver, Barbara, 1955 –) 美国作家

安娜 · 柯克帕特里克 (Kirkpatrick, Anna) 加拿大的图书馆读者

诺欧米 · 克莱恩 (Klein, Naomi, 1970 –) 加拿大记者、作家、活动家

迪恩 · 孔茨 (Koontz, Dean, 1945 –) 美国小说家

杰捷 · 考辛斯 (Kosinski, Jerzy, 1933 – 1991) 波兰出生的美国小说家

查尔斯 · 兰姆 (Lamb , Charles, 1775 – 1834) 英国散文家

路易斯 · 拉莫尔 (L' Am our, Louis, 1908 – 1988) 美国西部小说家

弗兰 · 勒波维茨 (Lebowitz, Fran, 1950 –) 美国作家

亨利 · 华兹华斯 · 朗费罗 (Longfellow, Henry

Wadsworth, 1807 – 1882) 美国诗人、教育家

约翰 · 鲁波克 (Lubbock, John, 1834 – 1913) 英国银行家、政治人物、生物学家、考古学家

诺曼 · 麦克林 (Maclean, Norman, 1902 – 1990) 美国作家、学者

阿奇巴尔德 · 麦克莱什 (MacLeish, Archibald, 1892 – 1982) 美国诗人、作家、国会图书馆图书馆员

纳尔逊 · 曼德拉 (Mandela, Nelson, 1918 –) 南非总统、反隔离活动家

阿尔维托 · 曼古埃尔 (Manguel, Alberto, 1948 –) 阿根廷出生的作家、译者以及编辑

威尔 · 曼利 (Manley, Will, 1949 –) 《美国图书馆》杂志专栏作家、图书馆员

弗朗西斯科 · 马尔奎斯 · 维兰纽瓦 (M á rquez Villanueva, Francisco, 1931 –) 西班牙出生的作家、浪漫文学教授

罗伯特 · S · 马丁 (Martin, Robert S.) 美国图书馆员、档案学家、管理者以及教育家

格罗克 · 马克思 (Marx, Groucho, 1890 – 1977) 美国喜剧演员、电影明星

伊丽莎白 · 迈克克拉肯 (McCracken, Elizabeth, 1966 –) 美国作家

查理斯 · 梅达沃 (Medawar, Charles) 英国作家，医药政策和药物安全专家

罗伯特 · 梅兰肯 (M é lan.on, Robert, 1947 –) 法裔加拿大人作家、学者

艾迪斯 · 帕特森 · 迈耶尔 (Meyer, Edith Patterson, 1895 – 1993) 美国图书馆员、编辑、儿童图书作者

迈克尔 · 摩尔 (Moore, Michael, 1954 –) 美国电影制片人、作家、政治评论员

珍 · 莫里斯 (Morris, Jan, 1926 –) 英国历史学家、作家、旅行作家

托尼·莫里斯 (Morrison, Toni, 1931 –) 美国作家、编辑、教授，诺贝尔奖得主

比尔·默亚思 (Moyers, Bill, 1934 –) 美国记者、公共评论员

萨缪尔·尼格尔 (Niger, Samuel, 1883 – 1955) 意第绪语文学批评家

巴拉克·奥巴马 (Obama, Barack, 1961 –) 美国参议员、第五十四任总统

艾瑞卡·奥尔森 (Olsen, Erica) “第二人生” (Second Life) 用户体验设计师，LibrarianAvengers.org 的创建者

何塞·奥特嘉·伊·加塞特 (Ortega Y Gasset, Jos é , 1883 – 1955) 西班牙哲学家

乔治·奥威尔 (Orwell, George, 1903 – 1950) 英国作家

威廉·奥斯勒 (Osler, William, 1849－1919) 医生、教授、目录学协会主席（1913-1918)

南希·珀尔 (Pearl, Nancy, 1945－) 美国图书馆员、作家、文学批评家

迈克尔·佩里 (Perry, Michael, 1964－) 美国幽默作家

亚瑟·普罗特尼克 (Plotnik, Arthur) 美国编辑、作家

葆拉·庞德斯通 (Poundstone, Paula, 1959－) 美国喜剧演员

劳伦斯·克拉克·鲍威尔 (Powell, Lawrence Clark, 1906－2001) 美国图书馆员、文学批评家、作家

安妮·普鲁 (Proulx, Annie, 1935－) 美国记者、作家

罗伯特·D·普特南 (Putnam, Robert D., 1941－) 美国政治科学家、教授

詹姆斯·奎因 (Quinn, James) 美国图书馆员

约翰·P·雷诺尔 (Raynor, John P., 1923 – 1997) 美国牧师、马凯特大学（Marquette University）校长

凯斯·理查兹 (Richards, Keith (1943 –) 英国吉他手、音乐词曲作者、滚石乐队成员

让·保尔·立克特 (Richter, Jean Paul, 1763 – 1825) 德国作家

埃莉诺·罗斯福 (Roosevelt, Eleanor, 1884 – 1962) 美国作家、政治人物、总统夫人

罗杰·罗森布拉特 (Rosenblatt, Roger) 美国记者、作家、评论员、教授

西奥多·罗斯扎克 (Roszak, Theodore, 1933 –) 美国学者、作家

菲利普·罗斯 (Roth, Philip, 1933 –) 美国小说家

卡尔·罗文 (Rowan, Carl, 1925 – 2000) 美国记者、公务员

乔纳森·伦德曼 (Rundman, Jonathan) 美国歌手、歌曲词曲作者

威利·拉塞尔 (Russell, Willy, 1947－) 英国剧作家、编剧、作家、歌词作者

潘·慕诺兹·里安 (Ryan, Pam Mu.oz, 1951－) 美国作家

卡尔·萨根 (Sagan, Carl, 1934－1996) 美国天文学家、天文化学家、作家

大卫·索亚 (Sawyer, David) 美国专栏作家、爱达荷州沙点市（Sandpoint, Idaho）市长

弗朗西斯·克拉克·萨耶斯 (Sayers, Frances Clarke,

1897－1989) 美国儿童图书作者、图书馆员以及教育家

米弗·夏夫 (Schaaf, Miv, d.1998) 历史文物保护者、《洛杉矶时报》专栏作家

亚瑟·叔本华 (Schopenhauer, Arthur, 1788 – 1860) 德国哲学家

小亚瑟·梅耶尔·施莱辛格 (Schlesinger, Arthur Meier, Jr., 1917 – 2007) 美国历史学家、社会批评家

玛丽·德·塞维尼 (S é vign é , Marie de, 1626 – 1696) 法国贵族

威廉·莎士比亚 (Shakespeare, William, 1564 – 1616) 英国诗人、剧作家

西德尼·谢尔顿 (Sheldon, Sidney, 1971 – 2007) 美国小说家、剧作家、编剧

杰西·谢拉 (Shera, Jesse, 1903 – 1982) 美国图书馆员和情报学家

西奥多·赛泽 (Sizer, Theodore, 1932 –) 美国教育改革领袖

雷蒙尼·斯内奇 (Snicket, Lemony, 1970 –) 美国作家、编剧

克利福德 · 斯托尔 (Stoll, Clifford) 美国天文学家、计算机专家、作家

贝亚德 · 泰勒 (Taylor, Bayard, 1825 – 1878) 美国诗人、译者以及旅行作家

罗伊 · 特南特 (Tennant, Roy) 美国图书馆员

梅根 · 乔 · 泰特里克 (Tetrick, Megan Jo) 美国图书馆读者

理查 · F · 托马斯 (Thomas, Richard F., 1950 –) 英国出生的作家、古典学教授

贝弗利 · 托娜 (Tona, Beverly) 美国记者

苏珊 · 艾伦 · 托特 (Toth, Susan Allen, 1940 –) 美国作家

马克 · 吐温 (Twain, Mark, 1835 – 1910) 美国幽默作家、演讲人

亨利 · 沃恩 (Vaughan, Henry, 1622 – 1695) 威尔士玄学派诗人、医药实践者

阿伦 · B · 维纳 (Veaner, Allen B., 1929 –) 美国图书馆、作家

库尔特 · 冯内古特 (Vonnegut, Kurt, Jr., 1922 – 2007) 美国作家

珍妮 · 瓦格纳 (Wagner, Jane, 1935 –) 美国电影制片人、导演、莉莉 · 汤姆琳 （Lily Tomlin） 喜剧的作者

罗杰 · 华纳 (Warner, Roger) 英国作家、Squiz.net 的导演

林顿 · 维克斯 (Weeks, Linton, 1951 –) 美国记者、编辑

蒂莫西 · C · 维斯科尔 (Weiskel, Timothy C.) 美国教授、历史学家、社会人类学家

杰萨敏 · 韦斯特 (West, Jessamyn, 1968 –) 美国图书馆员、博客作者、Librarian.net 的创建者

赫伯特 · S · 怀特 (White, Herbert S., 1927 –) 美国作家、图书馆和信息科学专业的教授

埃利 · 维瑟尔 (Wiesel, Elie, 1928 –) 犹太作家、教授、政治活动家以及诺贝尔奖桂冠诗人

D · C · 斯万 · 温特史密斯 (Wintersmith, D. C. Swan, 1839 – 1912) 美国邮政总长

维吉尼亚 · 伍尔夫 (Woolf, Virginia, 1882 – 1941) 英国小说家、散文家

查理斯 · E · 杨 (Young, Charles E., 1931 –) 美国教授，加州大学洛杉矶分校以及佛罗里达大学校长

来源

如果没有其他人编纂的作品，本书对名言的收集会更加困难。本书中材料的收集从以下图书和网站中得到了很多帮助：

Brainy Quote—www.brainyquote.com

Collection of Librarian Quotations—www.angelfire.com/tx/StatBook/libquot1.html

Favorite Library Quotes—http://homepages.gac.edu/~mtwait/favquotes.htm

Goodreads—www.goodreads.com

Imagi-Natives—http://imagi-natives.com

Library Jokes and Funs—www.librarybliss.com

Library, Librarian, and Librarianship Quotes—http://lis.gse.buffalo.edu/faculty/ellison/quotes/

Quotable Quotes About Libraries—www.ala.org/ala/aboutala/offices/ola/salquotablequotes.cfm

Quotations About Libraries and Librarians—www.ifla.org/I/humour/subj.htm

Quote Garden—www.quotegarden.com/libraries.html

Quotes on Reading and Literacy—www.literacyla.org/quotes.htm

Thinkexist—http://thinkexist.com

Valenza, Joyce K.—Power Tools Recharged. Chicago: American Library Association—2004.

Wikiquote—http://en.wikiquote.org

当你进入图书馆，准备好参加一场宏大的探险吧……因为在图书馆中有全部的世界，等待我们去发现。

塔季扬娜 · 埃斯克特兰德

编目员是少数自豪于细微末节之事的职业。

塔季扬娜 · 埃斯克特兰德

作者介绍:

塔季扬娜·埃斯克特兰德是位于康涅狄格州温莎的多诺霍小组（Donohue Group）的项目经理和资深编目员，多诺霍小组是一家服务于图书馆和博物馆的编目公司。在她二十年的职业生涯里，她指导过大学图书馆技术服务部门的建立。她从凯尼恩学院获得了文学士的学位，然后从布法罗大学获得了图书馆学硕士的学位。埃斯克特兰德参与编写了《同性恋艺术书目》一书，并且曾经参与加州大学圣迭戈分校的女权主义和同性恋研究的参考咨询工作。

青春之光

处世卷
CHUSHI JUAN

你的角落，别人的风景

一路开花／编

煤炭工业出版社
·北　京·

图书在版编目（CIP）数据

你的角落，别人的风景：处世卷／一路开花编．－－北京：煤炭工业出版社，2018（2021.7 重印）

（青春之光）

ISBN 978－7－5020－6658－1

Ⅰ.①你…　Ⅱ.①一…　Ⅲ.①散文集—中国—当代　Ⅳ.①I267

中国版本图书馆 CIP 数据核字(2018)第 097602 号

你的角落，别人的风景——处世卷（青春之光）

编　　者　一路开花
责任编辑　刘少辉
封面设计　宋双成

出版发行　煤炭工业出版社（北京市朝阳区芍药居 35 号　100029）
电　　话　010－84657898（总编室）
　　　　　　010－64018321（发行部）　010－84657880（读者服务部）
电子信箱　cciph612@126.com
网　　址　www.cciph.com.cn
印　　刷　唐山才智印刷有限公司
经　　销　全国新华书店

开　　本　880mm×1230mm $^{1}/_{32}$　**印张**　9　**字数**　240 千字
版　　次　2018 年 6 月第 1 版　2021 年 7 月第 2 次印刷
社内编号　20180308　　　　**定价**　58.00 元

CONTENTS 目録

第一辑

有信念就有好运气

他的朋友对他说："尼克斯，其实是你的信念带给你好运。是你的自信帮助了你，不是迷信。"的确，信心满怀地去做某一件事，成功的砝码在不知不觉中就增加了。相反，你对自己一点信心也没有，好运又怎么会降临到你的身上呢？

第二辑

做生活的“修补师”

我们总是在不断地追求更新鲜的事物，并在这种追求的过程中体会一种刺激和快感。可是，轻易地追求、丢弃，再追求、再丢弃，到最后我们会剩下什么？恐怕只有无以言表的失落和茫然。

第三辑

别把愤怒带回家

每天回家前，把烦恼、郁闷、愤怒，所有不开心的事，所有的坏情绪，全部丢开抛掉打扫干净，调整好情绪然后再回家。因为你把家里人弄得不开心时，你自己会更不开心。带上好心情回家，美好的生活需要大家一起去创造。

第四辑

占便宜其实是个套

其实，细细想来，占便宜说到底也不是什么好事，顾盼四周，大概还没有人因为占便宜而发家致富、飞黄腾达吧！但因为占便宜身败名裂、得不偿失的人却是大有人在。

第五辑

性格不决定人缘好坏

人际交往中，你话多话少没关系，性格内向外向也无关紧要，关键是看你品质如何，因此在我看来，一个人只要乐于助人，为人一副热心肠，不损人利己，懂得宽容与谅解，内心阳光正义，就能拥有好人缘。

第六辑

后退不一定失败

当我把实习锻炼当成人生积累，摒弃单纯追求利益得失时，我突然发现我的人生变了，变得开朗了，豁达了，也变得沉稳了，我也在这段时间里学到了职场里的很多东西，也学到了生命中的很多东西。

第一辑

有信念就有好运气

他的朋友对他说："尼克斯，其实是你的信念带给你好运。是你的自信帮助了你，不是迷信。"的确，信心满怀地去做某一件事，成功的砝码在不知不觉中就增加了。相反，你对自己一点信心也没有，好运又怎么会降临到你的身上呢？

父 爱

文/苏 童

父亲期望儿子比自己更加无可指摘，这是无可指摘的。

——普劳图斯

关于父爱，人们的发言一向是节制而平和的。母爱的伟大使我们忽略了父爱的存在和意义，但是对于许多人来说，父爱一直以特有的沉静的方式影响着他们。父爱怪就怪在这里，它是羞于表达的，疏于张扬的，却巍峨持重，所以有聪明人说，父爱如山。

前不久在去上海的旅途上带了一本消遣性的杂志乱翻，不经意间翻到了一篇并非消遣的文章，是一个美国人记叙他眼中的父爱的。

容我转述这个关于父爱的故事，虽说是一个美国人的父亲，但那个美国父亲多少年如一日为儿子榨橙汁的细节首先让我想到我的父亲。我父亲则是几十年如一日地早起，为儿女熬粥，直到儿女一个个离开家庭。

我一直在对比中读这篇文章，作者说他每次喝光父亲榨的橙汁后必然拥抱一下父亲，对父亲说一声我爱你，然后才出门。那个美国父亲则接受儿子的拥抱和爱，什么也不说。拥抱在西方的父子关系中是一门必备课，我从来就没拥抱过我的父亲，但我小时候每天第一眼看见父亲时必然会例行公事地叫一声：爸爸。

到我长大了一些，觉得天天这么叫有点烦人，心想不叫你你还是我爸爸，有时就企图蒙混过去。但我父亲采取的方式是走到你前面，用手指指着自己的鼻子，我就只好老老实实一如既往地叫：爸爸！

奇怪的是那美国儿子与我一样，他说他有一天也厌烦了这种例行公事的拥抱，喝了父亲的橙汁想径直溜出去，那个美国父亲就把儿子挡在门前了，说：你今天忘了什么吧？这时候我仍然在对比，我想换了我就顺势说，谢谢你提醒我，然后拥抱一下了事。

但美国的儿子毕竟与中国的儿子是不同的，他想得太多要得也太多，贸贸然提出了一个非常强硬的问题，说："爸爸，你为什么从来不说你爱我？"这个美国儿子逼着他父亲说那三个字，然后文章最让我感动的细节就出现了：那个父亲难以发出那个耳熟能详的声音，当他终于对儿子说出我爱你时，竟然难以自持，哭了出来！

我读到这儿差点也哭了出来，我仍然在对比我所感受的父爱。我想我永远不会逼着我父亲说我爱你，我与那个美国儿子惟一不同的是，知道就行了。父爱假如不用语言，那就让我们永远沐浴在这种无言的爱中吧。

载于《考试报》

古老相传，母亲给了我血肉，使我成长，而父亲却给了我骨骼，使我站立。父亲给了我一种启示，给了我教训，给了我一种暂时无法理解却受益终身的爱。而这种爱是父亲一生的付出。

不 急

文/寒　青

泰山崩于前而色不变，麋鹿兴于左而目不瞬，然后可以制利害，可以待敌。

——苏洵

人很容易急。自己吃亏了、上当受骗了、利益受损了……每每此时，人就容易急。而急的下一步，就是跟人言语相讥、针锋相对、据理力争、针尖对麦芒，一番刀光剑影下来，往往两败俱伤。自己不但没有讨回真理，却又白白惹了一肚子气，赔了夫人又折兵。有时由于愿望落空了，人也跟自己急，跟自己过不去，结果只能把自己弄得遍体鳞伤。所以，遇事不能急。

人生如行独木桥，一急，就容易慌张，一慌张就容易跌落下去，而桥下往往是急湍猛流或万丈深渊。人生亦如下棋。一着不慎满盘皆输。一急，就容易不慎，不慎就容易招致惨败。

不急。只能不急。

唐代名臣裴度在担任中书令期间，有一次，正准备和属下一起喝酒，就在吃饭前，一名手下慌张地跑来告诉他，大人，您的官印不见了！众人一听，也都着起急来，但他一点也不急，笑着对大家说，官印不可能丢，一定是放在什么地方忘记了，等想起来了自然就会找到了，并吩咐继续摆宴喝酒，欣赏歌舞。在整个过程中，他谈笑风生，好像根本就没发生过丢官印的事一样。深夜，酒足饭饱之后，众人正准备散去，这时，手下兴冲冲地来汇报，说那个官印还在，没有丢。大家都不明白是怎么回事，他笑了笑说，我一想啊，就是下面哪个小官把官印拿去盖私章了，如果大张旗鼓地去查，他一害怕，可能就把官印扔到水中或是火里，那时就真找不到了。如果先不处理，他就会悄悄地把官印送回来。众人听了，都称赞他遇事冷静，深思熟虑。

如果当时他十万火急，那么就不会有失而复得的局面，就不会有惊喜激荡他的胸怀，取而代之的是不可挽回的损失和挥之不去的郁闷。

可见，不急是一种心态、一种智慧和境界。有着不急之举的美国作家斯蒂芬·金，堪称我们学习的楷模。

20 世纪 70 年代，他发表了恐怖小说《魔女嘉莉》后声名鹊起。出版商里皮看中了他小说所含的巨大商机，对他说，只要你愿意写，我就会出高价买下你的小说版权。我敢保证，过不了多久你就会成为最富有的作家。他却答道，我还有更重要的事要做！两周后，他写出一个短篇小说，用笔名投给了杂志社。文章发表后，他兴奋地拿给大家看。当时，里皮也在场，于是惊诧地问，你拒绝我就是为了腾出时间写这个小东西？他点点头。里皮忍不住为他算起账来，你的稿费是 700 美元，这点钱和水管工的周薪差不多，值得你这个大作家花两周时间吗？他答道："当然。"之后，他用三个月创作出《玉米田的小孩》，经里皮出版后大卖，赚了不少钱。里皮希望他尽快再写一部，可他却摇摇头，我得停下来再写个小故事。他不顾里皮的催促，花了三周又创作了一个小故事，等发表后又开心地拿给里皮看，里皮终于不耐烦地说，你可是个有名的大作家，发表个豆腐块文章还这么开心。他说，人最怕的就是被成功冲昏头。所以我总是提醒自己要回到原点，以新人的身份再去写稿、投稿，这样才能保持创作的激情。

急功近利、急于求成……往往都是小人物之举，真正能成大器的人，不会如此慌张，因为他们懂得水到渠成、功到自然成的道理。这正好印证了《明心宝鉴》里的一句话："小家做事慌张，大家做事寻常。"

无论你有多急，每件事、每个事物都依然按照自己的速度前行，这就像两个人的约定一样，你早早地到了，而对方还没有到，你只能干着急，急着烦躁、抱怨甚至发疯……而就在你急的当儿，理智和冷静离你远去，而混乱和挫败则不请自来。

所以，不管你现在处境如何，不急，不急。要知道，不急者成事。

不急者犹如大海，经得起狂风暴雨的考验，而急躁者就像小水洼，就是一阵微风吹来，也能让他动荡不安。可见，要想做到不急，就必须拥有大胸怀和大境界。

载于《思维与智慧》

需要面对多少风浪，需要经历多少坎坷，我们才能学会去品这杯生活的酒？才能如此淡定从容？

台阶与人生

文/韩　松

人生并不像火车要通过每个站似的经过每一个生活阶段。人生总是直向前行走，从不留下什么。

——刘易斯

一

那天，带着三岁的儿子去县政府见一位文友。当我们到了一楼大厅后，我本能地朝电梯间走去，儿子却手舞足蹈地向楼梯跑去。我知道小家伙酷爱上台阶，那就满足他的心愿吧，虽然要见的文友在九楼。

儿子紧紧地抓住楼梯一边的栏杆，一步一步地向上挪移着。看着他吃力的样子，我用手扶着他，想助他一臂之力，结果他不领这份情，稚嫩的肩膀晃动着表示拒绝。小家伙，原来想玩自立啊。

于是我就“袖手旁观”，走在他后面，眼睛却时刻盯着他，生怕发生什么闪失，毕竟他只是三岁的孩子啊。

其实，人生也是这样。以为别人会需要我们的帮助，殊不知，那只是我们的一厢情愿，费力还不讨好，也就说该放手时就放手，给别人自立自主的机会，就像把天空交给鸟儿一样，给它飞翔的自由和快乐。

二

儿子也算是一个小胖子，当他吃力地到达四楼时，他那白皙的脸蛋早已变成了一个红扑扑的苹果。但他没有一丝一毫停下来的意思，一如既往地往上挪着，信心不减，热情不减。我把这叫作“向上的乐趣”。

其实，人生也是这样。只要有一个向上的目标追求着，生活就会撒满快乐的阳光，人生因此也变得温暖而美好。

三

儿子的额头已经渗出了细微的汗珠。看样子，儿子累得不轻。我有些心疼，想抱着他走一程，可是小家伙两手紧紧地抓住栏杆，表示拒绝和抗议。

我想起了英国思想家罗素。在20世纪30年代，有一次他在中国坐轿，他看到两个轿夫累得满头大汗，但他们谈天说地，有说有笑，于是他就问他们：“你们天天抬轿，不感到痛苦吗？”他们却说：“你看，我们不是很快乐吗？”后来他在《朴素的中国人》一书中写道：“不要自以为是地判断别人的快乐与幸福。”

其实，人生又何尝不是这样？

四

当我们到达六楼时，文友打电话催我，怎么还没有到吗？

我说，你再等一会儿。

他又问我，你在哪里啊？我说，我在等我儿子。他不解，继续问我，你儿子在哪里啊？我说，在台阶上啊，他走得慢，我们没有坐电梯……

其实人生也是这样，需要等待，就像此刻，文友等我，我等儿子。而这彼此的等待多像这一层一层的台阶，连接着我们的默契、快乐与和谐。

这使我想起了一组漫画：第一幅画上是一个缺了一只角的圆，由于缺角而变得不灵活，只能滚一下停一下，因此走得很慢，但是它一边唱歌一边欣赏路边的美景；第二幅画上还是这个圆，不同的是它找到了缺失的那只角，装上了角后，它再沿原路返回，可这次它却越滚越快，路边的景色欣赏不到了，歌也唱不成了。

我们就像这个圆一样，不停地在人生的道路上前行着，而等待就是那缺失的角，虽然看起来很碍事，占用了我们宝贵的时间，但是如果没有了它，我们的生活就会变得索然无味。

五

我们终于到达了九楼。这时儿子可能真的累了，他很听话地跟着我来到了文友的办公室。后来，我带着他坐电梯下楼时，他也没有“抗议”。可是我仍然在思索着台阶。

人生跟台阶多么相似啊，都连接着高处，而且每走一步都是进步，距离你的目标也越来越近。有谁不憧憬这样的人生？可是，人生又不同于台阶。罗曼·罗兰说：“人生不售回程的票，一旦出发，就绝不能返回。”而台阶可以自由地上上下下。因此，只有慎重地走好每一步，认真地做好每一件事，用心地珍惜好每一寸光阴，我们的人生才会远离遗憾与后悔。要知道，人生的台阶，只向前蔓延，绝不给你退路，哪怕仅仅是半步。

载于《思维与智慧》

人生就是单行道，不能复制，不能回头。我们能做的就是一直往前，不留遗憾。

与尘世握手言欢

文/梅　雪

我相信，现在未能把握的生命是没有把握的；现在未能享受的生命是无以享受的；而现在未能明智地度过的生命是难以过得明智的；因为过去的已过去，而无人得知未来。

——葛雷

走在黄昏的街头，有清幽的歌声轻飘过来：朝开而暮落的木槿花，月夜低头啊，心里想着他，记忆着已经流逝的那一段时光……是袁泉的《木槿花》。锦素年华时，爱情就是盛开在青春里的木槿花吧，大朵，明艳。若在多年以前，听上这样的歌，一定会泪眼蒙眬，情绪无端地低落，仿佛字字句句都是针，很有点“为赋新词强说愁”的矫情，那短暂的花期更易怅然若失。呵呵，多么沧桑的“多年以前”。而今，中年像洗得泛白的棉布衫，晾挂在光阴的风口，色渐渐地淡去，“潦水尽而寒潭清”般简素、清明。再次聆听，依然能触碰到心底最深处的柔软和脆弱。只是念起那些沉隐在岁月深处的点点滴滴，不再是满心霜意，而像这六月木槿般，淡淡的芬芳里有着贴心的暖。世间所有的苦痛与纠结，都被时光所收藏，像卵石散落在流年的河床。多年以后，拾起，放在手心里静静地赏，一颗，便是一个真情实意的记忆。

网上与友相遇，她笑问道：久不见人，亦不见文，哪去了？心顿生暖意，为这份陌生而熟悉的关心。微笑地敲下一行字："行走在烟火人生里。"

笃立在时间的长河里，回望来时路，感慨良多。蔼蔼红尘里，追逐着梦想的苦旅者，一路水迢迢，山遥遥，一程山水一程景，萧索失意的心情如影随形，纵然是美景良辰，也或浓或淡地染上袅袅的愁绪。快乐站在路口，像和家人失散已久的孩子，殷殷地等待一双手的温柔相牵。怨也罢，叹也好，追不回流逝的旧时光。不如重新上路，在庭院，在公园，在郊野，沐浴着阳光晴好，清风拂面，分享着草木的安宁静然。于一片青黄叶片上，寻找秋的痕迹；看一颗晶莹的露珠在荷叶上，来来回回地滚动；看珠光宝气的蚕不遗余力地吐丝结茧，化蛹成蝶，演绎着生命的神奇和价值。

自然万物如禅者无言，自斟自饮一杯岁月静好的酒，她们用绵绵无尽的绿意，把我们的一生温柔地牵绊，有什么理由不珍惜这烟火人生里的所有呢？

静下心来，坐看春深，细细回味那些如常日子里细小的美好。晚饭后，漫步到广场，儿子踩着彩灯滑轮随我左右。衣着明艳的大妈姐妹们跳着欢快的舞蹈，舒缓、强劲的旋律，整齐有致的舞步和脸上洋溢的笑容，无不感染着围观的人群。那是平凡的人们热爱生活的独特表达方式，和对幸福快乐的不懈追求。褐色的木椅上，家长们排成坐，关切的目光追逐着玩耍的孩子们。满头大汗的儿子娴熟地滑过来，赶忙递上水，叮嘱两句，又风一般溜远了。看这尘世间细碎的快乐，谁能拒绝快乐来敲门？下班绕到菜市场，经过一家豆腐摊，年轻的女摊主微笑地招呼，你不常买菜吧，没怎么见过你。嘴里应着，心里窃喜，菜市若是小江湖，莫非我这身衣袂飘然，不像这江湖中人？

流光抛人去，唯有这不咸不淡的缕缕烟火气息，才是人世间最朴素最恒远的生命背景。曾经有人问朱天文，为何不再写小说？她说我心里有一种就此不写了的冲动，因为再怎么写，也写不过生活本身。是啊，生活赐予了我们好时光蓬勃成长，然而，生活又强悍地追逐着年轻的容颜，一任花自飘零水自流。生活本无心，生者可有意。所以，让我们难以割舍的便是琐碎生活里这些不经意的种种。不经意的想起，依依心念的，仍是最初的本心。

渐走渐深的夜，与一些有着体温的往事一而再地重逢。且许我浮一大白，和尘世握手言欢，心随浮云，意赋花开，从此后，让快乐成双。

载于《散文百家》

社会何其喧嚣，逼仄的环境，鼎沸的人群，何不走出去，去感受自然的魅力。像飞鸟一样，飞到那明媚的山峦和蓝色的海角，只有风在飞舞，还有音乐做伴。

时来运转的登徒子

文/水玉兰

历史本身是自然史的一个现实的部分，是自然生成为人这一过程的一个现实的部分。

——卡尔·马克思

如果要说谁是这世上第一倒霉蛋，我想非登徒子莫属。打一次小报告，就落得个遗臭万年的下场。姑且不去猜测当年打小报告的登徒子究竟带着"君家事便是国家事"防患于未然的心态多一些，还是嫉妒成分多一些，总之一场口水战，让自己活时身败名裂，死后遗臭万年。足以见文人口诛笔伐的功夫丝毫不次于刀枪剑戟的杀伤力。

士大夫登徒子面奏楚王，说文学侍从宋玉，相貌俊美，能言会道，但为人好色，请大王以后不要让他任意出入后宫，以免生出不好的事情。楚王听了，很是震惊，唤来宋玉诘问。宋玉回答："容貌俊美，乃父母所生；口才好，得老师所传；至于好色，绝无此事。"为了刷清自己，宋玉苦思冥想写下了一篇流传后世的文章——《登徒子好色赋》。

大意是："天下的美女，要数楚国女子最美。楚国的美女，要数我家乡的女子最靓，而我家乡最美的姑娘还得数与我隔邻的东家小姐。东家小姐，貌美如仙，一笑倾城。这样一位姿色绝伦的美女，趴在墙上整整窥视我三年，我至今仍未答应和她相处。而登徒子呢，他的妻子蓬头垢面，耳朵斜，龅牙，豁嘴，弯腰驼背，走路一瘸一拐，满身的疥疾还有严重的痔疮。这样一位丑陋妇女，登徒子仍然和她生了五个孩子……请大王想想，究竟谁好色呢？”楚王想想应该是登徒子好色了。

至此后，宋玉便成了品行方正视美女如空气的正人君子，而登徒子便成了饥不择食大色狼的代名词。但凡有一点头脑的人，都可瞧出，宋玉对墙上美女无动于衷，却清楚美女偷看了他整整三年时间。知晓别人家老婆是豁嘴倒也罢了，竟然连痔疮也了解得一清二楚。这难免有点离谱，离谱到失去品味。

文人口诛笔伐，看似拼的是文采，实则拼得是一种看不见的内功。一个字一句话便可以变成利剑射向对手、射穿对方的心脏。头脑简单兼迂腐的登徒子真是有点不自量力，也不想想你挑战的是何等人。著名辞赋家，想象力惊人，一篇精美绝伦的《神女赋》，把天上的神女都请了下来和楚王缠绵了一把。可想而知，这灰头土脸还不是自找的？

换言之，如果登徒子挑战的是一位武将，顶多拳头耳光，落个鼻青眼肿，几日羞于见人。再糟糕也不过伤筋动骨卧床一百天，怎么着也不至于遗臭万年，害得子孙后代跟着抬不起头。想到此，猜想登徒老夫子临终咽气的时候肠子恐怕还是青的。

然而，世间事就是这么变幻莫测，倒霉蛋登徒子不会想到自己也有咸鱼翻身的时候。背负两千年臭名的他渐渐不再招人唾弃，甚至人气上浮有了粉丝。朋友的表妹，长相、学历、工作均属上乘，却迟迟待字闺中，朋友奉姑妈命向表妹打探心意。表妹回答得很干脆，想找一登徒子似的男人。朋友笑翻，说你何至于把自己想得如此不济。

表妹说，你想登徒子老婆如此不堪，他都不忍丢弃，还给他生了五个孩子，娶我为妻，还不把我视为天人哪。是啊，想那个时代，三妻四妾是男人身份的象征，即使不忍休了丢颜面的丑婆娘，束之高阁总可以吧，何以生出5个孩子来？可见登徒子即使不是弱水三千独取一歪瓢饮的痴汉，也算是有担当的男人。这担当二字的光芒丝毫不逊于豪宅与宝马车，日益丰饶的物质精神生活，给了你几多自信，就附加给你几多不安全感。担当怎能不让人求之若渴啊。

当年凭借一篇文章斗败了登徒子的宋玉，如何也不会想到，同样还是那篇得意之作，又把登徒子那老夫子捧上了天。此一时彼一时，世间事，就是这样变幻莫测。

人还是那人，文还是那文，事还是那事，评价却是随着斗移星转相差十万八千里。记不得谁说过的一句话：“世间事，往往是最近的距离看得最模糊，最远的距离看得最清晰。”千古事，好多不都是留给后人来定论的吗？

载于《知识窗》

滚滚长江东逝水，浪花淘尽英雄。是非成败转头空，青山依旧在，几度夕阳红；白发渔樵江渚上，惯看秋月春风。一壶浊酒喜相逢，古今多少事，都付笑谈中。

有信念就有好运气

文/庞启帆 编译

人生应该如蜡烛一样，从顶燃到底，一直都是光明的。

——萧楚女

尼克斯从来不迷信。

一天早上，尼克斯在刮脸的时候，注意到墙上的镜子有些歪了，便伸手去把镜子扶正，没想到镜子从墙上掉了下来，碎了。尼克斯记得有人曾说过，“打烂一面镜子，要倒霉7年”。但尼克斯认为这纯粹是胡说。

上班时，尼克斯把这事告诉了他的几个同事。“今天你要倒霉了。”他们都说。但什么坏事情也没发生。

下班后，尼克斯买了几注彩票。结果，他中了一等奖。这简直令人难以置信。大家认为在他身上所发生的事情会给他带来霉运，没想到竟然给他带来了好运！

第二天，尼克斯买了一本关于迷信的书，书上讲的都是世界各地关于迷信的说法。读完书后，他决定每件事都做一遍，看这些事是否会给他带来霉运。然而，随着他做的事情越多，他的运气就越好。他再次赢得了彩票。在酒馆玩骰子游戏，他几乎都赢。事情变得越来越疯狂。在某一天早晨，他还故意又打烂了几面镜子。

“你们看，”尼克斯对他的朋友说，“一切都好得不得了！那些荒谬的事情我做得越多，我就越幸运。”

“但是尼克斯，”他的一个朋友回应道，“你难道没察觉，其实你像我们一样迷信？当你看到打破迷信反而给你带来好运的时候，你更执着于去做那些事情，你的所为本身就是一种迷信。”

尼克斯认真想了朋友所说的话。然后，他承认确实是那样。他是那么执着去打破那些迷信，但在某种程度上，他确实是在注意那些迷信。第二天，他不再做那些迷信的事情。他又做回了以前的那个尼克斯，有时候运气好，有时候不好。

他的朋友对他说：“尼克斯，其实是你的信念带给你好运。是你的自信帮助了你，不是迷信。”

的确，信心满怀地去做某一件事，成功的砝码在不知不觉中就增加了。相反，你对自己一点信心也没有，好运又怎么会降临到你的身上呢？

载于《儿童文学·选粹》

信念就是最好的预测师，当你坚定一件事时，这件事更容易变成现实。

只问耕耘

文/思想者

锲而舍之朽木不折，锲而不舍金石可镂。

——荀子

就这样默默地埋头写作，辛勤地耕耘着自己的“一亩三分地”，至于收获则不是我们所能企求的。

不论是一国的总统、大公司的老总，还是个体从业者，抑或是一个普通的农民，都有自己的“一亩三分地”，虽然种的“庄稼”各不相同，但是每个人都渴望丰收。

有的时候，我们太看重结果，还没付出就妄想得到，总是好高骛远，而往往忽视了脚下的泥土，懈怠了每天的耕耘。因为心的力量分散了，我们三心二意地经营着自己的事业，到头来，收获寥寥，只有叹息。

同样都是“种地”，为什么有的人丰收，有的人总是歉收呢?

这里面有客观的原因。比如说，有的地在高岗上，土壤肥沃，遇到雨水大的天气也不会发生涝灾；有的地在低洼处，土质贫瘠，庄稼因先天不足而生长缓慢，收成当然不尽如人意了。此外，种地靠天，也非人力所能左右的。

可是，主观因素起着决定的作用，丰收还是歉收往往取决于你是否用心地耕耘。种地分人，再好的土地如果遇到懒惰的人，也不会有大的收获；再差的土地如果遇到勤劳的人，那么总有一年会丰收。

虽然每个人的事业有大有小，但是，相对来说，都是一亩三分地。土地是不会欺人的，它只青睐那些肯付出汗水的人。

你看台上演戏的人，他们把角色演得惟妙惟肖，殊不知，“台上一分钟，台下十年功”，他们成功的背后不知要付出多少汗水啊！

再看那些有成就的大作家，也并非一夜成名的。要知道，“板凳须坐十年冷”，“字字看来皆是血”，此中滋味又有谁能真正理解和体会呢？

冰心说：“成功的花儿，人们只惊羡它现时的明艳，然而当初她的芽儿，浸透了奋斗的泪泉，洒遍了牺牲的血雨。”

于是，我们懂得了成功与付出之间的内在关系，几分耕耘才能换得一分收获，这世上没有谁能随随便便成功。人生应抱着这样的态度，只问耕耘，莫问收获，因为收获正蕴藏在默默耕耘的过程中。

载于《档案天地》

对于一件事情的成败，不要去在乎，只是去努力做就好了。在意得多了就容易分散注意力，从而出现焦虑、失落、焦急、不耐烦等情绪。这样是不利于人的。

从普通人做起

文/李军民

不要光赞美高耸的东西，平原和丘陵也一样不朽。

——菲·贝利

煤矿工人被誉为开采光明的人，多年前我有幸成了其中一员。

16 岁初中毕业，考虑到我的学习成绩和家庭经济状况，父母一合计，给我报了矿务局技校，因为上技校既无经济负担，也无竞争之虞，而且三年以后我就可以成为煤矿的正式职工，何乐而不为！

一位与我一起放弃上高中考了技校的同学怕被别人嘲笑，见了同学绕着道躲着走。我设身处地安慰他，个人的实际情况和志向不同，不一定人人都要上大学，往一条道儿上挤。上大学是实现自身价值的一条重要途径，但不是唯一途径，也不是炫耀的资本，只要是通过正当渠道，做一个自食其力的人就是光荣的。并不是安于现状，而是量力而行；并不是没有追求，而是面对现实。为什么非到碰得头破血流、鼻青脸肿才知回头？有舍才有得，往一条路上挤，条件不具备，即使成功了也是侥幸。况且，那些嘲笑我们的同学自己也好不到哪里去，三年以后他们说不准还不如咱们呢！

三年的学习平淡无奇，半年的实习也按部就班，因为就在家门口上学，领略不到外面世界的精彩，与那些在外读书的孩子们相比可能我们缺少了对社会的了解，但是我们借助于企业的精心培养，拥有了足以养活自己及家人的一技之长。我入学时说的那句话最终得到了应验，真有同学三年以后没考上大学返回来上了技校，他们入学的时候我们已经参加了工作挣到了工资。

分配到煤矿以后，我和同学们被安排在井下一线。我的胆子比较小，下井以后跟在师父后面亦步亦趋，不敢跑远了。黑魆魆的巷道，冷飕飕的凉风。身上穿着宽大的工作服，脚上是笨重的黑胶靴。我一边走，一边抬头看顶板，低头看脚下。头上的塑胶帽壳被顶板的木板磕碰得“砰砰”直响。先开始坐“猴车”时怎么也跳不上去，钻液压支架时低不下头弯不下腰，割煤机开动后扬起来的煤尘呛得我直咳嗽。老师和师傅们讲过，煤矿事故不可预测，水、火、瓦斯、顶板、运输，各类事故稍不留神就会出现，死亡如影随形随时可能发生。因此，巷道一有气味我就担心有瓦斯涌出，顶板一有煤面子往下漏我就害怕冒顶。一个字，怕！后来慢慢摸准规律，对规程了解透彻了，各种情况经见得多了，也就不再害怕。

煤矿是一个高危行业，马虎不得，含糊不得，从事井下管理必须有基层工作经验、井下工作阅历，抓基层，打基础，苦练基本功，采、掘、机、运、通样样精通，不在每个系统干干，不知道工作流程绝对不行。事实就是这样，技校毕业以后大家不仅扎实工作，而且虚心好学，好多人上了各种函授刊授学校，使理论和实践得到有机结合，学的知识能够落了地，变成生产力，绝不是空中楼阁。有些人获得全省、全国科技进步奖，还有的获得政府津贴。大部分技校生从井下一线干起，许多人积累了丰富的管理经验，从队长、区长、科长、副矿长一路升上来，最后成了关键岗位的领导。在工余时间，我对知识的渴求也不曾懈怠，每年读各类书平均40多本，做不少于10万字的笔记，提升自己的思想修养。因为工作踏实，阅历丰富，我被组织选择从事煤矿办公室管理工作，后来又做了局里的人力资源管理工作。

当这个社会竞争日趋激烈，找工作成了难上加难的事情之后，许多大学毕业的矿区子弟回到矿务局安身立命，局里挤出就业岗位安排他们在矿上工作。大部分大学毕业生是好的，但也有一些大学生参加工作后，只想着如何评定职称，进入管理岗，当上技术员，提拔为科长，再一步步提拔为矿长、局长，完全忽略了从最基层井下一线干起，从一名普通的矿工做起打好基础。许多人在纠结中慢慢消磨了意志，丧失了信心，荒废了事业。作为煤矿的领导觉得最好用的一是退伍兵，二是技校生，然后才是大学生。人们开玩笑说，技校生出来当了领导，而大学生出来却当了工人。

实践证明，生存是第一位的，工作可能不是你理想的事业，但掌握一技之长是必需的。爱好是不可缺少的，在你陷入泥沼时它能拯救你，在你身处逆境时它能激励你，在你落寞无助时它能陪伴你。

追求的目标可以远大一些，但现实生活中必须脚踏实地。找一份工作养活自己，有一个爱好丰富的人生。不好高骛远，不华而不实。条条大路通罗马，做一个普通人未尝不可，从普通人做起，走得也许比别人还要远。

载于《才智》

每个人都应当在自己平凡的岗位上努力奋斗。就像平凡的世界里的孙少平。纵使生活中有太多荒芜，可是还依然要热爱生活。

知识点亮人生

文/林　子

知识就像烛光，能照亮一个人，也能照亮无数的人。

——谚语

人生需要用知识来点亮，才能终见光明。

或许很多年轻人有过这样的经历：最初对未来充满美好的憧憬，也想出人头地。可是，现实是残酷的，遭遇的失败和困惑常常让人苦恼，无论你怎样挣扎、呐喊，都不能摆脱命运的捉弄。就好像命运有一双看不见的手，无情地将你推进一个巨大的黑洞里，使你看不到人生的一丝光明。日子就这样在浑浑噩噩、跌跌绊绊中度过。

那么，朋友，不要悲伤，不要叹息，也不要忧郁，知识就是点亮人生的火炬，请你将它高高地擎起！

请相信，知识会让你聪慧。只要你肯努力地去追求，就能得到它。你会变得聪明，然后运用智慧去化解命运的魔力，从而摆脱困境。

请相信，知识会让你坚强，支撑你在人生的道路上无所畏惧地走下去，从容地笑对人生。

请相信，知识会让你充满力量。因为知识的里面潜藏着爱的因子，只要将它融入内心，就能使你焕发活力，释放生命的潜能。这力量足以撬动命运的磐石，让人生的轨迹发生偏转，我们怎能为之不动容？

请相信，知识会让你海阔天空。没有知识的人，他的路注定是窄的，也不能走得很远。倘若有了知识，海阔凭鱼跃，天空任飞鸟，你才能施展才华，人生的舞台将随心而变大，精彩的演绎会与众不同。

人生的路就是这样曲曲折折，有低谷，也有高峰。当你的人生不经意地走进黑夜的时候，请别忘记带上知识的火炬，因为只有知识才能让你走出无边的黑暗，迎来黎明！

载于《中学生》

一个人赤条条地来到世界，就像一只空的杯子，是没有根基的。而知识就好比是不断加入的水，有了知识，杯子才逐渐有了分量。

再多走一步

文/蒋光宇

在希望与失望的决斗中，如果你用勇气与坚决的双手紧握着，胜利必属于希望。

——普里尼

有一天，俄罗斯的著名作家克雷洛夫正在大街上行走，一个年轻的农民拦住他，向他兜售苹果："先生，请你买些果子吧，但我要告诉你，这筐果子有点酸，因为我是第一次学种果树。"年轻的农民很笨拙地说着。

克雷洛夫对这个憨厚、诚实的农民产生好感，于是买了几个果子，然后说："小伙子，别灰心，只要努力，以后种的果子就会慢慢地甜起来了，因为我种的第一个果子也是酸的。"

农民听了之后很高兴，认为自己碰到了一个"同行"，因而高兴地问："你也种过果树?"

克雷洛夫笑着解释说："我的第一个果子是我写的《用咖啡渣占卜的女人》，可是这个剧本直到现在也没有一个剧院愿意上演。"

与克雷洛夫的写作命运相近，海明威最初寄出的几十个短篇全部被退了回来；莫泊桑直到30岁才发表第一篇作品。

其实，第一个果实常常是酸的，这在生活中是一个到处可以看到的普遍现象。

曾被纽约世界美术协会推举为当代第一大画家的张大千先生，博采众长，独成一家，绘画技艺高超。他的许多代表作，都被世界各国的美术家们公认为世界美术宝库中的珍品。然而鲜为人知的是，在张大千先生的艺术生涯中，他第一次成功的画作卖出后仅换得80个铜板。在当时，80个铜板只能买2斤腊肉。张大千先生这一个成功之果并未给他带来丰厚的报酬，但他并未因此而放弃追求成功的决心和努力。

英国作家萧伯纳在初学写作之时，给自己规定每日必须完成5页稿子的写作任务。就这样苦苦写了4年，总共才得到30英镑的稿费。但萧伯纳并未因此而灰心丧气，而是鼓起勇气继续写作。又这样苦苦写了4年，陆续写出了5部长篇小说，先后向60多家出版社投稿，全部遭到无情的拒绝。在退稿信上，有的编辑甚至直言不讳地说，他根本不是写作的材料，并劝他放弃自己的写作生涯。但萧伯纳仍然坚持，坚持每天写一定数量的文章。又继续这样苦苦写了4年，天道酬勤，他终于成为英国20世纪最伟大的作家之一。

萧伯纳曾经说过这样一段充满哲理的话：

“多走一步，就可以缩短一步接近成功的距离。胜利就在前方，你的任务就是坚持，就是再多走一步！”

只要坚持，永不言弃，我们的明天就会充满阳光，充满成功的喜悦。因为我们都知道：坚持的昨天叫立足，坚持的今天叫进取，坚持的明天才叫成功。

神木底下难乘凉

文/贾子安

不管我们的成绩有多么大，我们仍然应该清醒地估计敌人的力量，提高警惕，决不容许在自己的队伍中有骄傲自大、安然自得和疏忽大意的情绪。

——斯大林

研究生毕业后，我到一家公司任职，具体工作是为大企业做广告策划。由于我学历高，头脑灵活，沟通表达能力强，办事效率高，所以被老板任命为策划部副主任。

对于一个初入职场的人来说，能受到老板如此青睐，自然心里非常高兴，我发誓一定要殚精竭虑，报答老板的知遇之恩。于是我全身心地投入到工作中，每天第一个到公司，最后一个离开。为了修改方案，我常常加班到深夜。有时候突然想到一个好的想法，我便会迫不及待地与同事商讨，不管是吃饭或休息时间。

刚开始，我能感觉到属下的兄弟们同我一样热血沸腾。大家都希望把这些策划活动做到尽善尽美，这样不仅提高公司的声誉，也会给自己增加收入。确实，对于这些漂泊异乡的打工者来说，再也没有比挣钱更重要的了。因此，他们都积极配合着我，不断地开展各种调查和研究，提各种建议和意见。

但不久之后，我就发觉情形变了：大家的热情似乎不那么高涨了，我提出什么想法，大家也不再热烈地讨论，当我休息时间给他们电话沟通工作的时候，我能感觉到他们语气中隐忍着的不耐烦。

我很苦恼。但我还是咬着牙坚持着，最后终于完成了企业策划。没有想到这次策划非常成功，吸引了各大媒体的记者纷纷前来报道，那家企业也非常满意，公司在业界也声名鹊起，来签订广告业务的大企业接踵而至。我们策划部集体受到老板的奖励，大家的奖金也翻了几倍。

原以为手下的兄弟们会欣喜若狂，会由衷地感激我，但没有想到他们对我的态度依旧冷淡，只要是我分配的任务，他们的积极性都不高，虽然没有消极怠工，但再也没有从前的热情和那种心心相印的感觉了。

我沮丧极了，愤然向老板辞职。面对职场第一次失败的经历，我百思不得其解，为何他们都因我而受益，但为什么非但不感激我，还竟然会排斥我呢？

回到家里，我向父亲倾诉自己的烦恼，原以为会得到父亲的安慰，没有想到父亲只是微微笑着，一言不发，拉着我的手向村口走去。

村口，那棵参天之木直插云霄，枝繁叶茂，旁逸斜出，郁郁葱葱，没有人能说出它的年龄，由于它实在太高大了，是普通白杨树的两倍以上，被村里人称为“神木”。但说也奇怪，鸟雀从来不在其上筑巢，而是将窝筑在普通的杨树上，东一个，西一个，远远望去，像村庄妩媚的眼睛。

走到神木下，父亲对我说：“孩子，天气这样热，让我们在神木下乘凉吧。”

“爸，神木这样高，它的枝叶虽然繁茂，但根本挡不住阳光，人是无法在它下面乘凉的。”我迷惑不解地望着父亲，心想，父亲是不是有些老糊涂了，怎么会忘记乡亲们是从来不在神木下乘凉的。

父亲爽朗地笑了。“孩子，你是知道的，神木底下难乘凉。你非常优秀，这是不假。在同事中间，你无异于一棵神木，你对待工作的热情和处理问题的能力令周围的人跟不上，你也很少采纳别人的建议和意见，于是少有人愿意与你合作，即使你取得成功，也少有人愿意与你分享。与其做一棵神木，不如让自己成为一片森林。孩子啊，你要学着广交朋友，有朋友的扶持和帮助，你才能更好地实现自己的人生价值。”

父亲的话不啻于醍醐灌顶，我豁然开朗，笼罩在心头的迷雾也消散一空。是啊，神木底下难乘凉。仔细想想，我们身边也常常有一些非常优秀的人，他们聪明，有能力，有激情，却不容易与之共事。因为他们太过聪明，所以不相信别人，听不进别人的忠告和提醒，这样就很容易陷入偏执的误区，导致困难来临时没有可以分享想法与分担压力的朋友，从而导致彻底的失败。

从此，我谨记“神木底下难乘凉”的教训，放低姿态，真诚地关心关注身边的每一个人，虽然在竞争非常激烈的职场，大家仍然与我交朋友，互相扶持与帮助，我的人生之路也越走越宽广。

朋友，别让你的生命里，只有自己这棵高耸的神木，神木巨大，但却孤单，认识更多的好朋友，聚集成一片森林，那才会成就你生命中更壮观的风景。

载于《人生与伴侣》

优秀本不是件坏事，关键在于优秀的时候，是不是记得回头看看，别人能否跟上自己的脚步。不然，就只能一个人越走越远，最终就会被孤立。一个人走远是远远不够的，一群人一起走远才是成功。

赤橙黄绿是生活

文/小　菁

生活的乐趣取决于生活的本身，而不是取决于工作或地点。

——爱默生

冬日的下午抑或夏晨，京城，常常可见一个人，衣着朴素，穿行在大小的书市，进去，出来，夹了三五本书，回家摆上书柜，“最近，新进的书都快满一格了！”他搓搓手，满足地说……

“真幸福呐！”我悠然神往，“这很正常，我身边的朋友几乎都这样。”他不以为然，“还得再去买，要不有一些看上的书会折磨我，一定要把它们买回来！”

不几天，这个人和他的书，又伴行在回家的路上，那书与屋，又飘散出纸墨的香。

这个人，在离我很远的地方，可是有一天，他突然出现在我面前：“小菁，我在博客上看了你的文字，所谓文如其人，我就以文看人吧。一、你是性情中人，敏感而细腻；二、你喜欢文字，特别是散文类，这与你的思维结构有关系，你感觉丰富，这样的文体正好适合你；三、你的外表和内心是矛盾的，外表看似有些冷，其实内心火热；四、矛盾的地方还不仅于此，表面看你做事一板一眼，很有章法，一般人会觉得你很有主见，其实，你经常缺少自信（抱歉）；五……”那一刻，我产生一种错觉，这人，难道是我的一个熟人？又或者，是我的哪位亲朋？好熟悉的陌生人。之后，每好奇问起此事，他都只淡淡说了两字：感觉！

“话不在多，关键是言之有物。”他说。所以他总是沉静、少语，可一聊起文字，就变得滔滔不已：“小菁，我完全被你浸透于文字中的真诚和你对文字的执着所感动，我有预感，你一定会成为一名好作者！”

心头窃喜，耳边却掠过这样的冷语：“你有自己的天赋，有许多别人没有的东西，可是有时候没有章法，显得有些‘疯长’。你需要越一个坎，把文章写得平实些，把人物写好，就特别好看！”

“你需要我这样一个读者，但是要有承受力，我是冷的。”

果真，新文一成，他就来对我说：“看了，顽疾依然。‘婉约’和‘悱恻’都是你写上去的，与女人无关。不是你说她看纳兰词，就‘婉约’了，也不是你写她在月夜下徘徊几圈，就‘悱恻’了。‘文是人样子’，情调一定是文中人行为举止的凝练，感觉一定要留给读者去品味。小菁，不能这样为文，太虚了。苛刻，见谅。”

我那时有点像《藤野先生》里鲁迅挨了先生批的情形，口里答应着，心下却想，文我写得还是不错的，至于道理呢，我自然知道，就和他争辩：“读者非得亲眼看到吗，他们不能直接进入我的情感世界吗？”

“读者是神仙吗？你说一句‘我很激动’，他们就能想象你激动的样子？你说一句‘我非常悲伤’，他们就能看见你泪流满面？因为是你的感受，光靠虚词和句子，读者感觉不到！我说100遍了，你不要去总结，就写具体的事情经过，就写细节、画面！”

“好作者，都是把虚词化作具体的景色和情境，蹩脚的作者才将精彩的场景用虚词来概括！特别拙！”“记住：你把画面交给读者，你就完成你的任务了！”

他稍稍停顿，又说：“小菁，有时间多看看书，不要忙着写东西，积累多了，感觉自然不一样，要不总觉得自己单薄。看看人家怎么写的，琢磨琢磨，你的文字，有时用的劲儿不对，比较硬，要注意柔韧。”

我有些疑惑，又惭愧，这么多年了，早不看书了，况且从哪儿看起呢，书那么多……

“不能不看，很多人拿时间来说事，翻几页书的空都没有，那该有多忙啊?!”

“我给你推荐几本书，我想想，给你列个书单子，让你闷头看一阵。”

“老师布置作业了！”我偷笑。

他不笑，严肃地说：“是！”

“不能急功近利，如果你希望文字纯净，心就要安静！”

是的，静下来看，沉下来看！他让我明白，读书、写作是人们的一种生活方式，它存活于人们的日子里，天天读书，天天生活！

赤橙黄绿是生活；酸甜苦辣是生活；读书、写作是生活；听曲、看片是生活……

他说：“书和碟是我生活中的最大消费，我有几千张碟，听了20多年音乐，这些，便是一个世界！每每看着，便觉得生活很美好！”

他有些沉醉："你知道喜欢是什么概念吗？就是没有不行！我反复地听，去大学给学生讲，到电台客座当主持。有外国乐团来演出，期刊会约我预先写稿子介绍演出的曲目。电影，也是这样，比较投入地看，从导演到摄影，体味妙境。"

我禁不住赞道："大哥，您可真算得上一位高人！"

"高人？没有，只有勤奋之人。"他很快回答。

随即又来一句："不是高人，而是喜爱生活之人！"

偶尔，他会打来电话说："小菁，忽然想念起你请我吃过的猪肚包鸡了。"隔一会儿，又来："好吃！真好吃！感觉那鸡的香气，直穿过话筒钻进鼻子了。"每逢这时，他就"原形毕露"话突然多起来："小菁，我要去你们那呢，不为风景，我要去吃小吃，排档那种……"

我想起他说过，新买了本汪曾祺的散文集《五味》，笑他："大哥，发现你特别喜欢谈吃的文章呢，汪曾祺的文字散淡、有味，是吗？"他呵呵笑，却又正色，说："你去看看，几乎所有的大师都有自己谈吃的文章，我喜欢汪的文字，不仅仅是有味，那更是千锤百炼的文字，大师之笔。"

民以食为天，我知道，这些早在他的文字间，"小时候，姥姥从老家来，曾经给我们做过这道鲶鱼炖茄子。记得菜端上来，喷香扑鼻，引得我和妹妹没了规矩。大人还没就位，我俩就你一筷子我一筷子地享用起来"；连声都有，"吃食好还得会吆喝，正月十五卖元宵，吆喝出来极豁亮：'筋道嘞滑透，桂花味的什锦馅的元宵啊，刚出锅的嘞！'"，朴实、悠长、醇厚、回香，这些原本就是生活的味道。

这人，俗得可爱，雅得可敬；有时可畏，却又可亲……

这么絮叨的时候，就看到他从书中抬头，皱眉："小菁，你又忍不住跳出来了，千万别自己去说，记住：就写画面，写生活！”

载于《做人与处世》

每个人都有自己的生活态度，只有亲近生活的人才是可以谈态度的。

学习是一种能力

文/好彩自来

在寻求真理的长河中，唯有学习，不断地学习，勤奋地学习，有创造性地学习，才能越重山跨峻岭。

——华罗庚

学习无论是对人还是对动物而言，最初都是一种本能。所不同的是，前者是有意识地去学习，而后者则无此意识。

雏鹰学习飞翔，羚羊学习奔跑，虎豹学习捕食，这种能力的获得都是自发的学习行为，只是为了生存的需要，体现了“物竞天择，适者生存”的自然法则。

而人从自然界进化出来以后，就有了自觉的学习意识。学习不再是自发的行为，也不仅仅是为了填饱肚子，更多的是为了认识世界，拥有掌握和驾驭自然界客观规律的能力。正因如此，人类才具有顽强的生命力，繁衍下去，生生不息。

学习对于人来说，是一种非常重要的能力。一个人若要在社会上立足，就必须具备一定的学习能力，否则将会被淘汰，无所作为，甚至连生存都成问题。

大凡成功的人，最显著的特征是具有较强的学习能力，不断地用知识弥补先天的不足，积累经验，发展智力，增益其所不能，才能成就一番事业。

然而，学习能力的获得，首先来自于我们主观上对学习的正确和深刻的认识。有的人对学习持不以为然的态度，认为不学习照样能赚钱，甚至还嘲笑那些爱学习的人。这样的观点是片面的，原因在于，赚钱也是一种能力，倘若不学习，怎能有那赚钱的本事呢？他们的这种说法岂不自相矛盾？所以，一个人只有对学习产生正确的认识，才能主动地去实践，获得他成长所需要的各种能力。

学习能力的获得并非是轻而易举的。学习本身就是一项艰苦的劳动，这过程要经历许多困难和挫折，就像小孩子当初学走路那样，免不了要摔几个跟头，之后才能走得平稳。

学习能力的获得也不是一蹴而就的。俗话说："一口吃不成胖子"，学习也是这样，需要长期不懈地坚持，循序渐进，日积月累，程颐说的好，"学至气质变化，方是有功"。

载于《思维与智慧》

学习是一个追索的过程，就像是去攀爬一座高山，总得跌倒几次才能到达。

钓 鱼

文/崔永照

生活中有两个悲剧。一个是你的欲望得不到满足，另一个则是你的欲望得到了满足。

——萧伯纳

那天清晨，心烦意乱的王海早早起床，匆匆赶到了老领导——已退休的原副县长刘佩家，刘佩正拿出昨晚收拾妥当的工具出门，要到秀山湖去钓鱼，王海便随同前往。

来到湖边，刘佩选中了湖东南角的一片水域，架好钓竿，就开始“做窝子”了。他说，“做窝子”用的原料是非常考究的，是用上等曲酒三两、“新农欢”原料一包、小麦半斤，浸泡一周后做成的。撒时得掌握好用量，太多鱼吃饱了不上钩，太少引不来鱼。他抓了三把均匀地撒向那片水域。顷刻间鱼贯而至，那片水域便活泛起来。

王海见缝插针说了自己遇到的一件棘手事。昨晚，自己的老同学——庞业建筑公司刁经理送来了十万元钱，说王秀要结婚，这钱正好置办婚礼用。王海正想说服刁经理把钱带走，他已夺门而出。自己先前从乡镇一步一个脚印干到富鸾县市政管理局局长已有九个年头了，上任以来，每年从笔下签过上千万元的市政工程建设款，自己都能做到心静如水，从没有雁过拔毛的念头，被县上树为反腐倡廉的典型。这次儿子王秀结婚确实需要一大笔钱，自己手头太紧了，若有了这十万元就高枕无忧了。可他知道刁经理来者不善……这是一把双刃剑。老伴当时也拒绝收钱，可刁经理说："这钱是我借给你们的，没外人知道，以前我也借过王局长的钱，我俩谁跟谁呀。我这钱咬手?"

刘佩听完，眉头拧成了疙瘩，神情严肃，沉思片刻，说："钓鱼!"

刘佩想钓些鲤鱼，便在钩上挂上了专买的很嫩的玉米粒，少顷，鱼漂动了一下，他迅速提竿，可什么都没有，看来鱼只是碰到了鱼饵。"这些鱼贼精，你得耐心跟它们耗着，要有'等得花儿都谢了'的那种心态。"刘佩笑眯眯地说。

"老领导……"王海刚开口，"嘘，鱼快上钩了。"刘佩打断了他。

果然，钓上了一条七八寸长的鲤鱼。那鱼在阳光下拼命挣扎。他很有成就感的样子："哈哈，这鱼咬了我的钩，便成了我的盘中餐了。"

湖四周是苍翠欲滴的绿树、青草，刘佩逍遥自在地哼着"采菊东篱下，悠然见南山"。王海也被这氛围感染了，心就像长了双翅膀在湖面上快乐地滑翔。淡泊名利，宠辱不惊，仙风道骨，物我两忘，陶陶然其乐哉!

刘佩在钓钩上换上了蚯蚓，他说："各种鱼口味不同，你得变着法子迎合它们的胃口才能钓到。钓鲫鱼要用蚯蚓做诱饵，钓草鱼要用鲜草做诱饵……"

"我……"王海又说。

"别说话，把鱼惊跑了。"刘佩摆摆手。

过了几个小时，他又在钓钩上挂上了鲜草。太阳西斜时，刘佩钓了一大筐鱼。

王海看着筐里的鱼，心头一沉，又想到了烦心事，说：“我该咋办?”

“心里装不下一点事！走，到我家喝几杯。”

“我哪有心思喝酒哇。”

到了刘佩家，王海用哀求的口气说：“老领导，您得帮帮我呀!”

刘佩反问：“你能告诉我对钓鱼有啥看法?”

王海心不在焉地说：“一、跑路多，锻炼身体；二、垂钓时没一点杂念，实为修身养性的良方……”

刘佩深深地叹了一口气：“人生沉浮，在时代的旋涡里，往往取决于一件小事或一瞬间。”

王海想起秀山湖的鱼争先恐后咬食鱼饵上钩的情景：“县城伏峰公园建设工程就要招标了，刁经理打着坏主意，想拉我下水。”

刘佩点了点头。

“刁经理这样煞费苦心与钓鱼有啥区别?”王海的话语里多了一分轻松。

刘佩爽朗地笑了，拍着王海的肩膀意味深长地说：“有悟性……”

载于《小小说选刊》

人生每一步抉择都是重要的，影响生命以后的走势。所以，在利益面前，保持自控力是很重要的。

第二辑

做生活的“修补师”

我们总是在不断地追求更新鲜的事物，并在这种追求的过程中体会一种刺激和快感。可是，轻易地追求、丢弃，再追求、再丢弃，到最后我们会剩下什么？恐怕只有无以言表的失落和茫然。

在何方

文/侯拥华

莫愁前路无知己，天下谁人不识君。

——高适

想起这个问题时，似乎觉得应该是一个伪命题。但转念一想，却不然。

在何方，不就是问你何时在何地吗？即便这样简单的问题，又有多少人能说得清楚呢？

静下心来，敛思细想，在何方，真不是一个简单的时间与地理的问题。即便是，要回答清楚，却并不容易。

幼年的时候，襁褓之中，你定然不知答案。但是到了你开始蹒跚学步，蹦蹦跳跳的时候，你却以为岁月是永恒的，美好是永恒的，连父亲与母亲都是永恒的。仿佛你一直那么小，他们就一直不会老——青春永驻人间。你以为那些你爱的，以及爱你的人，会永远与你同在，一直活在你青葱水嫩般的年华里。没有历经时光的淘洗，没有寒凉人世的侵袭，温暖且明亮的岁月中，你以为你就站在世界舞台的中央，阳光、雨露以及爱总是时刻包围着你，众爱一身，万物敬仰。于是，你便陶醉其中，沉醉不知归路，在爱与时光的长河中慢慢长大。当然，有时，也有一些小挫折、小打击，像一场小噩梦，天亮了，便统统忘却了，不在心里留下一点痕迹。早晨，出门的时候，你和小伙伴牵着手，蹦跳着，去寻找自己的乐园，直至夜幕降临，你们还沉浸其中，不知返回。那时，一个简单的游戏，一块湿润的泥巴，一枚圆滑的石头，一条浅浅的河流，抑或是一股云烟，一片花香，一声鸟啼，都会紧紧牵着你的目光与思绪，让你流连忘返，忘记周遭世界的存在。那个时候你一定忘记了时光匆匆奔走的脚步声，细雨开始落下来，打湿你的头发，鸟雀归巢了，站在枝头鸣叫，把夜幕一点一点叫成黑色，连远方，父母的呼喊声，都被你忽略了。那一刻，你怎知道你在何方呢？

青年的时候，世界的雨开始下得大起来，滂沱大雨，暴风骤雨，凄风冷雨，种种不一样的雨落在你的生命中，当然也有冰雹与暴雪闯进你的生活里。在拥挤的人群中，为得到一席属于自己的领地，你开始忘我奋斗与残酷厮杀。汗淌了一脸，血溅了一身，眼睛肿了，鼻子歪了，连牙齿都掉了几颗，可是那战斗还没有结束的意思，胜负没见分晓，你还要奋不顾身地闯进生活的激流里。偶尔，你败下来，会一闪念想到无忧无虑的少年时光，可是，短暂休息一下，多半时间，你在蓄势待发总结经验厉兵秣马，待找准时机杀他一个回马枪。如果胜利了，下一场冲锋又拉开了序幕。那时候生活总是充满变数，世界乱得一团糟。有时你沉醉于甜蜜爱情的浪漫游戏，有时痴迷于一掷千金的人生豪赌，有时纠结于纷乱如麻的人事关系之中正无力抽身。进退维谷，万事缠身，那一刻，你怎知道你在何方呢？

后来，人生迈入中年，烦恼种种，伤痕累累，无常与反复开始时常打扰你的生活，你才开始觉醒。你知道，人生并不漫长，现在已经半场。胜负，输赢，得失，快乐与悲伤，光荣与耻辱等都曾在你的生活中降临，你开始学会宽容，学会从容，学会忍耐，学会沉下心来思考一些事情。可是人生就像夜晚在大海上行舟，风雨飘摇，捉摸不定，有些事情你看透了却依旧放不下去，一些你想不在乎的人与事依然要放在心底反复掂量，人生依旧处在一团模糊不定的迷雾之中。那时候你又在何方呢？快乐的时候，你在高山上欢歌；苦恼的时候，你走进寺庙祈祷；痛苦的时候，你约朋友酒馆痛饮；彷徨的时候，你独自闷在房间里惆怅。你不停地追问自己，我在何方？我在何方？可是没人给你说得清楚，也没有人给你指明方向。这时候你怎会知道，你究竟是在何方？

再后来，人生暮年，天寒地冻，狂风肆虐，大雪纷纷，你残弱多病，走不了路，做不了事，连脑子都快成了糨糊。趁着还不太糊涂，你开始一点一点慢慢回忆往事，点点滴滴的过往像一场电影，一帧一幕，从你的心底里飘过，你知道真正的人生在感觉中时快时慢，悲喜交加，高低起伏。在回忆中，往事开始在时间的长河里与宽阔的生活地域中，一一建起了坐标，这时候你仿佛知道你曾在何方。可是，转念一想，你的那一小段人生岁月，于整个宇宙而言，不过是沧海一粟，狂沙一粒，你连自己的方位都找不到又何谈远方呢？

再后来，你脑子混沌成一片，难辨东西。在何方？你怎想得清楚。

想想，这一生的时光，其实你不停地在追寻，在追问，在求索——我来自哪里？将去向何方？又在何方？可是，答案在哪里呢，又有谁能给你说清楚呢？

难得糊涂，不问也罢。

载于《语文报》

我们就像是在一列火车上疾驰，它要开往哪里，在哪里停靠，我们都不得而知。

小肚鸡肠的书圣

文/幸运小嵇

紫罗兰把它的香气留在了那踩扁了它的脚踝上，这就是宽恕。

——马克·吐温

出生于东晋琅琊王氏望族的王羲之，是一个不折不扣的官二代、富二代。他的代表作《兰亭集序》冠绝群雄，达到了“贵越群品，古今莫二”的高度，因而有“书圣”的美誉。

就是这样一位书法大师，为人处世方面却颇有瑕疵，他最大的弱点，就是喜欢与人争闲气。看到有人哪方面比他好，就会生出嫉妒。王羲之有一位远方堂兄弟，名叫王述。

此人与王羲之同年出生，长得比较帅气，从小就被王羲之视作心中的“假想敌”。成年后，两王的名气都很响，论书法方面的成就，王述远不是王羲之的对手。可是官职、地位方面，王述却远胜一筹。

王述早先的声誉并不好，后来不知道使了什么手段，一路官运亨通。那时，王羲之在会稽郡当内史，相当于一个地级市领导；而王述已是扬州刺史，级别升到了省部级。更令人啼笑皆非的，是会稽恰好归扬州管辖，王述成为王羲之的“顶头上司”。王羲之彻底坐不住了，心里那股怒火熊熊燃烧。他不停地盘算着，怎样才能超过这个对手。

深思熟虑后，王羲之竟想出一个馊主意。他还为这个念头颇为得意，喝了一整坛酒，在微醺的状态下龙走蛇形地书写了一幅作品。第二天，他花了两个多时辰，完成了一份几千字的奏折。从政治、经济、文化、历史等角度，摆事实、讲道理，就是为了表达这个意思：把会稽郡从扬州中单列出来，并升格为越州，行政级别与扬州相同。

皇帝拿到这份奏折，气得哭笑不得。好你个王羲之，竟敢擅自妄言行政区域调整。如此狂妄之徒，一定要好好惩治。碍于当时王氏在东晋朝廷的势力，王羲之这才没有被狠狠修理。

一个多月后，批复送到这份奏折的始作俑者手中，上面只有短短的一句话："言论荒唐，不可行，望你好自为之。"王羲之的升官美梦，就这样被撞得粉身碎骨。他越想越生气，身体竟然被气出了毛病。风寒侵蚀本就不是很健壮的身体，他只得向朝廷称病回乡。

辞职后，按理说王羲之应该过上与世无争的日子了。他完全可以在书法、诗文方面多花些心思，以此证明自己的价值。可是，王羲之依然无法走出先前的阴影，他时刻关注官场中的动静，特别是王述的升迁情况。每当王述被提拔一次，他的愤怒就会增添一分。终于在59岁那年，王羲之在居所内愤慨致终。

一代伟大的书法家，竟因狭隘心气而英年早逝，实在太过可惜。拿自己的短处与别人的长处相比，那不啻就是存心与自己过不去。放下狭隘的比较心理，感恩已经拥有的一切，我们就会点亮一盏快乐的明灯，由此乐享幸福的人生。

载于《中国青年》

周瑜在临死前发出一句“既生瑜，何生亮”的感慨，心胸狭隘的人，迟早会因为这个毛病断送自己的前程。看不惯别人好的人，是不会有大出息、大作为的。

母亲的勇气

文/马朝兰

母爱是世间最伟大的力量。

——米尔

2006年12月14日，深夜11点24分，在美国洛杉矶国际机场，一位头发花白的东方女人引起了所有乘客的注意。

她挎着黑色的背包，背包上贴有一张用透明胶带层层缠绕的醒目的A4纸，上面用中文写着“徐莺瑞”三个字。

这些从萨尔瓦多飞到洛杉矶的乘客，几乎都是拉丁美洲人。他们根本不懂中文。这位衣着朴素的东方女人在等待了许久后，终于开始在人群中用蹩脚的普通话挨个询问：“请问你会说中文吗？请问你会说中文吗？”

临近午夜12点，她终于找到了救星。一位黑头发的男人驻足她的身前，低头端详她手里的纸条：“我要在洛杉矶出境，有朋友在外接我。”

其实，在这张揉得皱烂的纸条上，还有另外两行中文，每行中文下面都用荧光笔打了横线，方便阅读。

第一行中文：“我要到哥斯达黎加看女儿，请问是在这里转机吗？”下面，是两行稍微细小的文字，分别是英语和西班牙语。

第二行中文：“我要去领行李，能不能带我去？谢谢！”接着，同样又是英文和西班牙语的翻译。

原来，她的女儿在十年前随女婿移民到了哥斯达黎加。如今刚生完第二胎，身子虚弱至极。女人思儿心切，硬要从中国台湾过来看她，帮她坐月子。女儿执拗不过，便在越洋信件中夹带了一堆纸条。

如今，她已帮女儿坐完月子。原本女儿要陪她到洛杉矶机场，结果却因买不到机票而作罢。女儿为了让她有安身之处，特意请求远在洛杉矶的朋友帮忙。为了方便相认，女人便特意在背包上缠裹了醒目的 A4 纸。

很多人都以为，这不过是一个简单的行程。可深知航班内情的那位黑发男人，却不禁被这简单的描述感动得热泪涟涟。

从台南出发，要如何才能到达哥斯达黎加呢？

首先得从台南飞至桃园机场，接着搭乘足足十二小时的班机，从台北飞往美国，再次，从美国飞五个多小时到达中美洲的转运中心——萨尔瓦多，然后才能从萨尔瓦多乘机飞至目的地，哥斯达黎加。

她曾在拥挤的异国人群中狂奔摔倒，曾在午夜机场冰冷的座椅上蜷缩，也曾在恍惚的人流中举着救命的纸条卑躬屈膝……这一切的一切，不过只是想亲眼看看自己的女儿。

这是一位真实而又平凡的中国母亲。她来自中国台湾，名叫蔡莺瑞，67 岁；生平第一次出国，不会说英文，不会说西班牙语；为了自己的女儿，独自一人飞行整整三天，从台南到哥斯达黎加，无惧这三万六千公里的艰难险阻与关山重重。

她让我们看到了一位母亲因爱而萌发的勇气。这种匿藏在母性情怀中的勇气，从始至终都不会因距离和时间而改变。

载于《私人坊》

母爱是什么呢？我给不出确切的定义，我只知道出生之前它就急切地等待着我，在我成长中呵护着我，环绕纠缠着我，这种爱甚至渗入渗出入我每一个毛孔，直至耗尽它自己，而我却很晚才懂得。

做生活的“修补师”

文/暗香浮动

吾日三省吾身，为人谋而不忠乎，与朋友交而不信乎，传不习乎。

——孔子

前段时间，陪伴了我近五年的椅子光荣“下岗”了，看着掉落一旁的椅子腿儿，我无奈地叹了口气，搬起椅子准备处理掉。“妞儿，干嘛去?”父亲指着我手里的椅子问。我苦着脸回答：“椅子坏了，准备扔掉呗。”父亲起身，接过我手里的椅子，仔细看了半天，笑着说：“扔掉太可惜了呀，这把椅子修理后完全可以继续使用的。”说着，父亲在我惊疑的目光中，拿出工具箱，在螺丝刀和锤子的轮番修理下，本来只剩三条腿的椅子又稳稳当当地站了起来。“爸，您真是化腐朽为神奇啊。”我情不自禁地对父亲竖起了大拇指。父亲摆摆手笑了：“哪是什么神奇呀！不过是生活里的一些小经验而已。我们那时候，可不像你们现在，把什么东西都当一次性的使用，哪件东西没修补过，就是衣服也要新三年、旧三年，缝缝补补又三年的呢。”

看着父亲仔细端详旧椅子时那敝帚自珍的样子，我心中突然生出了一丝感动。其实，有些旧物于我们而言，不仅仅只是一件物品，它曾陪伴我们走过或长或短的一些日子，它上面更有一些我们关于旧时光的回忆和念想。也许正是如此，父辈们才会格外珍惜那些旧物，才会很认真地将有损坏的旧物一点一点地修补完整。我想，在修补的过程中，他们心中一定拥有着满满的感恩和知足。

不可否认，我们现在的生活条件好了很多。因此，我们对旧物也就越来越不在乎，坏了，我们可以扔掉再买，正所谓"旧的不去新的不来"。甚至一些明明可以修补好的东西，我们也不屑去修理，因为我们的心已经在不知不觉中变得浮躁、功利，缺乏耐性，我们不肯再去浪费过多的心思在旧物上。

其实，何止是旧物，在现实生活里，无论是工作还是情感，我们都失去了应有的耐心和珍惜。工作遇到一点麻烦，我们想到的不是战胜它，而是放弃；一段感情遇到了问题，我们没有尽全力去解决、去挽回，而是想着结束……我们总是在不断地追求更新鲜的事物，并在这种追求的过程中体会一种刺激和快感。可是，轻易地追求、丢弃，再追求、再丢弃，到最后我们会剩下什么？恐怕只有无以言表的失落和茫然。

在快节奏的今天，我们需要做的恐怕应该是慢下来，慢下来去"修补"生活，在对旧物的"修补"中，找到一种心灵的安宁和祥和，找到我们生命本身的意义和价值。

载于《哲思》

我们一路行走，一路停留，一路得到，一路丢失。适时的时候停下反思，自己是不是丢了什么，如此，才不会感觉没有安全感。

我的哥们儿是县长

文/崔 咏

你既然期望要过上辉煌伟大的一生，那么就应该从今天起，以毫不动摇的决心和坚定不移的信念，凭自己的智慧创造你和人类的快乐。

——佚名

马小多在上班路上接了一个电话。他的心马上如花儿绽放，就连脚步也多了几分欢快，然后趾高气扬地跨进办公室，用眼的余角扫一下小刘，把手一挥："去，给我倒杯茶来！"

小刘撇了下嘴，把不情愿的表情淹没了。心里却直犯嘀咕，他今天是咋了，从来没有过这样子啊？

茶香袅袅，飘散开来。马小多跷着二郎腿，呷一口茶，嘿嘿笑两声。翻翻报纸，歪着头想半天心事，喜形于色，溢于言表。

马小多，是固东县园林局一名普普通通的员工，眼见四十挂零的人了，还没混个一官半职。整天穿着朴素，走路办事慢条斯理，有人说他是属于磨磨唧唧那一类型的人。

在单位几十年了，从没见他给谁起过高腔，红过脸。有一次，单位刚来的一名小伙子曾试探着拿他开涮，当面给他起了个绰号叫"慢半拍"。马小多两眼露出怒色，脸憋得通红，一副剑拔弩张之势。

那小伙子自知理亏，做好了应对狂风骤雨的准备……但是，马小多刹那间竟像泄了气的气球，又恢复了平静，默默地走开了。同事们不由得暗自发出慨叹，真是八棍子打不出屁的人啊！那小伙子打着响指，吹着口哨，扬长而去……

“张局长！”马小多推门进了局长办公室，一改往日的畏畏缩缩。他挺直了腰杆，更多的是自信：“你今后有啥棘手的事，都可以给我说，没有我摆不平的事。要是在咱县不好办，我让巨峰县的高人来帮忙解决！”

张局长理理油光的大背头：“你发烧了，还是昨晚酒喝高了没醒？”

“看看，你咋一头雾水啊，我咋给你说啊……从哪儿说起啊……”马小多神神叨叨有点儿不知从何说起了。

张局长忙着接一个电话。

马小多退出局长办公室，心情出奇地好，特别特别好，他哼着的小曲，在走廊上回环飘荡。

江主任正在埋头看一份文件，马小多大踏步走进来，拿起桌子上的那包烟抽出一支燃着，狠狠地吸了几口，然后一屁股坐在沙发上，惬意地吐着烟圈。看主任诧异的样子，马小多别提有多得意了。

“我说主任，以后给我安排工作，请悠着点。繁重的、高难度的，在我这里统统绕行，一律免谈！”摇头晃脑的马小多，做出一副咄咄逼人的架势。

主任的脸有了猪肝色，出气也不大匀实：“有你这样跟我说话的吗，你啥意思啊？”

“我就这样跟你说，你要给我记清了，在咱县你要亏待了我，我到巨峰县搬救兵去！”

马小多斜溜主任傻愣愣的神态，心里真过瘾。他暗笑着走出主任办公室。

“呃！是谁帮咱们翻了身呃？是谁帮咱们得解放呃？……”马小多坐在回家的公共汽车上，眯着眼，哼着小曲，右手有节奏地打着拍子。

“哎，你干吗打我？”一名满脸络腮胡子的中年男子愤怒地瞪着马小多。

“干吗那样凶？我这不是打拍子嘛，又不是故意的！”马小多神气十足。

“吆嘿，打着我你还有理了？”

“我就有理了，咋的，有本事跟我到巨峰县走一遭，找人跟你理论理论！”马小多一字一顿地说。

“啥，在咱县你都输理，还想尿到外县去？我打……”那人一拳打在马小多的肚子上，又一拳打在马小多的右臂上。痛得他哇哇大叫，连声求饶，那人这才骂骂咧咧住了手。马小多情绪蓦然低落很多，有些惴惴不安。

马小多到了家，脚步又变得轻盈了许多。

“老婆，给我冲杯咖啡来！”

妻子从厨房出来，没好气地说：“今个儿长出息了，耍啥威风？没看我正忙着做饭！”

马小多瞪了她一眼：“我叫你冲！”

“趴一边去！”妻子一甩厨房的门，震得山响。马小多的心不由咯噔一下，半天缓不过神儿来。妻子又在喊：“快来洗菜，等一会儿扫地，再把地板拖干净了！”

累得满头大汗的马小多，吃饭时努力对妻子挤出笑脸：“我的铁哥们王真，你是知道的。”马小多搁下筷子又说，“他任职巨峰县政府副县长了，今天早上，他打电话告诉我的。还说我有啥难事他给解决，改日请我吃大餐。你说说，那可是我的铁哥们，我有啥事，他会一马当先帮我办好……”

妻子指着一脸喜气的马小多，怒气冲天：“哎，我说马小多，实际点吧，你要先搞清楚了，也不掂量掂量自己是半斤还是八两？那是你哥们升官了，你以为是你自个儿当县长了？”那高八度的女花腔，震得马小多心房一颤一颤的，甭提有多难受了。

载于《小小说精选》

别人就是别人，是跟自己有区别的，那个和朋友同穿一条裤子的年月早已经过去了。

两个人的战斗

文/朱向青

最好的朋友是那种不喜欢多说，能与你默默相对而又息息相通的人。

——高尔基

“让我们约定，彼此坚守吧，让我们在坚守中彼此知道：我们不是孤军！”

这句话是我的朋友程君说的，说这话时他的脸上显出很严肃的模样，几抹阳光恰恰伫足停留，使他的脸现出几分神圣般的光辉。我隐约觉得他的手马上要高高举起庄严宣誓了，不由轻笑出声：“你是在喊口号吗？”“呵呵”，他有点不好意思了，挠挠头，但随即认真地说：“我永远是一个理想主义者！”

这是一个雨过天晴的下午，天蓝得出奇，云彩似乎都躲起来了，阳光也久别了似的俏吻着大地，等不及地挤进果园里林子的缝隙，放纵地任自己星星点点洒满一地……

这时候，我正舒舒服服地坐在园子里，偶尔呷口清茶，漫不经心地听着，整个下午程君都一直在劝我要坚持写作，他热切地讲了很多很多……阳光懒洋洋地照着，我有一搭没一搭地应着，心里暗笑：我怎么会写呢，多少年没动过笔了，有什么可写的，再说哪有时间写呀……

面前的茶杯早已凉了，耳边飘来他的话语，却依然冒着滚烫的热气：

“你试试，写作能使人充实，体悟人生的真意，写作能内化人的各种素质。”

“不难，你就从写散文开始，再写评论、随笔，而后，不断提高……”

“写作的意义实在是太大了，至少，可以提升我们的思想，托举我们的灵魂！”

程君依然起劲地说着……

我把玩着手中的杯子，随着眼前这人的絮语渐渐地眯上眼睛，杯子也微微地摇晃起来……

写作，真的是很遥远的事了！

读大学的时候或许写过吧？那时，多喜欢看书呀，每每班上的男男女女手挽手，随着熙攘的人流，洒下欢声笑语走向各自神秘夜色的时候，自己就静静地躲在角落里，面前是一本摊开着的书。一任那些花自飘零水自流的清词丽句浸润自己的心田，一任那些一种相思两处闲愁的柔情漫绪轻舞自己的笔尖……

刚毕业的时候或许写过吧？那时，依然天真地认为，清风明月是一个人的事，依然迷恋独处的那份静谧与安祥，只是心中多了几缕对亲人的挂牵。那时多勤哪，一封封厚厚的书信如鸿雁般，穿梭于远方的兄弟姐妹间，年年月月，彼此思念……

记不清是什么时候，自己不再动笔，是工作渐渐的繁忙？还是心情慢慢的慵懒？或者什么理由也说不上，可是，却依旧心安……忽地，心里空空荡荡……手一松，杯子差点掉地，耳边没了声音。抬眼看，程君正不解地望着自己，猛醒到自己走神了。我有些不好意思，夺过他正要端起的杯子，“茶凉了，我再去倒一杯吧”。

一杯冒着热气的清茶端来了，放在了程君的面前，坐定，心里的彷徨、不安又涌上来，我忍不住问他：“这么多年了，你从未放弃过写作，它到底给你带来些什么呢？”

程君听了，沉吟半晌，坦然开了口：“其实，这样的问题也一度困扰过我。我曾经把写作视为生命，一直过着青灯黄卷、食不甘味的日子……可这条道路充满荆棘和艰辛，倾尽心血，有时却难有满意的收获。更何况，比别人多一份明白，也就多了一份忧患；多一份超脱也就多了一份寂寞。有时候，我真愿意过一种远离艺术的安宁日子。”

程君呷了口茶，眼睛渐渐亮起来了：“但也正因为有了写作，我觉得活着的每天都是一种新鲜的体悟，不再任文字搁置，任思维荒芜！”

“那时候，我挚爱着我的文学，我一直固执地认为，一个读书的人是幸福的。破书万卷、神交古人，读书恢复了我们的知性，使我们变得敏感而极易忧伤，但生命体验却因此更加丰富精彩。这实在是读书给予我们的恩泽啊，而笔耕不辍，舞文弄墨，更是苦中作乐……”

“我用笔记下世间一切普通的人及屑微的物事——

记忆里，初春，遍天遍地的雨丝似乎总在低低地为周遭萧瑟的乡村哭泣……耳畔是父亲长长的一两声叹息……

一样有风的冬季，当那个黝黑的小伙子蹬着堆满小山般蜂窝煤的三轮车出了小区的大门时，无声无息飞扬着的雪忽然就大了起来，胤弱的拉煤人的身形就和弥漫的飞雪裹在一起，模糊在我的眼睛里……

秋天的一次车祸，朋友来看我，我说这次你可以给我送这样一幅对联了——‘瘸腿走江湖，独眼看世界’，横批就是

‘如此人生’吧。闻言他竟噗哧笑出声来……

2006年夏季，我记下这样一件事，北京某报陈记者在救助一个少女时，被三个歹徒当场打得不省人事，现场有两桌食客和几个铺子的老板观望，但没有一个人报警打110，任由歹徒逍遥法外……

……一年四季酸甜苦辣就这样进入了我的文章里，文字，始终让我喜忧掺半苦乐与共！”

程君稍停，将杯中余茶一饮而尽，似乎意犹未足：“许多人都是有才华的，只是觉得不屑，于是在消磨中时光徒耗，才华渐尽，却浑然不觉，依然眼高手低，不以为然。再后来，与从前对比却已判若两人！”

“所以写作，赋予了我们无比高贵的灵魂，与常人不同的孤独高贵的灵魂——温婉而又冷酷、软弱而又坚硬、热情而又孤僻……在一种生与死的边缘矛盾、挣扎，只有亲近的人才知道啊。”

说着说着程君有些动容，他停下了，转头凝望着远处，我分明看出，他的眼角已微微润湿。我盯着他的侧影：这时的他，一个西北的汉子，表情竟是那么的柔和生动，与周围金黄色的阳光又是那么自然融合……

收回视线，程君继续坚定地说：“因为这样高贵的灵魂，我们便有了不竭的生命追求，我们的生活便有了求真求善求美的至高境界。普通及屑微的人物带给我更多的体悟与感动，写作就成了拯救我生命和灵魂的唯一手段。既然不能因诅咒黑暗而获得光明，那就燃起一截小小的蜡烛，为自己的生命照亮！”

“点亮心灯，为自己的生命照亮！”我反复念着这句，心似乎也跟着亮堂起来了！良久，程君沉默了，可他的话语却如同滚烫热水冲泡出的清茶，在空气里飘香，缕缕生烟，久久不散……

突然我有了一种冲动，我脱口而出："我愿意，我想写！"

程君笑了，带着鼓励，带点怜惜："文字其实是很累人的，文章写完还要欲罢而不忍，一直眷顾。呵呵，不过，文字的魅力也在这里，让你食无味，寝无眠……"

"享受幸福，忍受痛苦——这，是战斗的滋味，苦乐无穷，你，准备好了吗？"

滚烫的茶水触及我的唇，我深深地吸了一口气，是的，我记下了，我记住了这种味道，激荡的战斗的味道……

但我不害怕，因为这不是一个人的战斗，两个人的战斗，而是许多人的战斗！在我们的身边，有更多的战友，彼此注视，相互支持，一同站在了坚实的大地上！

"贴近底层，关注苍生，张扬个性，坚守信仰"是我们高展的文学旗帜，站在这面飘扬的旗帜下，我没有举手宣誓。与大家相比，我自觉渺小，但我却仰头，满心虔诚，小声而又坚定地说："我准备好了，时刻准备着……"

相约战斗！彼此坚守！——这一刻，是如此幸福，如此神圣！

载于《经典阅读》

友情是相知，当你需要的时候，你还没有讲，友人就已来到你的身边。他的眼睛和心都能读懂你，更会用手挽起你单薄的臂弯。由此你不会再感到孤独。

人心暖了，世界也就暖了

文/金　珠

爱之花开放的地方，生命便能欣欣向荣。

——梵高

一

李达买了一套新居室，便想把原来的旧居卖掉。他在网上发了一个帖子，一个叫孙强的人表示愿意购买，孙强看了李达的房子后觉得非常满意，两人的这笔买卖几乎没费什么周折就谈成了。李达在腾空房子时，阳台上一个大塑料箱里装满了他儿子小时候玩过的一些玩具，这些玩具虽然有些陈旧，但也没怎么损坏，只是孩子现在大了，他对玩具已失去了兴趣。

李达想起，孙强来看房子时，带着一个三、四岁左右的男孩，孙强说是他儿子。李达当即决定，把这些玩具留下来送给孩子。为了避免引起不必要的误会，李达特意给孙强打电话说了此事。孙强高兴地接受了，并一再对李达表示感谢。

过了几天，李达突然接到孙强打来的电话，孙强说，务必请李达过来一趟，有重要物品归还。李达去了，孙强拿出一条亮闪闪的白金项链给他看，“李大哥，你看这是不是你家落下的东西，我是在玩具里发现的。”李达眼睛一亮，这不是他给妻子买的那条结婚项链吗？当初妻子找不见项链，当是丢了，原来掉在了自家的玩具堆里。李达紧紧地握着孙强的手，感激之情不言而喻。

孙强倒是镇定地说："李大哥，您别这样，当初你把那么多玩具送给孩子，我提出适当给你点钱，你说什么也不肯要。你不知道那些玩具都好好的，我儿子可高兴了，当宝贝似的。我们是进城打工的，经济不宽裕，平时几乎没给孩子买过什么，难得您这片好心，我们对您感激还来不及呢！再说，这个链子本来就是你家的东西，我若不声不响占了去，还算是人吗。"

听了这话，李达心里热乎乎的，同时也是感慨万千，他没想到，这些对他已毫无用处的玩具，却帮他找回了最宝贵的东西。

二

表嫂给一家单位做饭，这家单位规模不大，也就十来个人，每月工资1800元，4天休假。

前一阵子，我的几个同学合伙开了家公司，让我帮他们找个做饭的，每月工资2500元，双休日照常休。我一下子想到了表嫂。不料当我把这个好消息乐滋滋地告诉她时，却被她一口拒绝了。我不解劝她，这里收入要比你过去每月多700元，而且还多休4天假，按市场行情已经很好了。

表嫂不为所动，微笑着说："是不错，可我在那里时间久了，呆出了感情，让我突然离开，我还真有点不舍得。再说，他们吃惯了我做的饭，离开了，总觉得心里欠下人家什么似的。"我笑她糊涂，人走茶凉，有谁会记得你的好？

表嫂摇头道：“我来给你说几件事吧！有一次，我感冒了，硬撑着去做饭，他们一看我不舒服，赶紧让我回家休息，晚上又带着礼品来看我，这令我很感动；逢年过节，他们发慰问品，总要给我备一份；每次吃饭，如果我正好忙着炒菜，每盘菜刚一出锅，他们就单独拨出些留我一部分；有人外出旅游，带回来的纪念品总少不了我的，可以说他们从没把我当外人看！你说，人家对我这么好，我如果因为别人给我工资多了就离开，良心上能过得去吗?”

三

家里装修新房，图方便，我把房子钥匙交给了装修师傅。一天，我正上班，送灯具的打来电话，说东西到了，可家里没人。由于一时走不开，我给装修师傅打电话说了情况，装修师傅说，他这就回去开门，让送灯具的稍等一会。

本以为事情就这么完了，但过了一阵，送灯具的再次打来电话：“师傅，我还和别家约好要去送货，你能不能让装修师傅快点，麻烦你了。”我有些意外，原以为门早就开了呢！赶紧给他解释：“你先别着急，装修师傅应该正往回赶，这样吧，如果过十分钟门还没开，你再给我打电话。”

跟他通完电话，我正想给装修师傅打电话问问，凑巧，办公室来了一位同事，我们又谈起工作上的事。同事走后，我去接水，看到外面骄阳如火，行人稀少，突然心里一动，也不知道给送灯具的打开门没，如果让人家大热天还在太阳底下干等着，实在就说不过去了。

心念至此，我决定再落实下情况。拨通电话，送灯具的爽朗地说道：“送到了，送到了，我这会正给别人去送货，没事啦！”我也放下心来。

几天后，我正在新房查验，门外响起敲门声，打开一看，门口站着一位穿劳动服的陌生人，他自我介绍：“我是前几天给你家送灯具的，那天给你家送的灯具在库房装车时外包装破了，掉出一包螺钉帽，今天我给你送来了。”哦，怪不得安装灯具的师傅说如果固定灯具的螺钉有个装饰帽就更美观了，原来是漏掉了。

我连连向他道谢，他却略显腼腆地说：“你那天还最后打电话问我进门没，说明你一直把事放在心上，很少有人对我们送货的这么在乎和尊重，有时我们催促紧了还讨人嫌。其实这包东西我送不送都无所谓，但我还是觉得应该给你送来。”

人心都是肉长的，只有当我们心里装着别人，自己的言行举止能让对方充分感受到温暖和尊重，对方才会用同样的态度和方式回报你，世界也会因此变得更温暖和明亮。

载于《人生与伴侣》

在这个钢筋水泥构筑的城市里，除了阳光给予的温暖，还有人心传递的爱呢。

戴维斯的“背叛”

文/凤　凰

别人都走开的时候，朋友仍与你在一起。

——谚语

戴维斯开了一家公司，却因为经营不善倒闭了。他的朋友马克也开了一家公司，生意做得风风火火，大把大把地赚钱。马克见戴维斯走投无路，便让他加入自己的公司，当然，为了不让戴维斯感到难堪，他说他的公司需要一笔钱周转，如果戴维斯愿意投资的话，那将是对他极大的帮助。戴维斯信以为真，于是将自己所剩的钱都交给了马克。为了对戴维斯的帮助表示感谢，马克给了他公司一定的股份。

戴维斯加入马克的公司后，才知道公司的生意做得风风火火，但马克告诉他，这是因为他的加入，才给公司带来了转机。戴维斯为此非常高兴，他希望公司的生意做得更好，为此，他努力工作，和马克配合默契。后来的一段时间里，公司的生意果然因为他的努力而变得更好。马克非常高兴，戴维斯加入公司真是对了。公司有钱了，壮大了，于是马克把生意做得更大了，甚至做起了别的生意，他想赚更多的钱。

这天，马克告诉戴维斯，他准备跟另一家公司合作，买一批古董，他说只要这笔生意做成了，公司会赚一大笔钱。戴维斯听了摇头，说他不同意做古董生意。马克说道：“公司是我的，我决定了，就这么做。虽然你占了一定的股份，但一切还是我说了算。我告诉你一声，已经是对你最大的尊重了！”戴维斯见马克坚持，也坚持自己的意见，坚决不同意买下这批古董，他说如果马克一意孤行的话，他就退出公司。

马克见戴维斯不支持他不说，还要退出公司，非常生气，说道：“在这关键的时候，你居然要退出，好，你要退出就退出，到时候，我赚了钱，你可别眼红！”当天，马克就筹集资金，交给了戴维斯，叫他立即就走。戴维斯走了，马克非常难过，戴维斯在关键的时候退出，这是对他的背叛。想当初，戴维斯落难的时候，是他叫他加入公司，还给了他一定的股份，才让戴维斯“起死回生”，赚了一笔钱。

戴维斯拿着属于自己的那笔钱，又开起了公司。让马克没想到的是，戴维斯居然跟他做的是同样的生意，他很想去找戴维斯理论，但想想还是算了。不过，马克十分生气，戴维斯不但背叛他，还跟他对着干，简直就没把他当朋友了。气归气，马克回过头来还是得做自己的生意，他想，只有把自己的生意做好，才是对戴维斯最大的打击，只要戴维斯失败了，到时候，他就又得回头来找自己。为此，马克斗志昂扬。

就在马克与那家公司合作，准备买下那一大批古董的时候，突然却传来一个不好的消息，戴维斯也想与那家公司合作，也想买下那批古董。马克这时明白了，戴维斯口口声声说不能做这笔买卖，还坚持要退出公司，原来并非这生意不能做，而是为了独吞这笔生意。马克说：“戴维斯啊戴维斯，我真是看错了你！我把你当朋友，你却一再跟我作对。想跟我争这笔生意，没门！就你那点资金，人家根本瞧不上眼！”

虽说戴维斯现在的公司不起眼，但马克也不敢大意，为了避免夜长梦多，他连忙与那家公司签订了合同，并且一手交钱一手交货，把生意给做成了。就在马克以为自己发财了的时候，事情发生了意外，原来这是一个骗局，这是对方精心设计的骗局，那些古董都是赝品。守着一堆赝品，马克哭了，对方早已不见了踪影，自己的那笔钱，也追不回来了。这下，公司全完了，马克从富翁一下子又变回了穷人。

这时，伤心的马克想到了戴维斯，他又露出了笑容，戴维斯开了公司，找他帮帮自己，自己就一定可以重振旗鼓。没想到，马克还没有去找戴维斯，戴维斯就主动找上门来了。马克心想，他肯定知道我的事了，该不会是来羞辱的我吧？不过，马克还是接待了戴维斯，他想看看戴维斯到底会怎么对待他。戴维斯握了马克的手之后，开门见山就说道：“马克，你的事我都知道了，对不起，我没能阻止你的这场交易！”

看着一脸内疚的戴维斯，马克顿时糊涂了，戴维斯没有羞辱自己，便问道：“你这是怎么了？”戴维斯告诉马克：自己见他一意孤行，非做要那笔古董生意，为此他很是担心，于是他决定退出公司，自己开一家公司，抢着做那笔古董生意，如果自己失败了，那么就挽救了马克的公司。当然，如果他成功了，那也有马克的一半。如果马克失败了，至少还有他的公司存在。因为从一开始，他的公司就有马克的一半。

马克听了恍然大悟，拍着戴维斯的肩膀说：“原来你退出公司，其实是为我着想啊，我还以为你真的背叛我了呢！你别自责，你退出公司，就是帮了我的大忙。我见你开公司，知道你困难，于是通过别人，悄悄地向你的公司投了一笔钱，没想到你现在生意做得风风火火，我也跟着赚钱了！”戴维斯笑了：从前马克帮他，自己“背叛”他后，他还帮着自己，而自己“背叛”他，也是为了他，他们是真正的好朋友！

原载《知音·海外版》

背叛和爱傻傻分不清，是我们经常犯的错误。应该懂得哪些人是虚伪的，而哪些人却一直站在自己身边。

七年之“养”

文/孙道荣

在一个崇高的目标支持下，不停地工作，即使慢，也一定会获得成功。

——爱因斯坦

七年之养？没错，是七年之“养”，营养的养，培养的养。

有一个理论，一个人如果要熟练地掌握一门知识，或者一项技能，大约需要七年的时间。

对一个人来说，这是什么概念呢？假设一个人可以活到80岁的话，那么，从12岁开始，你有差不多10次的机会，在某个领域出类拔萃。

这真是太鼓舞人心了。

我认识一个本地的作者，是个农民，也是个家庭主妇。每天闲暇的时候，就在房间里写东西。开始是日记，后来是故事，反正每天都写。也没投过稿，甚至没给别人看过，纯粹是兴趣。若干年之后，一次偶然的机会，她的文字被一个出版商意外发现，得以出版，淳朴的文风，一下子打动了无数读者。如今，这位女农民，已经发表出版了近百万字的作品。而我认识的很多比她有才气得多的作者，却一直没什么成就，只是偶尔写几篇豆腐块，发泄发泄，他们的才情，像久未深垦的土地一样，慢慢荒芜了。

小区里有一块平地，每天傍晚，都会有一个老人，在那儿用巨大的毛笔，蘸着水在地面上写字，从几年前我搬到这个小区，就看到他了，而听说在此之前，他就已经写了好多年。把整个地面都写满字，大约需要个把小时。等他写完的时候，前面写的字迹，差不多快干了。他的字遒劲有力，路过的居民，都忍不住停下来，看几眼。每年过年的时候，他都会在平时练字的地方摆张桌子，为居民们免费写对联，求者云集。他的书法到底怎么样，我不敢妄评，但他的故事确实打动了我，你根本想象不到他不识什么字，而且还是个中过风的老人，好多年前，半边身子就失去了知觉。开始写字时，是为了恢复训练，此后，慢慢在一笔一画中，找到了一份宁静和快乐。他坚持了十多年，从未间断，即使下雨天，他也会在地下车库的地面上练习，才有了这一手的好字。

坚持七年，对许多人来说，似乎并不是特别困难的事。可是，为什么很多人，做了十年的公务员，还只是一个小职员？做了20年的会计，还只是一个小单位的出纳，而没有成为经济学家？在家里天天围着厨房转，做了30年的饭菜，也没有成为特级厨师？

那很可能是因为你只是像陀螺一样地旋转，而并没有自己明确的方向。

并不是说，无论什么事只要你坚持了七年，就一定能够超出别人。七年时间，可以让你熟练地掌握一项技能，但要命的是，七年之后，你也可能就此陷入一种疲惫期。在婚姻里，有一种说法叫“七年之痒”，婚姻的新鲜感和热度都消失了，曾经热烈的感情变得寡淡无味。不仅婚姻存在着七年之痒这道坎，工作是这样，学业是这样，事业也是这样。很多人花了七年的时间，掌握了某项技能，却又陷入七年之痒的泥淖，如果不能自拔，不能及早挣脱，就会像很多婚姻一样，了无生气地延续。这就是为什么很多人一辈子都在做某件事，却永远只能是掌握了熟练技能的匠人，而不是大师。

所以这个“养”，是需要悉心培养，需要源源不断的营养补给的。七年只是一个平台，平台之上，仍有无数台阶。

人生只有一次，但人生的路，绝不是一条。假设生命是一条河的话，那么，人这辈子，差不多有十次改变方向的机会。有机会的时候，你想转弯，都还来得及。

因此，如果想改变我们的人生，不需要再给我们一辈子，只需要一次七年，一切就能从零开始。还犹豫什么呢？

载于《智慧背囊》

人常常感叹自己没有时间做某些事，或者抱怨生活一成不变，于是，时间就在这些抱怨声中匆匆流逝。七年足够让人生改变一次，就看你是否有改变的决心。

手写的运气

文/散风落涯

要从容地着手去做一件事，但一旦开始，就要坚持到底。

——比阿斯

安德鲁·戴维斯是一名作家，每天他要给报纸专栏写稿，收入颇丰，他对自己的工作和生活自信满满。

但自从互联网盛行，报刊行业朝不保夕，有的甚至干脆倒闭，这直接影响了安德鲁的收入。他不仅担心自己的收入，更担心报纸的发展，于是他有了复兴报纸业的想法。而自己多年写专栏，对报纸有深刻的了解，有一些自己认为可行的办法。但他这些办法怎样才能付诸于实践呢？当然是通过媒体大亨和报纸出版商了，只要他们接受自己的办法，就可能实现自己的抱负，但具体从谁开始呢？

搜集了大量资料后，安德鲁确定从巴菲特开始，因为他了解到巴菲特在过去几年间购买了几十家时报，巴菲特不仅仅是一个投资家、一个股神，也是报业巨头，巴菲特需要新的盈利模式。他认为只有让巴菲特了解自己这些想法并认同，就能够实现让报业更大的盈利，从而使更多的报纸企业恢复生机。

安德鲁明确了自己的目标：和巴菲特讨论提高收益的办

法，复兴报业。制定目标容易实施难，巴菲特是全球最大的投资人，是人们心中的股神，每天有忙不完的工作，怎么会抽出时间和一个普通作家讨论自己的企业呢？除非自己撞了大运！他决定不等运气上门，而是要给自己制造一个运气。

怎样开始呢？这让安德鲁很困扰，但他相信只要自己的方法得当，一定能够得到和巴菲特会面的机会。他研究了很多方法：打电话，接线员根本不可能把陌生的电话转给巴菲特；写邮件，但现在邮件就像一个问候短信一样，很容易让人忽略，何况对方是大投资家巴菲特，不用想也会知道自己的邮件会淹没在千万封邮件当中。要想脱颖而出，真的让巴菲特看到，必定要用一种很特别的方法才行。他看到自己手中的信件，于是有了一个大胆的想法。

从 2012 年 10 月开始，安德鲁每周一都给巴菲特手写一封信，在信里他记录着帮助报纸商盈利的新想法。他把自己给巴菲特手写书信的事情告诉给朋友和同事，大家都很好奇，请他把书信内容公开，大家看到后都认为他的那些想法很实用，有人直接问是不是可以借用，他很痛快地就同意了。

为了让更多的人看到信件内容，安德鲁把信件在微博上公布，并把链接分享给大家，很快他的微博就得到了很多人的关注。有人点赞，也有人嘲笑他痴心妄想，股神怎会降临人间呢？他的每一封信都石沉大海，巴菲特没有一点反应，但他依然坚持每周一都写，他坚信机会是自己制造的。

安德鲁拥有的大批的“粉丝”，其中有一百位出版商每周都读他写给巴菲特的信件，他们有的是 CEO 和总裁，有的是媒体界的推动者和颠覆者，在媒体王国有着自己特殊的地位。他们邀请他面对面讨论：如何在新媒体内推动新的赚钱的点子。他从不懂商业，到慢慢学会了把商业企划转变成商业利润的方法，这时候他的很多想法趋于成熟和实用了，信件里的观点更加精辟。很多出版商都对他产生了浓厚的兴趣，甚至远在意大利的出版商都想了解关于书信的内容，有的人想借鉴他的想法，有的人更直接想用他的书信出一本书。他感觉自己的信在一点点靠近巴菲特的大门。

安德鲁的感觉很对，一周年之后，就是在 2013 年 10 月，他接到了 NBC 今日秀演播厅的邀请，去做一期关于市场营销的节目，当他推开演播厅的大门，坐在嘉宾席位上的时候，惊讶地发现巴菲特就坐在对面。他一阵狂喜，在写了 42 封信之后，自己终于成功地和巴菲特坐在一起了，经过讨论巴菲特接受了他的想法，并付诸于自己的报纸企业。巴菲特对他说：在你写到 20 封的时候，我就每周都看你的信件了。你很快就会看到自己的想法变成现实，相信这一定会给报业带来新的革命。

现在的安德鲁不仅是一名畅销书作家，更是一名市场营销演说家，他的事业又拓宽了一个领域，他在自己的新书中写道：我确信如果你也给一位“巨头”写信，你将脱颖而出。但你要想好，谁是你的“巨头”？你应该写些什么？

让我们好好想想自己需要什么样的运气，谁是自己的“巨头”，应该写给他们一些什么？最关键的是拿起“笔”给自己制造一个运气。

载于《山东青年》

一切成就都是经过大风大浪，也许你触过礁，甚至翻过船，只要用心坚持，就能到达彼岸。

没有被摘走的南瓜

文/李代金

凡事当有远谋，有深识。坚忍一时，则保全必多，一时之不忍而终身惨矣。

——胡林翼

主人屋后有一片荒坡，坡上零星地长了些野草。主人见这山坡荒着太可惜了，种点什么肯定有所收获，最后，主人在坡上栽了些南瓜秧。

南瓜秧一天天地长，并向四处蔓延。后来，那片荒坡上爬满了绿色的南瓜叶，很是好看。

不久，南瓜藤上开满了南瓜花，这儿一朵，那儿一朵，很是喜人。蜜蜂、蝴蝶在花丛里飞来飞去，热闹极了。

不久，南瓜花一朵朵地凋落，一个个南瓜出现了。

南瓜长得很快。没过多久，主人去看，发现南瓜长大了，可以摘下来吃了。主人看着这儿一个那儿一个南瓜，便数了起来：“一、二、三……”不数不知道，一数吓一跳，共有一百多个。主人还发现有个南瓜特别大，应该就是南瓜王了。主人摸着南瓜王，很是喜欢。

主人开始一个一个地摘南瓜，把摘了的南瓜放进背篓里，然后拿去卖。这么多，他吃不了。主人摘的都是大南瓜，但主人摘来摘去就是没有摘南瓜王。南瓜王心里嘀咕起来："怎么不摘我呢？快来摘我呀！"主人摘了半背篓南瓜，走了。

南瓜王很是委屈，它实在弄不明白主人为什么不摘它，它想，也许下一次，主人会摘我了吧！

第二天，主人又背着背篓来摘南瓜。主人还是在挑选着摘大南瓜，可主人就是不把手伸向南瓜王。南瓜王着急了，它叫起来："主人呀，你快摘我吧，我能卖很多钱！"可是主人没有听到它的话。主人摘了半背篓南瓜后就走了。

南瓜王更加委屈了，这主人什么意思呀？为什么他就不摘我呢？我可以为他换很多钱的啊！下一次，主人应该会摘我吧！

第三天，主人又来摘南瓜，这一次，主人又摘了半背篓大南瓜，但还是没有摘南瓜王。

南瓜王看着远去的主人，绝望了。南瓜王想，原来我是没有用的东西啊！那么活着还有什么意思呢？在这里只能丢人现眼！南瓜王挣脱南瓜藤，骨碌碌地滚下了山坡，它被摔成了几大块。

第四天，主人又来摘南瓜。主人发现了山坡下被摔成几大块的南瓜。主人蹲下身子，摸着摔碎的瓜片，惊叫起来："天啊！这不是我的南瓜王吗？我还准备把它留作南瓜种，让明年的南瓜都长得像它这么大，没想到它却摔成了这样！"主人十分惋惜。

南瓜王听了主人的话哗啦啦直掉流泪。它一直认为主人不摘走它是嫌弃它，原来主人是看重它啊！是要重用它啊！

我们有一些人，就像这个南瓜王一样，不敢相信自己，没有耐性，一遇到冷遇就自暴自弃，最终失去了被人重用、成就自己的机会。

载于《思维与智慧》

是金子总会发光的，做最好的自己，自有人赏识，并得以重用。

替身

文/李岱蔚

反腐败就亡党，不反腐败就亡国。

——陈云

现实社会，时兴替身，干什么都有替身。这不，我就是个替身，说也难怪，谁让咱跟领导长得像呢？

我们局长名叫项利民，四十多岁，比我大两岁。可我俩说不上是怎么长的，比双胞胎还像，就连我俩的爱人有时也辨别不出来。

我原来在养路段工作，后来交通局党办缺写材料的人，就把我抽去写材料。见我做事严谨，干活勤快，又能胜任工作，党办吴主任就留下了我。刚开始，我只能帮助主任续写本县县志，不过只用了半年时间，我们的党办主任就不写材料了。局里的大小材料都出自我一人之笔。

这年春天，项局长报考党校，要我替他去考试。很不幸，当场就被监考老师认出来了。这是个中年妇女，一见考卷上的名字，气就不打一处来，忿恨地说："哎，我说，你在替谁考试？这小子，他能提拔你呀！"

说着就把我往外推，我苦苦哀求，别让我出去。可她很倔，竟抡起拳头，对着我的后背打了十几下。虽然打得很疼，可我还是没出去。

考试成绩下来了，我被录取了，准确地说是项局长被录取了。一共五个学期，两年半时间一到，我终于替他考完了十四门全部课程。毕业论文——《三讲是领导干部的起码要求》被评为优秀论文，还获得了全县五个一精品工程精品奖，奖品是一套高档炊具。当我把党校法律本科毕业证书、学历证明和领奖卡交到项局长手上时，他说了声谢谢我！

学完了党校法律本科，县政府要培养后备干部。我们项局长也在后备干部名单之中，培训地点在地区湖平市，他又派我去了。教师是由省里派来的大学教授，教室设在地区党校。不愧是大学教授，课讲得就是地道。

通过学习，使我知道了什么叫 GNP、什么叫 GDP、什么叫恩格尔系数，我从不缺课。早上七点半，湖平地区组织部宣传科的侯科长要来点名，每当念到项局长名字时，我就答应一声。

我没有手机，一同学习的同学虽然跟我年龄相仿，可人家都是正牌的局长和公司老总，而我只是一名普通科员。他们中有的跟我处得很好，不过，也没发现我这个冒牌局长跟他们的区别。相反，觉得我有学识，有水平，还有晋升的机会。

学了两年，要毕业了，我写完论文交了上去，就等着论文答辩了。后来教授为了方便起见，就不搞答辩了只需要合影就毕业了。这次，我不能再替了，因为结业证书上有他照片。项局长要去湖平地区的前一天晚上，还给我打来电话，问是否要论文答辩。我告诉他放心吧，不会答辩的。拿到硕士研究生结业证书那天，项局长拍了拍我的肩膀，又说了声谢谢我！

为了得到提拔的机会，他主动要求赴西藏参加援藏工作。因为干部任免有新规定，只有援藏的局长，才有提拔为副县长的可能。上西藏，条件那么艰苦，他真的肯去吗？就在我想这个问题时，这天晚上，他又找到我说："兄弟，我是上有老，下有小，心脏又不好。再替我去西藏一次吧！谁让咱俩长得像呢！"望着他那恳求的目光，我真是不好拒绝。

时间过得很快，三年援藏工作结束了。我因成绩突出，工作上取得了显著成效，而受到上级政府的表扬。藏民们给我送了5面锦旗，还要把我留在当地。我也舍不得朝夕相处的藏族同胞，可我是冒牌的干部，不回去怎么能行呢？当我戴着哈达回到阔别三年的县城时，项局长亲自到火车站接我，我一下火车，他就伸双手握住我的手说："谢谢！真是太谢谢你了。"在后来的日子里，项局长还参加了援藏事迹报告团，拿着我写的材料巡回演讲，一时间，他成了电视媒体的热点人物。一个月后，项局长被提拔为我们县的副县长，县委常委。

可我，仍然在交通局干着文字将的工作。第二年3月份，交通系统实行改革，我所在的养路段工程队开始下岗分流，我一下又成了下岗工人。

"你那个项局长真不够意思，连个编制都没给你解决。"一回到家，媳妇就不无埋怨地说。我默不做声，有时见她说个没完，就劝她几句："下岗人太多，他想照顾也照顾不过来呀！"家里又没什么积蓄，孩子今年考大学，学费还没着落呢。下岗三天没待上，我就开始蹬三轮拉客赚钱了。

一天晚上，我开了一天电三轮，刚回到三间砖平房的家，就听见有人敲门。我打开院门一看，这不是项局长的夫人吗？我把她让到屋里。项夫人神色慌张，我忙让她坐下，她刚要开口说话，院外又响起了敲门声，她神经又紧张起来，原来是媳妇回来了。进了屋，我给她们作了介绍，坐了好半天，项夫人才说："老项被双规了，他想让你把他替出来。"媳妇一听，皱了皱眉，项夫人说：“我也知道你们生活困难，这3000元钱，就算是我给孩子的一点学费吧！”媳妇一见，忙笑着说：“行，替就替呗！还拿钱干什么！”我半天没有说话，可项夫人就是坐着不走。见她眼里浸满泪水，最后我说：“好吧！我再替一回。”

次日一早，我来到县纪检委，我一进屋，就把案件审理室的人吓了一跳。“项利民，你，你是人是鬼！”原来，项县长被双规后，被留在纪检委接受审查。不久，因心脏病突发死了。为了找到他贪污款的下落，县纪检委没有通知家属。

项利民贪污好几百万元工程款，弄得我县新建大桥坍塌。可是纪检委找不到他钱藏在哪儿，她媳妇也不说。

想了好一会儿，我站起身，附在纪检干部耳边说了几句话……

晚上，我来到项县长家，项夫人一见我，惊恐地问：“哎呀，你怎么回来了？”“他们放我回来了，我还没吃饭呢？”“那我给你做去。”我端起酒杯说：“哎，咱俩不如到南方买栋楼，过几天安闲日子。”“行啊，那我明天把钱收拾一下。”“一共咱能有多少呢？”“不多。”“那，明天，你存几张银行卡。”

第二天上午，当项夫人把银行卡递给我后，我就立即去了纪检委，交给纪检干部。经查，五张卡共计人民币498万。

项局长的葬礼我参加了，除了直系亲属，外人就是我了。

这天，我坐在三轮车上等生意，一位拄着拐杖的老人上了我的车。我回头一看，呀！是项利民的老父亲，他70多岁。他是找我打架的吗？我和气地问：“老人家，你上哪？！”“啊，我去敬老院。”我跟他聊了一会儿天，等转到项局长的话题时，老人气愤地说：“他死了，我一个眼泪疙瘩都没掉。早年他跟公安局长打得火热，我跟他说，给你那公安哥们说一声，帮你大哥的孩子办个农转非，他说，拿 5000 块钱来。我说，算了，我不办了！”听了老人的话，我不寒而栗，亲爹都不行啊！这样说来，项局长对我还算不错，那次，不是看我生活困难，还送给我 3000 块钱吗？

载于《2014 年中国微型小说精选》

恐怕任何人对于腐败都是气愤的，这样的官场，这样的官员，真是让人汗颜！

反应能力

文/庞启帆 编译

只要我们具有能够改善事物的能力，我们的首要职责就是利用它并训练我们的全部智慧和能力，来为我们人类至高无上的事业服务。

——赫胥黎

一个炮兵部队的侦察连即将挑选一名士兵升任侦察中士，中选的士兵要求必须具备敏锐的观察能力和迅速的反应力。本次的人选有三名，分别是：布莱特、鲁本和安德拉斯。考核内容分为两部分：笔试和面试。如果笔试不合格，直接淘汰。

让人意想不到的是，笔试结束，三人都获得了满分。战友们都想：这下可有好戏看了。因为大家都知道，三个候选人都很机警。

面试这天，大家都去看热闹。当然，为了公平和公正，三名候选人都必须在考场外等候。

首先被叫进场的是鲁本。考官，也就是侦察连的连长手指1英里外的一座小山，问鲁本：“士兵，请你告诉我，你能看到那边的那座山吗？”

“当然，长官！”鲁本大声回答道。

“士兵，请你告诉我，你能看见山上的无线电天线吗？”

连长接着问。

“是的，长官！”鲁本又大声回答道。

“那么，”连长继续问：“你能看见蹲在天线上的那只小鸟吗？”

场内看热闹的士兵不禁都愣了。因为大家都知道，如果不借助望远镜，是很难发现1英里外的一根天线上的一只小鸟的。

只见鲁本努力向前倾着身体，眼睛也眯成了一条缝。许久，他沮丧地答道：“不能，长官！”

第二个上场的是布莱特。连长问的问题跟提问鲁本的一样。大家都竖起耳朵听布莱特怎么回答最后一个问题。只听布莱特答道：“能，长官，如果有望远镜的话。“

连长笑了笑，喊道：“下一位。”安德拉斯进场后，他问了之前同样的问题。最后，他又问道：“士兵，你能看见蹲在天线上的那只小鸟吗？”

安德拉斯探了探身体，然后答道：“看不见，长官！但是我能听见它在唱歌。”

还用我说，是谁荣升侦察中士吗？

载于《东方少年·作文与阅读》

其实每一个人都拥有智慧，但有些人做了智慧的傀儡，而有一些人则做了智慧的主人。

第三辑

别把愤怒带回家

每天回家前，把烦恼、郁闷、愤怒，所有不开心的事，所有的坏情绪，全部丢开抛掉打扫干净，调整好情绪然后再回家。因为你把家里人弄得不开心时，你自己会更不开心。带上好心情回家，美好的生活需要大家一起去创造。

容纳不同意见

文/沈岳明

真正的虚心，是自己毫无成见，思想完全解放，不受任何束缚，对一切采取实事求是的态度，具体分析情况对于任何方面反映的意见，都要加以考虑，不要听不进去。

——邓拓

三国时期，张辽与乐进一同效力曹操。两人同是将军，但张辽常打胜仗，乐进却总打败仗。乐进觉得不可思议，便常去向张辽讨教。

讨教的结果，又总是令乐进不满意。因为张辽所讲的，乐进全都知道。事实上，两人的才能是不相上下的。就连曹操也早就看出了这一点，所以才没责怪乐进，而是依然重用。只是因为没有做出成绩，乐进自己却不好意思了。

一天，苦恼的乐进，又去向张辽讨教。刚走近张辽的帐营，乐进便听到了激烈的争吵声。乐进不想多事，便准备离去。可是，听着听着，他的脚步便迈不开了。因为他分明听到张辽的部下在他面前，一个个就像面对敌人般针锋相对、剑拔弩张。乐进第一次知道，张辽与部下的关系，竟然是这样紧张。

乐进想，这样下去，还怎么打仗啊，没打倒敌人，自己倒先打起来了。于是，赶紧让人将张辽叫出来，并直接说出了自己的担忧。没想到张辽不但不以为意，还反问乐进："你与部下又是怎样相处的呢？"

乐进一拍胸脯，说："当然是和睦有加呀，我们天天在一起喝酒、吃肉，亲如兄弟呢！俗话说，打虎亲兄弟嘛，如果我与部下都不和睦，那还怎么打仗呀？"

张辽却摇了摇头，说："那么，我问你，究竟是我的胜仗打得多，还是你的胜仗打得多呢？"乐进一时语塞，犹豫着说："这正是我不明白的地方啊，你跟部下的关系这么紧张，还老打胜仗，我跟部下亲如兄弟，却老吃败仗！"

张辽说："表面上，我跟部下的关系紧张，其实是容纳了他们的不同意见。只有充分考虑不同意见之后，做出的作战计划才有必胜的把握。而你每天与部下喝酒、吃肉，看起来亲如兄弟，久而久之他们便失去了直言的机会，每次拿主意的人总是你一个，所以在实战中，就出现了诸多问题。"

乐进听了豁然开朗，并且很快便采用了张辽的做法，终于成长为一个与张辽齐名的大将之才。

一个家庭是这样，一个公司是这样，一个国家也是这样。如果所有人的想法都一样，那么就变成了一个脑子，而他们做出的决策，也会存在各种盲点，其中一定潜藏着非常危险的问题。但是，凡是经过激烈争论之后做出的决策，实施起来，反而更有成功的把握。

载于《少年文摘》

兼听则明，偏信则暗。大山不拒细壤方能成其高，大海不辞小流故能成其大。集体的力量是无穷的！

先抱荆棘后拔刺

文/张燕峰

极度的痛苦才是精神的最后解放者，唯有此种痛苦，才强迫我们大彻大悟。

——尼采

在一次酒宴上，我认识了一位叱咤风云的企业家。家乡的各级报纸曾对他有过连篇累牍的报道，因此对他的故事我早已耳熟能详。

少年时，父亲常年卧病在床，生活的全部重担压在母亲孱弱的肩上。一天，母亲上山为父亲采集草药时，不慎滚落山崖，当场昏厥过去，再也没有醒来。闻听噩耗，父亲一口气没缓过来，也去了。一天内痛失两位至亲，遭此沉重打击，15岁的他一下子沉闷了许多。乡亲们看他孤苦伶仃甚是可怜，于是纷纷接济他。可要强的他不肯接受大家的帮助，一个人苦苦地熬过了生命的第一次寒冬。

18岁时，他去县城的大修厂做学徒。由于心灵手巧，加之刻苦好学，不到三年，他就掌握了全部的修理技术。可好景不长，大修厂很快倒闭，他空有一身本事，却失了业，不得不赋闲在家。

后来，别人看他技术好，拉他入伙共同办修理厂。几年下来，积累了丰厚的资金。合伙人巧舌如簧，借口要进新设备，卷走了全部的积蓄，逃得无影无踪，只留给他一个破破烂烂的院落。

他的心灵，又一次遭遇了重创。乡亲们很为他担心，以为他会从此一蹶不振，失去生活的信心。那段时间，他整天不言不语，着了魔一般拼命地干活，头发蓬乱，满身油污，30 出头的年纪落魄得像个 50 岁的老者。

由于他的修理技术已至炉火纯青之境，很快便东山再起，有了自己的修理厂不久，修理厂规模越大越大，许多小修理铺都主动投到他的旗下。后来他又涉足食品加工，近几年又搞房地产开发。每一次的创业都险象环生，可他就是凭着顽强的信念，一路披荆斩棘地走过，终于获得了巨大的成功。

他从小命运多舛，人生可谓跌宕起伏，他的创业史更是血泪斑斑。然而，每次陷入人生的低谷后，他总是及时收拾残破的心情，重整旗鼓，走出困境。

席间，我好奇地询问："是怎样强大的信念在支撑着您，使您成为打不倒摧不垮的钢铁斗士，虽历经艰难却仍像巨人一样屹立在人生的风口浪尖?"

他微微一笑，淡淡地说："尝的苦水太多了，便学会了先抱荆棘后拔刺。"

"先抱荆棘后拔刺!"这句蕴含深刻哲理的智慧之语猝然击中我心底最柔软的角落，心弦蓦地颤动不已。

是啊，每个人的人生都不是一帆风顺的。当我们遭逢人生的"滑铁卢"，遇到无法选择无法逃避的命运时，是满含忧愤地诅咒命运的不公，终日怨天尤人、自暴自弃，还是坦然地接受它，义无反顾地把荆棘抱入怀中，然后忍着身体和心灵的剧痛，把侵入肌肤痛进骨髓的那些尖利的刺一点点地剔除干净，一面自我疗伤，一面坚韧执着，将生活的苦难酿成芬芳醇香的美酒，敞开胸怀，迎来生命的春暖花开。无疑，这位令人尊敬的企业家交出的是一份优秀的人生答卷。

路漫漫其修远兮，谁都无法预知前路会发生什么。当坎坷泥泞、风雨凄迷之时，一定要以沉潜淡定之心、从容豁达之态，以坚不可摧的勇者之姿，直面惨淡的人生，将荆棘抱入怀中，勇敢地挑战厄运，咬紧牙关，迎难而上，把那些扎人的刺一根根拔掉，这才是真正的勇士，才会在人生的历史上书写浓墨重彩的辉煌篇章。如果选择退缩，不战而退，实则是辜负了命运的馈赠，荒芜了大好人生。

载于《思维与智慧》

拥抱荆棘，就是拥抱困难，拥抱痛苦。在生活面前，我们就需要这种敢于流血的精神。就像鲁迅先生说的那样：敢于直面惨淡的人生，敢于正视淋漓的鲜血。

一张 VIP 卡

文/怜　子

画龙画虎难画骨，知人知面不知心。

——蒲松龄

那年春节前夕，叔叔和几个朋友开了一家宾馆。开业前，他特地给我家送来一张刚做好的黄金 VIP 卡，也邀请我们全家去参加他们的开业典礼。

在开业仪式上，叔叔骄傲地向人们介绍了他的哥哥我的父亲，那时候父亲正和几个朋友合伙开着一家粘土矿，正值火爆。人们都在羡慕他们兄弟俩：哥哥有那么好的弟弟，弟弟有那么好的哥哥。

那年夏天我要参加高考。考前一个月，叔叔就在宾馆准备了一间套房专门供我复习和休息用，直到高考结束。那时候我们家庭聚餐或者是父亲矿上的应酬都在叔叔的宾馆，但是都没用过叔叔给的那张 VIP 卡，因为叔叔特地交代他们宾馆只要父亲签个字便可。那时候，叔叔有空就会去家里看我们，包括我要去南方上大学时，也是他送我到学校，还帮我办理好入学手续。同学们都说我有一个好叔叔，我自己也觉得有时他给我的依靠比父亲还多。

大学里第一个假期回家的时候我特地为叔叔买了一些南方

的特产，叔叔把它们带在车上，放在家里最显眼的位置，逢人就炫耀说是他侄儿在南方读大学买给他的。

大学第一个暑假回家的时候，出了车站，发现只有父亲一个人在等我，让我更惊讶的是，父亲竟然是骑自行车来的。原来在两个月前，父亲的粘土矿突然发生地陷，所有的开采设备在一夜之间全部陷入地下。后来请了很多挖掘设备开挖，结果在挖到一半的时候又发生了第二次地陷，部分挖掘设备也陷了下去。就这样短短的两个月间，不但父亲赚钱的粘土矿没有了还欠下了一些债务。父亲跟我说这些的时候推着车子看着前方，我看不到他的表情，看不到他的眼神，他平淡的语气像是在述说别人的事。那天，我们用自行车驮着行李箱从车站走回家，但是我感觉是从一个世界走到了另一个世界。我清晰地记着，父亲那天穿了件白衬衫，记着他后背微微沁出了一点汗印，记着他推着自行车跟我说话的样子。

过了两天，父亲的那几个朋友决定举家到南方去闯荡。走的那天，他们一起吃饭，就在叔叔的那家宾馆。饭局结束时几个人都哭了，我第一次见一群大老爷们泣不成声。最后结账的时候被告知父亲的签字不再有用，我给叔叔打电话他没有接。后来还是妈妈去找邻居借钱过来结的帐，她还带了那张黄金的VIP卡，享受了最大的折扣，这也是我们第一次用那张VIP卡。

后面就再也没有见过叔叔，也没有电话联系，也没有听到父母提起过他，就好像从来都没有过这个叔叔一样。父亲进了一家企业做了一个普通员工，我们家就过起了靠父亲薪酬度日的小日子。虽然不如从前充裕，却更有幸福感。

大二暑假的时候，远在乌鲁木齐的阿姨回来探亲，父亲安排他们住在叔叔的那家宾馆，当然是用了那张VIP卡。在阿姨的记忆中叔叔跟我们很亲，所以还特地给他带了礼物，结果那份礼物最后也没有送出去。看到我们现在的处境，阿姨走的时候留了张卡给妈妈，当然是她回到乌鲁木齐才告诉妈妈放卡的地方和卡的密码。那天父亲拿着那张银行卡和那张 VIP 卡看了好久。

转眼之间就到了我大学最后一个寒假了，我们全家在家正准备着过春节呢，突然涌进来一帮人。原来是父亲当年一起开矿的朋友，他们现在又发了家，现在回来给父亲拜年。其中一个居然是在我读大学的城市，还说让我毕业后直接去帮他管理公司。过完春节，他们就张罗着在我们市为我父亲开一家公司，还利用他们之前开矿时候的关系帮父亲开了一家运输公司。挂牌开业的那天，叔叔突然来到我家，死缠硬磨地让父亲去他的宾馆举行了开业仪式。

大学最后一个暑假回家的时候，一出车站就看到叔叔在出站口，上了车才发现父亲也在他车上。到了家母亲才告诉我，知道要放暑假，叔叔便天天来问我什么时候回来，见今天父亲去接我，便非要一起去。见家里堆满叔叔送来的东西，我知道他又像以前一样对我们亲热了，但我们却并没有因此觉得高兴，特别是父亲。那天叔叔还请我们全家吃饭，席间他边喝酒边讲起小时候他和父亲的故事，讲到小时候父亲怎么带他出去玩，怎么在爷爷面前护着他，还有在他读书时候老去学校偷偷给他零花钱。讲到这些的时候他一个人拿着酒杯不断地喝着，脸红红的，但眼神很迷离。

大学毕业后我最终留在了上大学时的城市，那年父亲突然说他和母亲要来陪我过年。等他过来才知道他已经转让出那家运输公司，准备在这里做点小生意陪我。南方的春节没有雪，但有比雪还要冷的雨。那天父亲要我陪他散步，走到离市中心不远的一个路口，他指着一个商铺说以后他和母亲就在这开一家小商店，安心地过他们的小生活。说完，父亲从我手中接过伞，递给我一张卡，并要我随身带着，在得意的时候多看看它。我接过卡来一看，正是叔叔当年送我们的那张 VIP 卡，我看了下办理日期，正好五年，不差一日。

载于《青年博览》

人心隔肚皮。我突然觉得这不就是赤裸裸的讽刺吗？总是有这样的人嫌贫爱富，阳奉阴违，在别人发迹的时候靠拢上来，在别人落魄的时候悄然离开。有些人的嘴脸注定是丑陋的，我们需要认清。

别把愤怒带回家

文/王晓宇

能控制好自己情绪的人，比能拿下一座城池的将军更伟大。

——拿破仑

傍晚下班时间，大街上车流滚滚，一辆接着一辆，却慢如蜗牛。

大赵夹杂在车流中，心急如焚，可能是中午吃的东西不干净的缘故，这会儿肚子疼痛难忍。偏偏那车被十字路口的红灯挡住了，过了好几分钟，车子仍然被挡在那儿不动，大赵心中有些生气。

自从买了这辆车，天天有很多时间都耗在路上，久而久之，便患了“路怒症”，只要一堵车，他就弹簧一样跳起来。鼻子眼都碍事，怒气像着了火一样，从心头冒出来。

原来前面有两辆车发生了轻微的亲密接触，车主互不相让，发生了口角，所以后面的车堵得像长龙一般。好不容易警察赶来了，才把纠缠不休的两个人分开。大赵舒了一口气，赶紧打道回府，谁知到了家门口，自己的车位又不知被哪个临时停车的占住了。他情急之中，把车子停在花坛边，赶紧回家去 WC。

刚刚打开家门，儿子冲过来，扑到他的怀里说："爸爸、爸爸，早晨我让你买的奥特曼，你给我买了吗？"大赵说："乖儿子，爸爸忘了，明天再给你买。"孩子不干了，"哇"地一声哭了，一边哭一边嚷："爸爸骗人，爸爸是坏蛋。"

一直急于去 WC 的大赵，至此，坏情绪终于被全面引爆了，他怒不可遏，大骂："这是什么破路？这是什么破车？这是什么破家？还让不让人活了？"

孩子哭得更凶了，大赵的爱人以为他打孩子了，从另一间屋子里冲出来，指着大赵嚷嚷："嫌破车不好你别开啊！嫌破家不好你别回来啊！嫌孩子不好你把他扔了啊！"

至此，好好一个周末，以为全家三口可以聚在一起，加两个菜，吃个轻松舒适的晚餐，结果全被破坏掉了。两个人来言去语，吵得翻了天了。

大赵的妻子本来心里就堵得慌，她在公司里生了气，和同事闹别扭，上司偏袒，心里有气，像被摇晃了的可乐瓶。结果大赵又把愤怒的坏情绪带回家，点燃了她这只待爆的汽水桶。

原本一个轻松愉快的周末，结果孩子哭，老婆叫，大赵愤怒到想跳楼，一个家乱成了一锅粥，这日子还怎么过？

生活像一个万花筒，每个人在生活中都会遇到一些开心或不开心的事儿，遇到不开心的事儿，心中难免会抑郁愤怒。可是回到家中，把在外面遇到的不开心的事儿或者愤怒带回家中，那种场景，你自己都能想象出来。

任何人都会有情绪低落的时候，任何人都会有不开心不快乐的时候。这种时候，最好的办法就是自己克制一下，忍耐一下，别把坏情绪传染给别人，别做引爆家庭战争的杀手。

家是一个温暖的港湾，我们每天都要在这个港湾里休养生息。家里的人都是我们最亲的人，我们每天都要和家里人在一起。

每天回家前，把烦恼、郁闷、愤怒，所有不开心的事，所有的坏情绪，全部丢开抛掉打扫干净，调整好情绪然后再回家。因为你把家里人弄得不开心时，你自己会更不开心。

带上好心情回家，美好的生活需要大家一起去创造。

载于《智慧背囊》

每个人都有坏脾气的一面。工作不顺利，恋爱不顺利，就把这种糟糕的情绪带到家里，传递给每一个家人。这是不好的，一个环境就该有一个环境需要去做的事，不要把坏情绪带回家。

表现

文/崔永照

没有独立精神的人一定依赖别人；依赖别人的人一定怕人；怕人的人一定阿谀谄媚人。

——福泽谕吉《劝学篇》

马成一直想表现，表现的机会终于来了。

表现，当然是在自己的顶头上司汤兵面前。

那是初春的一个上午，暖洋洋的春风亲吻着公司大院的几株桃树，那娇艳的桃花好像禁不住缠绵，不时洒下花瓣雨，地上便是缤纷一片。

马成端着一杯茶，一杯飘着浓浓茶香的茶。抿一口，咂咂嘴，回味半天，显得悠闲自在。不过大脑在想着好多事儿。比如，这次公司中层干部选拔，总经理汤兵力排众议，把自己从一名普通职员提拔为财务部长。

想想几千号人的大公司，财务部长是管钱的，是万众瞩目的重要岗位，有人还在私下议论这可是个肥缺。自己已经上任两个月了，可还没给汤经理任何表示。

上个月到外地出差，他精心挑选了一套精品茶具，送到汤经理家里。汤经理淡淡地说，小马呀，别这样，我从来不接受别人的财物。还有，当前中央都提出了《八项规定》，纠正

"四风"，咱更得廉洁自律，以身作则。

可是，您提拔我，我不表表心情，过意不去。

你来公司四年了吧？我看重的是你的人品和工作能力，好好干工作就行，别想那乌七杂八的。你去吧！汤经理抬抬手，就把马成打发了。

这时，马成眼睛一亮，看见汤经理的大奔从外回来，少顷，他扶着一位老人下了车，朝自己的住宿楼走去。那老人是谁呀？他想。

听说，孝顺的汤经理把他七十八岁的老父亲汤超接到城里来，要住段日子。刚从外回到办公室的小刘，在和小谢嘀咕，这个消息如台风，顷刻间刮来。马成笑了，把茶杯放下，踱到窗口，狠狠地吸了一口新鲜空气，他就知道自己处心积虑想表现的机会终于来了。

他在汤超到城里的第二天夜里，带着几件高档营养品赶到汤经理家，可敲了半天门也没人应声，无奈回到自己的住室，盯着院子看。很晚了，才见汤经理和爱人搀着汤超慢慢地进了院子了，不用说，他们陪老人出去散步了。

汤经理，给您汇报个事儿。马成第二天到汤兵办公室，急急地说。

说吧。汤兵呷了一口茶。

我听说老爷子来城里了，我想请老爷子吃顿饭。马成一脸虔诚。

哦，小马呀，谢谢你的好意，不用了。汤经理漫不经心地说。

汤经理，您听我说，您那么关照我，我又是您的下属，我请老爷子吃饭是应该的。

我是你的领导，在城里你请我爹吃饭，也显得我很有面子？汤经理说。

不是的，是您给我面子。马成在心里说，你要的不就是这个效果嘛。

呵呵呵，汤经理笑了。

嘿，看来有戏。马成异常高兴。

算了吧，不用，你去吧。

马成感觉自己一下子跌进了万丈深渊。

他惆怅了好几天。

从量变到质变的规律马成掌握得不错，半月后，汤经理经不住马成泡蘑菇，终于答应了。

那个傍晚，马成搀扶着汤超穿过酒店金碧辉煌的大厅，感觉自己宛如走在幸福的大道上。

在豪华包厢就坐，汤经理，他的妻子和孩子围着汤超递水、夹菜，唠嗑聊家常，温馨幸福，一家人其乐融融。连马成都羡慕不已。

汤超还一个劲夸菜很可口，马成不禁为自己周密的安排而有些沾沾自喜。他们不知道为了让老爷子吃好饭，他专门找到酒店经理，从菜要做得淡些、熟透、适合老人口味多方面进行了嘱托，还给经理了几张大票表示感谢呢。

看他们兴致很高，马成不失时机提出了一个大胆的想法，无酒不成席，咱们喝几杯酒吧？

汤经理迟疑了一下，算了吧。

哦，哦。老爷子反应比较明显，分明有渴望的眼神。

老爷子年龄大了，不敢喝酒的。

这个我知道，不过咱不喝白酒，就喝葡萄酒。这是既养生又保健的，咱少喝点？马成解释。

那，那就少喝点儿。汤超抢先答应了，汤经理没再说啥。

服务员打开葡萄酒，倒到高脚杯里，这红色的琼浆玉液，愉悦着大家的眼神，氤氲出诱人的香。

很快大家推杯换盏，把晚餐引向高潮。

喝高兴的老爷子对汤经理说，我看这个小马很精干……

我敬您一杯酒，祝您福如东海，寿比南山。马成受宠若惊，来到汤超面前，毕恭毕敬端起一大杯酒，一仰脖就下肚了。

我再敬汤经理一杯酒，祝您事业辉煌，前程似锦。马成端着满满一杯酒，来到汤经理面前。汤经理满意地拍了拍马成的肩膀，马成一激动，又喝下了一杯酒。

大家都喝得醉意朦胧，这才打着饱嗝离席了。

马成觉得这是一次成功的宴请，在心里为自己欢呼和自豪。

走出酒店，马成小心翼翼地扶着汤超下台阶，他两腿软绵绵的，汤超也踉踉跄跄的。汤超一步没有走稳，马成还没反应过来，他就重重地摔倒在地。

大家惊慌失措，乱成一团。当把汤超送到医院检查后，医生严肃地说，病人胳膊和腿三处骨折，需要住院治疗，是喝酒喝高了吧……

马成听到头顶响起了一声炸雷，震耳欲聋。

载于《小小说选刊》

有些人总觉得世间所有的事情都可以用巴结奉承可以搞定，这样的想法一旦根深蒂固，那就跟祈求恩赐没什么区别。

你曾经说过的最温暖的话

文/安　宁

人之为善，百善而不足。

——杨万里

人若是舟楫，那信任大约是助其向前的波浪；反之，则是阻其行走的大风。信任越多，舟楫越快；信任越少，舟楫则有可能倒行逆施，背离要抵达的目的。这就犹如偏执一些的孩子，母亲如果对他微笑宽容，不去修剪那些旁人以为芜杂的枝杈，倒是让他生出冲天的枝干；但如果怀疑，猜忌孩子，反而会让这孩子原本无关紧要的小性子，放肆地向四下里伸展开去，一直到只顾着反抗，而忘记了那主干向上的姿态。

所以看到那些上课迟到的学生，信誓旦旦地在我面前说谎，总是大度一笑，想起十年前的自己，也是这般将大学过得鸡飞狗跳、喧嚣一团的模样，对老师所撒的谎，写下来可以编成一本《迟到早退理由之大全》，供师弟师妹们参考或者效仿。

我清晰记得那些学生撒下的谎，犹如记得自己在老师面前的小心计。有一个学生，在我讲到一半的时候，气喘吁吁地闯进来，又风一样跑到我的面前，报告说他的舍友生了病，他刚刚将他送到校医院回来。然后还擦了一把额头的汗，飞给我一个做了好事没留名的羞涩表情，便匆匆归了位置。但他不知道我在下课后恰与他的其中一个舍友一起下楼，相聊间，便得知了他上课迟到，不过是因为与女友闹了小别扭，为了讨好，去学校门口买了她爱吃的热薯条，又怕冷掉了，惹女孩不悦，便一路飞奔，做了速度最快的“快递员”，送至女孩自习室，在外面偷偷看女孩吃下一口后，这才穿越整个校园，赶自己要上的课程。我没有在又遇到男孩后，揭穿他为自己“贴金”的小把戏，更没有像他的舍友们那样，在知道了前因后果后，封他个“情圣”的称号，而是微微笑着问他你舍友的病好了么？他果然红了脸，低下头去，说好了，谢谢老师。这一个“谢”字，他没有加上“关心”的后缀，但我们彼此却心知肚明，他会因此记得我这一次的善意，而我亦会自此得到他的信任。

想起自己读书的时候，一次跑去看一场日间的老电影，忘记了上课，等到想起来时，课已经快要结束。本来可以完全逃掉，因为那个总是一脸淡漠的老师，未必会对我有深的印象，但出于尊敬，还是快马加鞭地奔跑过去。从后门悄无声息地溜进教室，打算课下再对老师解释一个合理的迟到原因，但老师锐利的眼睛，却即刻化作无情的鞭子，越过全班同学的头顶，重重地抽在我的脸上，并起了红色的印痕。她几乎是把我喊叫起来，让我这从后门进去的学生，重新绕到前门，并在我解释完是因为给学校校报帮忙而耽误了上课后，她毫不留情地便当场斥责我撒谎，并罚我一直站到课下。但在她上课结束离去时，她已经完全忘记了我，或者是故意将我冷落掉，擦着我的肩膀过去。我几乎能感觉到她胳膊上传过来的静电，咝咝地烧伤了我的肌肤，连同里面裹着的一颗试图请求她谅解的心。

此后我对这个老师，再也没有产生过兴趣。她的课像是一张被揉皱了的纸，我看也不看，便随手丢进了记忆的垃圾箱。

她未曾给予过我谅解与宽容，在我这里也同样没有为她留下一个温暖长久的位置。

我的一个同事是教舞蹈的，那些每天 5 点早起辛苦练功的孩子们，常常来不及吃饭，就要赶赴早晨 8 点的课程。所以每每她上课的时候，下面便可以看到一张张啃食面包的嘴，时不时地，还会发出有节奏的咀嚼声。同事站在讲台上，若不回头，那些声音听上去便像一群酣畅饮食的小猪般可爱，也让人哭笑不得。许多老师，一再严肃申明，上课不准吃饭，曾经有一个老师，因为将一个正在偷吃饼干的女孩叫起来训斥，差一点让女孩当场噎住了喉咙，因在同学面前丢了颜面，她再也不敢来教室上课。而同事则巧妙地在点名的几分钟里，让孩子们一起吃完手头的东西。孩子们果真听话，迅速地消灭掉买来的早餐，并因为老师给他们时间吃早餐，给予他们信任与宽容，在听课时就格外认真，毕业后都还念念不忘老师的好。

同事一直用心记着一个女孩的话，她说，老师，你知道吗，你说过的最温暖的一句话是，“孩子们，慢点吃”，这比你讲过的任何一节课，都更能打动我们的心灵。

载于《中学生》

你曾说过最温暖的话是什么呢，恐怕连你自己都不记得，或者你压根儿就不知道，因为你说过的话，在别人心里。总之，多一点善良和爱吧，别人总会记得。

老先生的课

文/安　宁

教育者应当深刻了解正在成长的人的心灵，只有在自己整个教育生涯中不断地研究学生的心理，加深自己的心理学知识，才能够成为教育工作的真正的能手。

——苏霍姆林斯基

学院里有一老先生，教授舞台表演。听说他是当地话剧团的团长，退休之后，闲极无事，便成了学院的外聘教师。我不知道他有着一份正职的时候，是否也如此敬业，或者一丝不苟，热爱他的下属，并将他们当成自己的孩子一样深爱。我只知道当我开始工作的时候，他就已经在这个学院里教了多年，有一批喜欢他的孩子。他对这份工作，有一种失而复得的珍爱。

第一次见他，是学院里一个讲座，他恰好坐在我的旁边。我是新人，对于周围的热闹与熟络，觉得陌生而且孤单。他是一级演员，有着很好的洞察能力，看出我与周围人的隔阂，便主动地与我说话。我们谈及各自的故乡、家人、爱好。他的两个女儿，均在日本做着与专业无关的工作，其中一个，大约是医生，有着不菲的薪水。每年的暑假，他都会飞去日本，与女儿相见。在他说到山东话剧界的一些朋友时，又热情地问及我的创作，说如果有可能，我们合作一部话剧吧。他已经老了，头发灰白，但精神却矍铄，掸去岁月的尘埃，可以看得到他年轻时英姿飒爽的身影。声音是台柱子的洪亮与大气，当是不需话筒，在台上表演许久，也不会沙哑。

讲座结束的时候，他转身去给后面听讲的学生，布置下堂课的作业。不知道他说了什么，学生们齐声高呼："好!"他果然有很好的号召力，又大约是个人魅力的光芒很盛，他只是在学生面前一站，自有一种将散沙汇聚在一起的力量。我站在旁边，安静看了一会儿，心里有微微的羡慕与嫉妒，对于这样有着浓郁艺术家气质的老先生。我想起高晓松的《冬季校园》里，所唱的白发的先生和漂亮的女生，这样苍郁与青葱的组合，在校园里，犹如法桐之于玉兰，和谐到你觉得他们天生就应该是生长在一起的。

之后，我时常会在上完课后，于教室门口、走廊里、办公室内或者校园的小道上遇到他。有时他会带着与自己同样白发苍苍的夫人，我猜测学生们会称呼她师母。她也是一位笑意盈盈的老人，有不服老的天真与单纯。他们称呼我"王老师"，我常常因此羞涩，觉得这一称呼黯淡了光泽。他们一来，办公室里便格外地热闹，似乎他们两人是一个火炉，可以融化掉冰冷的空气，和同事之间刻意保存的距离。我喜欢听老先生说起课上某个爱叽叽喳喳的男孩，或者总是迟到的女孩。他提及他们的时候，言语里满是爱怜，没有丝毫的责备。曾经有老师，抱怨一个冷门专业的学生们集体闹情绪，大约觉得找不到未来的方向，不知道学了之后，在所需极少的社会上能有什么用武之地。他听后便宽容地笑笑，安慰那上课的老师，说："孩子们有情绪，很正常，等过了这一年，他们慢慢热爱上这门艺术，自会留恋和懂得它对于人生的好，到时怕是你让他们转系，都不肯了呢。”

据说，这话每个刚刚接手这个专业的新老师都会听到。他很少说这样语重心长的言语，只是这样站在走廊上，与年轻老师闲聊似的，安慰一阵，然后继续去和学生们说笑。那些学生，全将他父亲一样地爱着，热爱中又没有距离，会和他开开玩笑。有时候遇到学生与女朋友约会，那牵着小女友的手并不会松开，好像知道他会慈爱地看一眼，而后带着一点羡慕说：“每天看到你们两个在一起，真开心。”

想起见过的一个老师，远远地瞥见一对牵手走路的男孩女孩，不屑道：“那两个学生，学习不怎么用功，谈恋爱倒是起劲得很。”这个老师大约从未觉得他们从美好的爱情中学习到的其实相比于用来谋生的专业，对其一生的影响，更为深远长久。而另外一个老师，看到一个上体育课偷偷从队伍里溜走的女孩，即刻愤愤地追过去留下一句臭骂。那一刻，他也忘了，他自己曾经也是一个爱从队伍里逃走，去寻找新天地的孩子，这样的出逃不是要小心计，也不是偷懒，而是一时兴起，想要旁观一下某个暗恋的男孩，或者哪个好脾气的体育老师。

我常常想去听一下老先生的课，就像一个刚刚读了大学的学生，隐在角落里，看他在台上那让我心生仰慕的飒爽的英姿。我想那一定很美。

载于《疯狂作文》

一个人心是明朗的，不管年岁多么无情，脸上却也是明朗的。一个人完全可以影响一大批人。

此心安处是吾乡

文/叶浅韵

昔我往矣，杨柳依依；今我来思，雨雪霏霏。

——《诗经·小雅》

每一方山水都有自己独特的走势，依偎在这种地脉中长大的人也就有了自己独特的禀赋。在同一方山水中孕育出来的人们除了血脉相连的亲情，一定还有许多剪不断的乡情。而这些情怀，只有远离故乡才有被检阅的机会。

我在离故乡不远的小城里居住，我的存在，成了故乡的人从村庄通往城市的一个驿站，更像是一个桥梁。无论是孩子上学、老人看病，还是借钱、购物、托人办事。因为有我，他们就觉得与这个城市的关系不至于那么陌生，尽管有时我显得那么力不从心。

因为他们一直对我寄予着的种种希望，有时，我就特别害怕自己对不住故乡的山水，所以一直保持手机昼夜开通的习惯。我曾在深夜的电话里听到鸡鸣狗叫的声音，及时知道村庄失火的消息，用最快的速度把车开到家里，与父老们一起面对着可怕的灾难。以至于我对一些信息有了免疫的能力，陌生的号码打进来，早早的电话，深夜的电话，我都保持着高度的敏感。不是让我难过就是让我耗费精力的事情。

这些年，我习惯了，习惯了把自己当成一头耕牛，艰难地行走在故乡贫瘠的土地上。

我知道自己只是不小心成了游离在故乡怀抱的人，故乡的山水草木，故乡的亲人邻里，就成了梦里别样的画卷。

在男人们忙着寻根问底时，女人对于故乡的概念像一根水草，根基不稳地守望着故乡。当我在祖先的墓碑上看清自己的来路时，我却成了不能走在这条路上的人。即使后来我坚定地走向一座桥，我也必须不时地回望着那条路。

在异乡的时间长了，就如寄生在某种植物身上的另一种植物，自然或是不自然地生长在一起。渴望有朝一日回到自己的故乡，可匆匆几日却又逃离了故乡的怀抱。故乡仿佛只适合存在梦境里。

可以割裂故乡的景物，而对于故乡的人，无论我梦着还是醒着，几个数字之后的铃声，再有一辆从故乡通向城市的班车，我的全身就必须投进故乡的怀抱。

明知道有些债从借出的那一天开始就知道它打了水漂，有些人明明就是落井下石的小人，而心中留存的那份情，却容不得我拒绝。我忍不住要伸出手去，不，我恨我不能长出千手。

夫取笑我说，我不是强大的美利坚合众国，却要充当世界警察。也不是千手观音，救不了人间苦难，更不是玛莉娅、特雷莎修女。其实，我知道我是那么渺小，常在心力不足之间抱愧不止，而我却拒绝不了，忍受不得。

在疲惫乏累的夜里，梦是一片沉睡的海平面，这时，我忘记了故乡的一切。我梦见清澈的小溪，静静地、轻轻地淙淙向前行走着。醒来，想起苏轼的那首词："试问岭南应不好？却道：此心安处是吾乡。"

我不知道在明天，那片山水之间生存着的人，他们会给我喜讯还是悲伤。但我知道，我永远无法割舍与故乡连接的那条线，即使在闭上双眼时，我成不了故乡山水的一部分，我的灵魂也一直行走在故乡的土地上。

载于《知识窗》

故乡的一切都映在我的脑海里，那停滞的云、流动的风，故乡的一草一木，都是我永恒的记忆。总是在梦里看到自己走在归乡路上，而你站在夕阳下面容颜娇艳。

犟松

文/林振宇

何当凌云霄，直上数千尺。

——李白

生命的树种被风吹落了，有的落在平坦、肥沃的泥土里；有的落在山坡树林间；有的不幸落在险崖峭壁的石缝中，谁也无法选择。

落在平坦、肥沃泥土里的树种，沐浴着充足的阳光、雨露，茁壮生长着；落在山坡树林间的树种，虽没有前者环境优越，但也长得顺当；而落在石缝中的树种就没有那么幸运了，恶劣的环境让它几乎窒息，但它还是顽强地活了过来。由于缺肥少光，生长缓慢，十年过去了，居然变化不大。

又过了十年。

这时候，它的同伴们已经长成了参天大树，挺拔、伟岸，而它才从石缝里斜斜地挺出头来，柔柔弱弱的样子，刻着先天不足的烙印。

所有的不幸，它都默默地承受；所有的苦难，它都化作内在的斗志。它太犟了，不肯向命运低头，也不屑于自己外表的瘦小和同伴们的嘲弄，紧紧地抓住泥土，把身子斜向上伸出来。因为它知道，如果生存环境无法改变，那么只能改变自已。它以无法想象的坚韧和命运顽强、持久地抗争着……

转眼已是百年。

有一天，山里突然来了一群游客，他们被险崖峭壁的石缝中斜伸出来的奇松吸引住了，虽然它只有碗口那么粗。导游小姐提醒大家，这棵松树已经在那里生长一百年了，当地人给它起了个名字叫“犟松”。游客们听了叹为观止，站在犟松面前，不由产生一种对生命的敬畏之情。

这是怎样的一棵树啊！在石缝里，历经百年风雨，硬是挺立出来，还长成了一道奇绝、瑰丽的风景。然而这背后，有谁知道它到底经历了多少世事沧桑啊！

犟松，你像一位世纪老人一样站在那里，虽然什么也没说，却告诉了人们应该以怎样的姿态活着。

载于《知识窗》

大雪压青松，青松挺且直；要知松高洁，待到雪化时。生命的坚韧顽强来源于内心对生的渴望。

会走路的植物

文/瞿幼芳

在世界上出人头地的人，都能够主动寻找他们要的时势，若找不到，他们就自己创造出来。

——萧伯纳

常言道：树挪死，人挪活。可是大千世界，无奇不有，这世界上就有不怕死的植物，不但会走，而且活得还很滋润呢。苏醒树和步行仙人掌就是典型的代表。

苏醒树，生长在美国东部和西部地区，生物学家经研究发现，它的行动和土壤中的水分含量有关。当土壤中有足够的水分时，它便扎根土壤，长得郁郁葱葱，枝繁叶茂。但一旦天气干旱，土壤缺水时，它就会自动把根从土壤中抽出来，形成一个球状体，任凭风吹来吹去，当吹到有水的地方时，它又重新将根插入土中，重新生活，又长得非常茂盛。

这种苏醒树是有灵性有感应的植物，它能不断适应周边的环境，比一般的植物都要高级。它还能有意识地控制自己的身体从而帮助自己更好地生存，虽然不能像人类一样改变环境，但它能让自己找到所需的环境并在那里生活下来，简直就是植物中的奇迹！

据传，在神秘的羽族部落，苏醒树的树液还被用于制作出征统帅所穿的祈福胸甲上的薄盾片。在将事先制作好的木盾片完全去除水分后，秘术师们将其完全浸入苏醒树的汁液中，然后晾干，加持上明月系的祈福秘术。七浸七晾之后，轻薄小巧的胸甲片便会覆盖上一层坚硬的半透明的白色玉质层，在夜里会发出淡淡的白色荧光。传说，这种祈福胸甲通常为统帅出征时提前三天佩戴。如若胸甲片颜色清明，则象征着凯旋；颜色黑浊，则象征着战事不利，需要更换主帅。事实上这种传说并非毫无依据，据羽族的御医检测，这层玉质层能检验人的健康程度，颜色重浊则表明主帅身体不适，不宜出征，更换主帅也在情理之中。

苏醒树生长起来后，缩卷身体，沉睡；又张开身体，苏醒。但是在这个不断进化自己的过程中，苏醒树总是努力使自己重生，这也是它名字的由来。

同样在南美洲秘鲁的沙漠中，有一种自己能徒步行走的植物——步行仙人掌。这种仙人掌能将自己的根系当成腿和脚，慢慢地向别处行走。

步行仙人掌的根是由一些软刺构成的，能随风在地面上移动，随遇而安。沙漠本来荒凉贫瘠，缺少水分，这种仙人掌为了觅取自身需要的水分和养料，以便维持生命，当在某一地区生活不下去的时候，只好随风一步一步地移动，当遇到适宜的生活条件时，便停下来。用它那些软刺构成的根，吸取水分"安营扎寨"，继续生长。步行仙人掌需要的营养大部分是从空气里吸取的，故能短时间离土而不死。

苏醒树和步行仙人掌是植物中的天才，当扎根的土壤不能再维持生命时，它们便毅然离开，去寻找更为适宜的土壤。

在我们的周围，也有一些人，整天抱怨环境的不如意，但他们又鼓不起勇气开创新的生活，对过去的眷恋总会成为往前走的障碍。既然过着混日子的生活，不如向苏醒树和步行仙人掌学习，去广阔天地寻找更为适合自己的环境。

载于《知识窗》

学会变通，学会随遇而安，就像一株生命倔强的草，虽然微小，但不可被藐视。

与劫匪一起高歌

文/ 庞启帆　编译

爱是生命的火焰，没有它，一切变成黑夜。

——罗曼·罗兰

几年前的夏天，我和妻子朱迪斯以及我们两岁的女儿雷拉开着一辆小型野营车，在墨西哥的下加利福尼亚州的巴扎半岛旅行。在返回圣迭戈的前一晚，我们在海滨附近停车过夜。

半夜时分，朱迪斯猛地推醒我，大声叫我起床。迷迷糊糊中，我听到一阵喧哗声和撞击声。我光着身子跳了起来。我们的野营车被几个蒙面人围住了，他们正在猛烈敲打车窗。

我扑向驾驶座，发动引擎。野营车在整个旅途中已经顺利启动至少50次了。这一次，它却在响了几声后，熄火了。这时，我听到了玻璃破碎的声音，然后一只手从车窗外伸了进来。我再次转动钥匙时，一把枪顶住了我的脖子。

一个劫匪会说一点英语，他叫嚷道："钱！钱！"枪仍然顶着我的脖子，我只好从司机座下面取出我的钱包，递给其中一个劫匪。我希望他们拿到钱就离开。但他们没有。

拿枪的那个劫匪从破窗口伸手进来打开了门，然后将我拖出车外。劫匪共有四个人：一个拿着枪，一个拿着一把生锈的杀猪刀，一个拿着一把大砍刀，一个空着双手。

拿枪的劫匪继续用枪顶着我的脖子，我被迫躺在地上。另外三个劫匪开始在车上乱翻，同时用西班牙语大声叫喊着。

我的脑海里开始出现强奸和谋杀的景象，但不知怎的，一会儿后，一个新想法猛地把那些可怕的景象赶走了。他们也是上帝的孩子。我曾在公众面前多次宣称我以服务他人为乐。现在，这些人就在我面前！我看着那些劫匪，心中响起了一个声音："别害怕，他们不是强盗！他们是上帝的孩子！"

我对那个会说英语的劫匪说："嗨！你错过了最好的东西！在司机座下面有一部很好的相机。"

他奇怪地看了我一眼，朱迪斯和雷拉也惊奇地看着我。

那劫匪用西班牙语跟另一个劫匪叽里咕噜了几句，很快，他们在司机座下找到了我的索尼相机。

我爬起来，走过去从副驾驶位上拿起我的吉他，一边向他们展示一边说："很棒的吉他！"我拨了几下琴弦。"谁来弹一曲？嘿嘿……还有，索尼随身听、耳机、磁带！你们想要吗？"我想真正的美国人在紧要关头会放弃那些该放弃的东西。我努力在想我的所有物品中，他们最喜欢什么呢？

很快，我有了主意。我问道："你们想吃点什么吗？"

那个会说英语的劫匪向他的同伴翻译了我的话。然后，四双眼睛愕然地看着我打开了食物袋。我看见了一个漂亮的红苹果。"哇，多可口的苹果。"我拿起苹果，递给那个拿着大砍刀的劫匪。

虽然我们无法沟通，但我知道在不同的文化中，分享食物是一种交流的方式，友谊的信号，或者和平的传递。那个劫匪看着我手中的苹果，犹豫了一会儿，然后微笑了一下，接过了苹果。这一刻，我知道他已经放弃了我们刚见面时所扮演的角色。

我们已经送出礼物，并且与他们一起分享了食物。然而，吃饱之后，说英语的那个劫匪说，要我们跟他们一起驾车离开这儿。我们一家又回到了恐惧状态中。我无奈地说："好吧，我们跟你们走！但请你们不要伤害我们。"

我穿好衣服，爬上车后座，与朱迪斯和雷拉坐在一起。拿杀猪刀的那个劫匪扭转钥匙，启动引擎。见鬼，这次竟没有熄火。

大约半个小时后，车子驶进了沙漠地带。一路上我都在心中盘算，当车子接近人群时，我就踢开车门，把朱迪斯和雷拉推出车外。

车子不知行驶了多久，我突然问自己："如果我与朋友一起开车旅行，我会怎么做？"当然是唱歌啦！

我和朱迪斯、雷拉放声唱了起来："听，听，听我心中的歌。我永远不会忘记你，我永远不会抛弃你……"

雷拉的脸上一直挂着可爱的笑容。她吸引了两个劫匪的目光。好几次我看见他们努力地保持严肃的神色，仿佛在说："省省吧，孩子，别跟我们来这一套，我们可是劫匪。"但是，他们最终情不自禁地笑了起来。

我松了一口气，但我很快意识到他们并不懂我们所唱的歌的意思。我想了一会儿，灵感就冒出来了。

"卡塔那美拉，卡塔那美拉的姑娘啊……"

成功了，他们开始跟着高声唱了起来。这时，再也没有什么劫匪和受害人了。我们脚上踏着节拍，在夜晚的沙漠中一路高歌。

不知过了多久，我们进入了一个偏僻多山的村庄。车子在开进一条黑暗的土路后，突然停了下来。我和朱迪斯互相对视着，都猜想他们可能就要杀死我们。我们紧紧抱住了我们的女儿。

他们打开车门，下了车。我等着他们来拖我们下车，没想到他们竟跟我们说“再见”。然后，那个会说英语的劫匪说道：“请原谅我们。我和我的同伴，我们是穷人。我们的父亲们没办法帮助我们。你知道我们得挣钱，这是我们的法子，很抱歉！你是一个大好人，你的妻子和孩子也都很好。”

他一遍又一遍地道歉。“你们是好人，请不要把我们当作坏人。”

他从口袋里掏出了我的钱包。“给你。”他把我的信用卡还给了我。“这个我们用不着，你最好拿着。”然后，他又把我的驾照还给了我。最后，在他的同伴惊讶的注视下，他抽出了几张墨西哥纸币。“给你，你的车可能需要加点油。”

我像他的同伴一样诧异，好一会儿，我都没有接那几张钞票。

他微微一笑，把钞票塞到我手中，然后说：“再见。”

很快，他们消失在夜色中。我们一家三口紧紧拥抱在一起，哭了。

载于《情感读本》

这世间一切的丑恶，唯有爱可以化解。因为每个人都是上帝的孩子，人性本善，谁都不是一下子变成了邪恶的魔鬼的。

“体验”瑞典

文/徐 伟

民主使每个人成为自己的主宰。

——詹·拉·洛威尔

休年假了，在瑞典的弟弟一家邀请我去玩玩，我愉快前往。我很快喜欢上了这个国度，因为她平易近人，即使去政府部门办事，也能处处让人感到温暖。

一天，弟弟说他还完房贷了，请他岳母陪我去房管局做抵消。我们步行去车站，差不多十米远就到车站时，一辆车迎面驶来。快到近前时，我发现正是我们要乘坐的那班车。我连忙挥手，车子缓缓停下来，我们上了车，我向司机道谢，然后要买票。谁知，司机让找座位坐下，说不用买票。

怎么回事呢？我不解。弟弟的岳母说：“在瑞典乘公交车，要在车站的自动售票机上买票。而公交车上是没有售票机的，后上车的乘客只是顺路捎带，不用买票。”“车上的客人不多啊，司机为什么不等等客，多赚些钱？”我问。“每个人的时间都是宝贵的，公交公司不能因为自己的利益浪费乘客的时间。所以，即使车上只有一名乘客，也要准点出发，不耽误乘客哪怕一秒钟的时间。这是对已买票乘客的尊重。”“那么，这样的捎带，会不会使一些人滋生逃票心理？”“不会的，逃票是要重罚的；人们很自觉遵守乘车准则。”我不禁为充满人情味的变通和严格的规定叫好。

到了房管局，一进门，便见一张方桌上醒目的温馨提示，“请自己取号，等待叫号办理。”弟弟的岳母从桌上的一个盒子内取出一个拇指见方的小号码递给我，我们坐到大厅里等候。

很快到我们了，弟弟的岳母示意我去办事。我来到服务窗口，一位四十几岁的先生微笑着，彬彬有礼地问：“您好！有什么让我效劳的?”我连忙说明情况，交出资料。“请稍等。”那位先生说。不一会儿，他递给我两张表格让我填。我接过表格，他请我坐下，并指了指面前的电钮，按了下去。忽然，桌面的高度降了下来，恰好与坐着的我齐胸，正是方便写字的高度。这小小的细节使我心下一暖！

可表格上的术语让我如坠云端，什么“抵押权利人”“抵押人”“房地产权证”“土地他项权证”，等等，看得我头都大了。正当我不知所措之际，那位先生问：“有什么不明白的吗?”我尴尬地说：“怕填错。”他笑着说：“不要急，很容易的。”接着，他耐心地逐一空格指点我怎么填。两张表填好后，他又告诉我去几号窗口继续办理。在后面的三个窗口，迎接我的都是笑容可掬、热情周到的办事员。就这样，在我印象里程序繁杂的房产证赎回手续，在这里不到半个小时就办好了。回到家，我感慨万千地对弟弟说，国内提倡的微笑服务，我在万里之遥的异乡切切实实体验到了。弟弟说：“瑞典是高税收国家，个人所得税在所缴纳的各种税收中比例高达三成多。这就意味着公务员是在花纳税人的钱，那么，为纳税人提供称心的服务，是理所当然的。”

几天后，因为淋了雨，我去看医生。那次，弟弟告诉我就诊的一般程序，帮我预约了医生。到医院挂了号后，我在候诊区等待叫号。也就五分钟的工夫，一位医生走上前，问了我的名字后，热情地握着我的手，说她就是我预约的医生，来迎接我去诊室。这让我大吃一惊，同时感到心里暖暖的。

到了诊室，医生耐心细致地询问我的身体状况及感冒原因。了解了一阵子，医生说没什么大事，吃点药就能好。“这么简单?”我暗想。想起在国内，即使比我症状轻的，只要进了医院，就要做多项检查，还要打四五天的吊针。“打几天吊针会好些吧?”我不大放心地问。“那等于慢性自杀！我不能对您的身体不负责任。”笑容和蔼的医生忽然严肃起来说，弄得我很尴尬。医生见状，抱歉地笑着拍了拍我的手，请我放心。还就饮食等注意事项，做了详细说明。之后，送我出诊室。

回到家，和弟弟说起在瑞典的就医体验：“整个诊疗过程给我的感觉，就像老朋友的亲切关怀，令人如沐春风。不过，这里的医生很傻——很少做检查不说，还不给患者打吊针，哪里能赚钱?”弟弟笑了笑，认真地说：“把患者当傻子的医生，才是真正的傻子。因为在瑞典，医生倘若敷衍患者，或者对患者滥用药物，将会被吊销行医执照，终生不得行医。也就是说，百姓的强有力后盾是政府，公务员必须全心全意为其服务。”

载于《做人与处世》

一个国家如果把个体的舒适度、利益等放在第一位的话，那它一定是很进步、很人性的社会集体。

为国家留点生机

文/段奇清

致天下之治者在人才，成天下之才者在教化。

——胡瑗

1947年9月初，沈从文收到一封信，写信人在信中说了自己的处境，并请求沈从文预先支付一些稿费。

写信人叫柯原，早在这年的夏天时，他陆续给沈从文寄去了一些诗歌作品。此时，沈从文从抗战期居留的昆明回到了北平，在复校的北大继续任教，并受邀担任了天津的《益世报》文学周刊的主编，北平的《平明日报》等报纸文学副刊的编辑。

柯原投稿时署的是“路苇”的笔名，诗作反抗黑暗、渴望光明、追求未来，充满激情，沈从文很是喜欢。7月19日，沈从文在《益世报》文学周刊上发表了路苇的《飞吧，我的心》等两首诗作，这一下点燃了路苇的创作热情。

编辑和作者之间是有缘分的，自打刊发柯原的作品后，沈从文是来稿必回，能发表的告诉其优点、特色所在；凡是满意的，沈从文还争取发在他任编辑的《平明日报》等副刊上。不刊用的也会一一退回，并在每篇稿件附上具体意见。

这让柯原成了既写得多，见报率又高的作家，如仅在

《益世报》上每月都会有他的诗作刊出。无论是收到了发表作品的样报，还是退稿信，柯原的心中都会是暖暖的，他也就把沈从文当作值得信赖可亲可敬的人。

柯原这时只有 16 岁，是天津河北高等工业学校的一名学生。虽说学习的是化工专业，却尤其喜欢文学。文学创作之路顺畅，可家庭却遭到变故：他的父亲是一个小职员，因年纪较大被工厂裁减而失业。这时他们 6 口之家就只有柯原的姐姐在一所小学当教员了，微薄的薪水根本不足以撑起这个家。也许是出于对生活的焦虑，他的父亲失业没多久就得了急性肺炎，更不幸的是治疗不久就去世。因当时物价飞涨，治疗费用昂贵，他们家欠下一笔债务。日子艰难时就会想到最信赖的人，于是柯原写信向沈从文求助。

接到柯原的信后，沈从文忧心如焚，因为他知道，以当时柯原的知名度和文章，是很难获得报社预支稿酬的。无奈当时他们一类的知识分子日子也很艰难，即使沈从文同时做了几份工作，也没能有余钱去帮助柯原。

其实，虽说沈从文对柯原多有文字交往，让柯原视作亲人，可他与柯原未曾谋过面，本来力所不及是可以写信让柯原原谅的，对方虽说失望也不会对他说些什么。可沈从文对柯原的遭遇寝食难安，最后，他想到用手中的笔来给予柯原一些真正的帮助。

“有个未谋面的青年作家，家中因丧事情形困难。我想作个‘乞醯’之举，凡乐意从友谊上给这个有希望的青年作家解除一点困难，又有余力作这件事的，我可以为这作家卖二十张条幅字，作为对于这种善意的答谢。这种字暂定最少为十万元一张，我的办法是凡要我字的，可以来信告我，我寄字时再告诉他如何直接寄款给那个穷作家。这个社会太不合理了，让我们各尽所能，打破惯例作点小事，尽尽人的义务，为国家留点生机吧……”于是，1947年9月20日他在《益世报》文学周刊上发了这样一则启事。

也许人们被沈从文“为国家留点生机”的情怀所感动，所激励，柯原家中陆续收到20多份“买字者”寄来的款项，不过这些人并非大款阔佬，多是一些善良的普通人。有的人还写信表达问候之情。凭着这些钱，这些温暖的信，柯原走出了困境。

其实，在沈从文做出卖字的决定时，也是在思想上经过一场交锋的。由于沈从文身上那种强烈的中国文人知识分子的傲气，以前他的日子即使再窘迫，也没曾卖过字，在他看来，文人卖字就卖掉了自尊心。但为了帮助一个身处困境的青年，他也就顾不得许多了。

但沈从文在启事中，并没有公布这位“未谋面”青年作家的姓名，只是要求买字的人写信给他，在按对方所说的规格、内容写好字寄去时，才告诉“未谋面”青年的地址，让买字人将钱寄去，他这样做为的是给柯原留有一份尊严。

因种种原因，这“未谋面”一过就是30多年，直到1980年夏天，柯原才去北京看望了一直渴望见面的恩人沈从文。此时，一位是在中国现代文学中卓有建树的文坛老前辈，一位是才气横溢的当代诗人。这第一次见面，第一次握手，情形感人至深！

为给国家“留点生机”，不惜以牺牲自己的尊严帮助一个“未谋面”的青年，却又千方百计维护这位青年的尊严，沈从文善良的心性和崇高的风范尽显无遗。

载于《做人与处世》

现代好多人都有恶习，自以为是、倚老卖老。如果我们每个人，尤其是地位相对高的人，肯把机会留给年轻人的话，那将是民族的荣幸了！

时光柔软

文/范泽木

流光容易把人抛，红了樱桃，绿了芭蕉。

——蒋捷

时光是单行的列车，上了这车，便永不能回头。即使是硬着头皮，也还是得走下去。

在刚出发的时间里，我们总是欢欣雀跃，一路欢喜。这大概如我们坐车去春游，途中总是特别激动。

时光赐予我们少年的不羁，那时，我们浑身有使不完的劲，在操场上飞奔，在赛场上驰骋，有张扬的个性和挥洒的激情。

那感性大于理性的岁月，我们可以因为梦想而奋不顾身，可以因为一时脑热说收手就收手，也可以因为所谓爱情而哭天喊地。

18 岁那年，朋友小 A 借了叔叔的摩托车。我们在宽阔的操场练了一下午后，觉得得心应手，于是载着同学在公路上疾驰。我后座的同学不时惊叫，还吹着响亮的口哨。由于我们的张扬跋扈，我们的第一次骑行以人仰车翻宣告结束。

的确，时间确实如此，让我们去欢笑，也让我们去思考，然后我们在时光里慢慢变得胆小。从那之后，我们再也不敢放肆地骑车。

前段时间，在闹市看到几位血气方刚的少年，骑着电瓶车横冲直撞。现在的电瓶车动力够好，载了三四个人还是身轻如燕。看他们摇摇晃晃地绝尘而去，恍然看到多年前的自己。也是这般年纪，也是如此放荡不羁。如今却陡然后怕，殊不知，如果父母看到那时的自己，会担心得怎样。

如今越来越能站在父母的角度去看问题，所以多年前的嗤之以鼻，总能变为现今的不令而行。以前，父母对我三令五申，比如要穿暖，夏天睡觉要盖住肚脐，但我总是我行我素。如今我反而经常给他们打电话，要穿暖，要记得带雨伞。

在时光的河流里，每个人都是石头，慢慢被磨去棱角，渐渐变得温润。有人说这是失去个性，变得中庸。事实上个性并不是玩世不恭、锋芒毕露，而是内在的执着与张力，是坚毅与坚韧。能被时光轻易带走的，往往不是真个性。

时光让曾经外显的，变成内在的。它慢慢褪下我们的浮华，尘埃落定；让我们变得越来越谦逊，越来越温和，越来越坚韧与执着。

多年前，我写过一篇文章，叫《成长是一个妥协的过程》。但事实上，时光给我们的不是妥协，而是让我们成为越来越好的自己。

载于《语文周报》

时光带给我们什么呢，伤痛、惊喜、失落、收获。其实都无所谓，因为这些都会令自己成长。

第四辑

占便宜其实是个套

其实，细细想来，占便宜说到底也不是什么好事，顾盼四周，大概还没有人因为占便宜而发家致富、飞黄腾达吧！但因为占便宜身败名裂、得不偿失的人却是大有人在。

在心里种下一首歌

文/顾晓蕊

若是每一个孩子的诗情画意都能得到人们的欣赏鼓励，从而获得健康的成长，那么，世界将成为一个富于诗情画意的世界。

——般庆功

那是一个秋天的黄昏，斜阳渐落，红霞染红了天边。我和家人一起吃晚饭，偶一抬头，见窗外冒出两张粉脸。再一看是阿美和小胖，挤眉弄眼地朝我招手，我会意地冲他们点点头。

妈妈在一旁说道："别着急，多吃点饭。"我心里跟猫挠似的，胡乱扒拉了几口，就站起来说："吃饱了，我要出去玩了。"话音刚落，人已跑远。

不一会儿，院里的小伙伴陆续聚拢过来。我们开始跳方格、捉迷藏，玩累了，阿美提议说："咱们来开演唱会吧。"大家一致举手赞成，靠墙的一块青石板成了临时舞台。

阿美清了清嗓子，唱了一首《蜗牛和黄鹂鸟》，清亮的童音传进耳畔，引来我们的阵阵掌声。轮到我上场了，学着歌星的样子先鞠了个躬，然后故作陶醉地唱道："我爱你，塞北的雪……"

“哈哈哈……”二胖妈不知何时走过来，双手掐腰，笑得花枝乱颤，“这一嗓子号的，吓了我一大跳，简直比哭还难听。”她是位大嗓门的东北女人，边笑边夸张地比画着。我羞得满脸通红，扭身跑回家中，趴在床上抽泣起来。

那年我10岁，正是敏感而脆弱的年纪，被一句无意的嘲笑，淋湿了心空。我将墙上的明星海报撕掉，缺少了歌声的陪伴，感觉生活变得单调了许多。

读高中时，学校举办“庆元旦”文艺会演，老师要求全班同学排练大合唱。回想起难堪的童年往事，我灵机一动，想到个好主意。站在队伍中，跟着低声附和，没想到很快被老师识破了。

“你——站出来，单独唱一遍。”老师用手一指，厉声说道。当时我的脑子一片空白，木木地走到前面。刚唱了几句，老师摆了摆手说道：“我看还是算了吧，你就对对口形，千万别唱出声来。”

全班哄堂大笑，笑得乱成一团，难过与羞愤混杂在一起，我恨不得找个地缝钻进去。

我变得愈加孤僻内向，正是从那时起，喜欢上了阅读。我独自坐在花树下，捧着一本书，安静地看着。青春如悠长又寂寥的雨巷，而我，仿佛是那个丁香一样的结着愁怨的姑娘。

刚参加工作那几年，每逢闲暇时，同事们三五成群地闲侃，或去唱歌跳舞。我依旧一杯茶，一本书，静静地打发时间。后来，我尝试着写作，渐渐地文字不断出现在报刊上。

有一年夏天，我去海滨小城参加笔会，晚饭后，我和美女作家茉莉沿着海边漫步。月光洒在银色的沙滩上，海面上波光潋滟，一切如梦如幻，恍若置身仙境。

茉莉说：“这么好的美景，咱们来唱歌吧。”我不好意思地说：“我唱歌很难听的。”然后，我跟她讲了因唱歌闹笑话的尴尬往事，她微笑着说：“其实，不用太在意的。不管是快乐时光，还是悲伤瞬间，歌声都是最好的陪伴。”

那天晚上，我们并肩坐在沙滩上，轻轻地唱着歌。那些从心底淌出的音符，有一种让人安定的力量，仿佛置身于另一个世界，感到从未有过的轻松和愉悦。

她说：“在人生的舞台上，你永远都是自己最好的听众。”我听了，惊住，一时感慨不已。只因别人的几句嘲笑，我的生活被罩上一层阴影，现在回头去看，才发现过去的想法是多么荒唐可笑。

从笔会回来以后，我们偶尔会在网上聊天，她说最近迷上黄梅戏了。我告诉她，我报了个古筝班，闲时写文章，弹古筝。她在那边欢呼道，可以想象，你弹古筝的样子，肯定会很优雅的。

再后来，有一天，我应邀到一所中学做文学讲座。这要放在以前，是想都不敢想的事。

因为在人多的地方讲话，我会脸红紧张，手足无措。可这一回，我鼓起勇气，欣然前往。当台下响起热烈的掌声时，我起身鞠躬致谢。

想起曾经看过的一句话：你学过的每一样东西，你遭受的每一次苦难，都会在你一生中的某个时候派上用场。如此说来，那些嘲笑过你的人，那些忽视过你的人，也是生命中的“另类贵人”。

而今，在月光如水的夜晚，我喜欢听听音乐，喝茶看书。不抱怨，不张扬，像一株植物一样安静地活着。有朋友说，你变得更明媚了，有着动人的芬芳。只有我自己知道，在心里种下一首歌，是件多么美好的事。

载于《新作文·初中生适读》

曾经我们都是孱弱的，就像流浪的小猫，到了陌生的环境，遇到陌生的人就害羞得紧张得不行。后来，慢慢有了勇气，有了自信，因为遇到了鼓励自己的人。

弱者也是强者

文/张燕君

内心如果平静，外在就不会有风波。

——谚语

古诗云："独立三边静，轻生一剑知。"能够独立的"弱者"内心最宁静。

澳大利亚的动物学家戴维森一直研究猴子的生活习性。一次，他来到亚马逊河流域，将两只猴子带了回去，分别关进两个笼子里，每天精心喂养，并随时观察它们。

一年后，一只猴子健健康康的，另一只却不幸死掉了。戴维森百思不得其解，按一般人的眼光，如果两只猴子一定要死掉一只的话，死掉的应该是还活着的这只。因为带回时，死掉的那只猴子又大又壮，活着的这只却瘦小羸弱。

为了知道这是为什么，戴维森又让人从亚马逊河流域带来一只更大更健壮的猴子。这只猴子却死得更快，只半年工夫就撒手人寰，倒是那只小猴子依然健在。

难道说这是偶然吗？戴维森又进行过两次类似的试验，强壮的大猴子依然在一年内死去。

戴维森坐不住了，再次来到亚马逊河流域，这次他索性住在了猴子非常多的巴西。经过半年多的观察研究，他终于弄清楚了被关进笼子的大猴子必死的原因。

原来，凡是体格健壮的猴子容易被其他猴子接受，它也乐于和其他猴子在一起。一旦有空，它就在猴群中来往穿梭，同时还能得到其他猴子供奉的食物。这样的猴子最怕孤立，一朝失去自由，被关进笼子也就往往活不过一年。

那些瘦小的猴子则不然，没有同类愿意搭理它们，久受孤立，也就学会了独立，或者说适应了被孤立，被关在笼子里时丝毫也影响不了其生活质量，且吃的不愁，反而会健壮起来。

一个有趣的现象，或者说生命的悖论出现了：强者沦为生存的弱者，而弱者反倒成为生存的强者。

我不禁想到发生在二战时期的一个故事，在德国东部布痕瓦尔德纳粹集中营，看守人员创造了一种独特的死刑执行方式。

在集中营附近有一座埃特斯山，山间有一道深不见底的峡谷，峡谷上拉起了一条钢索。在死囚将行刑时，看守就押着他们来到峡谷前，对他们说，谁能赤手空拳爬过钢索，谁就能获得自由。

按说比起挨枪子儿或刀子来，这样有着一定的生存希望。但是，一名男死刑犯爬着爬着就坠入了深渊，两名，三名……十名……三十名，无一例外。这也是看守人员敢玩这种“死亡游戏”的原因所在，因为这根钢索足有2公里长，这些囚犯已被折磨得够呛了。

然而，到底出现了一个奇迹。

一天，纳粹看守又押来了一个死囚，这位犯人爬过约三分之一时，两位行刑人员就开始喝酒聊起天来。只因为爬钢索的是一位叫艾米丽的女子。他们想：连男性犯人都没有一个能爬过去的，更别说这位瘦小羸弱的女子了。

俩看守喝着酒，其中一个谨慎者也免不了不时拿眼看一下随着钢索上下抖动的女子。女子约爬过一大半了，“谨慎者”对同伴说：“奇迹会不会发生在这个女子身上?”同伴连连摇手说：“不会的，我们只管喝酒聊天。”

“谨慎者”到底害怕女子成功爬到对岸，他们会受到上司的处罚，喝得醉眼朦胧的他于是向女子开了枪。此时峡谷中的雾越来越大，连女子的影儿也看不到了，艾米丽终于成为一位逃过死亡魔掌的人。

有人说艾米丽之所以能创造奇迹是因为母爱：家中有一个3岁和一个2岁的孩子。其实，那些在“死亡游戏”中坠入谷底的男性，也有孩子盼望着他们回家。而父爱和母爱同样是爱的两座高山，没有谁比谁逊色。

最后研究人员认定，艾米丽能爬过钢索，是由于她内心的宁静。男性囚犯开始时并不将钢索放在眼里，再加上求生心切，一到钢索上便拼尽全力爬动，终于力所不支，不得不绝望地松开求生的手。艾米丽则缓缓爬动，一开始就能做到爬一会儿再伏到钢索上闭上眼睛歇息一会儿，或看一看峡谷中缓缓飘动的雾岚。因为属于弱者的她根本没有逞强的资本。

“鸣鹘直上一千尺，天静无风声更干”。静是一架无形的天梯，它能让你站立于境界的高端。因为没有包袱，“羸弱”者反倒能让灵魂变得轻盈，内心获得宁静。“心轻者上天堂”。内心宁静者也就能避开地狱，到达生命奇迹的彼岸。

载于《知识窗》

孤独是本领，平和也是，最后能走向成功的，往往是那些不显山不露水的人。所以，孤独是成长的必修课。

把夕阳当饭吃

文/王晓宇

我们走得太快，灵魂都跟不上了。

——佚名

多年前，我曾经看过一张照片，是一张逆光的摄影图片：圆型的拱门配方格子玻璃落地窗，窗内有一张精致的方形桌，桌上有两杯咖啡，一杯尚满，一杯已空。

夕阳斜照在窗棂上，呈暖暖的桔黄色，远处是欧式的洋房。画外音是：口袋里只有五个便士了，我不喝咖啡，请给我来一份夕阳。

看图片的时候，我的心怦然而动。先不说构图的精致与完美，单单那一份意境、那一份从容与豁达就令我痴迷。如果是我没有钱了，会不会很慌张？会不会很失落？像一只丧家犬一样，夹着尾巴跑来跑去，忙着找工作，忙着找朋友借钱度过饥荒？怕失业，怕生病，谁还会有闲心看夕阳？

跟朋友说起对这幅图片的感受，朋友忍俊不禁地笑了，说："口袋里没有钱，还有心思看夕阳。吃饱撑着了才会干这种傻事，没有钱哪还有心情干这种傻事啊？"

我张了张嘴，生生地把想说的话咽了回去。他不是缺乏艺术修养的人，可是他还是用惯常的思维和大多数人的角度去解构这个问题。他不缺钱，多年的奔波操劳和兢兢业业，让他已经积攒下一份不小的产业，可也不见他放下手里的事情去休闲看书、看夕阳。

他天天忙着打理手上的事情，谈合同，签合约，一会儿国内，一会儿国外，忙得脚打后脑勺。因为不能按时进餐，他患上了严重的萎缩性胃炎。不过是刚刚进入中年的人，额头上已是沟沟壑壑，两鬓青丝已早生华发。

看见他，我便跟他开玩笑："你的钱多得在仓房里都招耗子了，何必呢？拿出点时间，享受一下生活，调整一下身体，岂不比什么都好？"

他摇了摇头笑了，说："你不懂，当你看到那个数字一天一天不断地水涨船高时，那种幸福感和成就感简直难以言喻。"我明白，他说的数字当然是指银行账户上的数字。为了那个数字，他疯狂地工作，像一个工作狂一样没日没夜。为此，妻子说和他已经三年没有一起吃回烛光晚餐了，儿子则说父亲从来没有去学校替他开过家长会。

后来，妻子爱上了别人——一个肯和她一起看夕阳的人，顺便也把他的儿子带走了。他成了孤家寡人，一个人抱着一堆的钞票欲哭无泪。看见我，他抱怨说："你说我有什么错？我拼命地在外面打拼，不就是为了妻子和孩子能过得好一点吗？我容易吗？看人脸色，饥一顿饱一顿，图什么啊？"

我也笑了，说："她图的是那个人能陪她一起看夕阳。"他怔住了，呆呆地看着我："看夕阳有那么重要吗？那个男人哪儿比我好？每个月挣那么几张有数的钞票，想去一趟欧洲都得攒好几年。看夕阳，晒月光，风花雪月论斤买，能当饭吃啊？"

我听了，无言以对，滚滚红尘中，有多少人和他的想法一样？两只眼睛里除了钱，什么都看不到，那是他们人生唯一的目标，也是人生终极的理想。物质带给他的满足和喜悦远远超越了人间的一切，不言而喻，结果肯定是凄凉的。

如果有一天，我失业了，没有钱了，我会不会很从容、很镇定，甚至底气很足地对餐馆里的服务员说：“我不吃饭了，请给我来一份夕阳。”

夕阳当然不能吃，只能慢慢欣赏。不太如意的人生，会因为这份夕阳变得美丽生动起来，惆怅不安的心境也会因为这份夕阳变得温暖舒畅起来。当人生走到绝境的边缘时，我们不妨从容对待。洗个澡，美美地睡上一觉，明天之后，一切都会是一个新开始。

载于《文苑》

生活的本质是什么呢，这是我们应该思考的问题。那些看似光鲜的背后，是不是也隐藏了很多令人不安的因素？比如，不着家；比如，经常冷落了孩子；再比如，跟妻子不和，等等。我想说的是，看清生活的本质和自己所肩负的责任是很重要的。尽量，不要做一个太俗套的人。

抬起我们的头

文/嵇振颉

预防胜于治疗。

——狄更斯

公交、地铁车厢内出现了专注于手机、平板电脑屏幕的“低头一族”。这究竟是科技进步为人们带来的福利，还是时代带给我们的无奈？

君不见在拥挤的地铁、公交车里，众多年轻一族都作“低头看屏幕”状。手机或平板电脑上的网页、视频、小游戏，让这些上班族找到了打发往返途中无聊时光的有效途径。他们关注的范围，仅限于屏幕那方小小的空间。至于周围有其他异动，很难引起他们的注意。时间就在屏幕不停地闪动中悄悄溜走，如同潺潺的流水静静地从他们身边流过。

低头族现象不仅止于流动的公共空间，更多地表现在“人坐在一起，而心却各在他处”。无论是工作会议、朋友聚会，甚至是恋人约会，许多人都会觉得和身边的人无话可讲，反而对网络上的信息更感兴趣。当人们没有继续交流下去的兴趣时，这样的会议、聚会、约会也就成为一种鸡肋和例行公事。

低头族的产生，有着深刻的背景。城市化进程的加速，生活节奏越来越快，客观上造成私人时间碎片化。不少年轻人希望抓住这些零碎的时间，通过数字终端进行娱乐休闲，以此放松紧张的身心。上网浏览、玩游戏、看视频等，“低头一族”在页面的不停切换中玩得不亦乐乎、乐在其中。

我并没有贬低“低头族”的意味，一个不懂得休息的人，不会拥有一个幸福的人生。可是，这一动作习惯的弊端还真应该引起我们的重视。有研究说，每天长时间接触电视及电脑，脑部会受到海量信息的过度刺激，由此导致注意力不集中，这势必会影响一个人的工作和生活的效率。

其次，过分依赖手机、平板电脑，会造成人际关系的冷漠。人间的真情，绝不是冷冰冰的数字和符号可以替代的。亲情、友情、爱情，正是在面对面沟通交流中不断加深、升华，而不是面对闪烁的屏幕时就可以擦出火花的。低头族好像大海中的孤岛，只专注于自己的“一亩三分地”，而忽视了自己的社会责任。如果任由这样的现象发展，整个社会将成为一盘散沙，而我们又可能退回到“原子式”的状态。

最后，低头一族会带来健康上的隐患。清晨的朝阳、落日的余晖、蹒跚学步的孩童、饱经岁月的老人、小草上的露珠，这些都是上天对我们的恩赐。如果埋首于数字终端，那么我们就错失了让身心愉悦的机会。低头注视液晶屏幕时，大脑依然处在高度紧张的状态。这哪是放松？依然是一种异化的“工作模式”。长此以往，无论是生理上还是心理上，都很难摆脱亚健康的状态。

如果数字终端被我们适度、合理地利用，它们将是我们获取信息、娱乐休闲的强大助手；反之，我们就将成为它们的“奴隶”，在紧张刺激的画面中渐渐迷失真实的自我。

抬起我们的头吧！身边有很多美好的事物，等待我们去发现、去欣赏。

载于《文苑》

普及一个小知识：研究表明，低头看手机时，颈椎所承受的压力是平常的三倍还要多，时间久了，颈椎病就会找上门来。所以，尽量减少对电子产品的依赖是很有必要的。

“半”字人生

文/李　玲

人之心胸，多欲则窄，寡欲则宽。

——谚语

“半水半烟著柳，半风半雨催花；半沉半浮渔艇，半藏半见人家”，这是明代诗人梅鼎祚的咏春诗《水乡》。4句24个字，连用8个“半”字，把一个半隐半现、烟雨迷蒙的江南春景图描写得惟妙惟肖，恍惚迷离、飘渺散逸的美感呼之欲出。

在湖南长沙岳麓山爱晚亭至麓山寺之间的山道旁有一座六方形单檐凉亭，名曰“半山亭”。在很久以前，此地原为半云庵之所在，为麓山寺里的僧人们上下山的必经之处。

传说，寺里有一烧火僧以“半”字为题，赋诗一首。“半山半庵号半云，半庙半地半崎嵚；半山芳草半山石，半壁晴天半壁阴；半酒半诗堪避俗，半仙半佛好修心；半间房舍半分云，半听松声半听琴。”18个“半”字将一事一物、一景一地、一心一行的分寸拿捏得恰到好处。住持赞叹不已，立即收该僧人为衣钵弟子，“半”字诗也一直流传至今。

明末清初的李密庵，有一首为人称道的《半半歌》，“看破浮生过半，半字受用无边；半中岁月尽幽闲，半里乾坤宽展；半郭半乡村舍，半山半水田园；半耕半读半经廛，半士半姻民眷；半雅半粗器具，半华半实庭轩；衾裳半素半轻鲜，肴馔半丰半俭；童仆半能半拙，妻儿半朴半贤。心情半佛半神仙，姓字半藏半显；一半还之天地，让将一半人间”，倡导一种豁达从容、知足常乐、随遇而安的生活状态。

“半”是一种人生智慧。晚清名臣曾国藩将自己的书房取名为“求阙斋”，意在持满戒溢，知足自省，“盛时常作衰时想，上场当念下场时”“有福不可享尽，有势不可使尽”是他常诵的格言。中和谦恭，虚怀若谷，顺其自然，日积月累，才能兼收并蓄，为之大成。

“半”是一种处世哲学。月满则亏，水满则溢，人满则骄，是先辈留下的至理名言。说话留有余地，做事掌握分寸，把握一个“度”，“中立而不倚”“味让三分，路留一步”，不顾此失彼，不剑走偏锋。

“半”是一种心灵状态。“半贫半富半自安，半取半舍半行善；半聋半哑半糊涂，半智半愚半圣贤；半人半我半自在，半醒半醉半神仙；半亲半爱半苦乐，半欲半禅半随缘。”人生中苦乐得失参半，善恶悲喜参半，常抱平常心，不消极遁世，不饮鸩止渴，张弛有道，游刃有余，如此才能得“自安”求“自在”。

载于《品读》

一个人的快乐，不是因为他拥有得多，而是因为他计较少。原谅别人，就是善待自己。未必钱多乐便多，财多累己招烦恼；清贫乐道真自在，无牵无挂乐逍遥。

最高奖赏

文/李　玲

爱是世上的幸福，但幸福并不是爱的全部礼遇。

——劳伦斯

8 岁的小侄子正在摆弄他的新玩具，玩得正尽兴的时候，他 4 岁的小弟弟哭着嚷着要将玩具据为已有，母亲闻声过来："他毕竟比你小，让着点他吧。"将玩具让出的小侄子跑来问我："小姑姑，所有好吃的我都已经给了弟弟，为什么还要拿去我的玩具呢?"

他扑闪扑闪的黑眼睛里写满了委屈。

我想和孩子说，他做得已经很好了，虽然他只有 8 岁。

他把自己的压岁钱积攒起来给小弟弟买喜欢吃的糖果和巧克力，从不向家里人提任何他认为会超出我们预算的要求，还会在客厅被那个小捣蛋搞得鸡飞狗跳时安静地捡起散落一地的瓜果纸屑。

这样一个懂得隐忍克制、不吝啬分享、并且有爱的孩子，不是应该得到更多的关怀和照顾吗?

这件事让我想起了母亲常说的那句话："会哭的孩子有奶吃。"这真是一句至理名言，它容不得你不信，至少它在我们童年的记忆里带有相当大的普遍性。我们的父母大人总是用暂时的给予来求得耳旁片刻的安宁，却无意中一次次中伤了好孩子的心。

长辈们都比较喜欢听话懂事的孩子，但这样的孩子得到的可能只是虚幻的口头嘉奖，而那个令所有人头痛、烦恼、泼皮的孩子也许会受些皮肉之苦，但得到的物质却是实实在在的。

1963 年，一个叫玛莉班尼的女孩给《芝加哥论坛报》写信，她帮妈妈把烤好的甜饼送到餐桌上，得到的只是一句夸奖，而那个什么都不干只会捣蛋的弟弟戴维得到的却是一个甜饼。她问，是不是上帝把好孩子都忘记了？

西勒库斯特是儿童版栏目的编辑，十多年来他收到很多类似的来信，却不知道如何回答。正好他去参加朋友的婚礼，新人在交换戒指时，因为激动把戒指戴在了右手上。牧师幽默地说，右手已经非常完美，还是用戒指来装饰左手吧。

牧师的话使他茅塞顿开。在那封著名的回信里，他这样说，上帝让右手成为右手，就是对右手最高的奖赏。同理，上帝让好人成为好人，也是对好人的最高奖赏。

面对正在长大的小侄子，我该怎样把这个故事说得通俗易懂呢？

载于《芳草·经典阅读》

对啊，怎么告诉孩子这个比较难懂的道理呢？你已经很优秀了，你的优秀就是上帝对你最好的奖赏，你不需要用物质或者别的东西来填补。那些得到物质的孩子，比你欠缺一点优秀，所以才要给些玩具激发他们。

占便宜其实是个套

文/高小宝

世界上没有便宜的事，谁想占便宜谁就会吃亏。

——徐特立

有一个人去街上买布料，布料68元，他给了商家100元，理应找回32元，但不知商家大意还是眼拙，竟错把一张50元当10元找给了他，那人暗喜，接过钱也没声张，赶紧离开了。路上他去买肉，可是当他把那张50元给卖肉的时，对方立刻拉下脸来："师傅啊，这张是假币，你给我换一张。"假币？那人一愣，不会吧！刚才卖布料的找我的，卖肉的同情地对他说："你被人骗了，他给你的是假币！"岂有此理！那人气得脸都变绿了，不行，我得去找他。

他气势汹汹来到卖布料那里，"啪"地把假币往柜台上一拍，愤怒地说，你怎么能坑人呢？这张钱是假的，你给我换了。围观的群众窃窃私语。岂料，卖布料的不气不恼，哂笑道："这位师傅，你先别着急，有事咱们慢慢说。"那人脖子一梗："我买了你68块钱布料，给了你100块钱，你找给我的这50块钱是假的！"他话刚说完，卖布料的不乐意了："师傅，这话可不能随便说，你买了我68块钱布料，给了我100，我应该找你32，怎么能把50块钱假币找你呢？你让大家给咱评评理。”是啊，这个账谁不会算，到底怎么回事？围观的群众向那人投去鄙夷的目光。那人自知理亏，却哑巴吃黄莲有苦说不出，憋得他满脸通红，本是来兴师问罪的，反倒让人家抓了把柄，他只好打掉牙往肚里咽，悻悻地走了。

他便宜没占成，自己吃亏不说，还坏了名誉，惹了一肚子气。

还有一个小伙子在路上无意捡到一张手机卡，他把这张卡装进电脑的无线卡槽，发现竟能上网，小伙子欣喜万分。然而让他高兴的事还在后面，一般手机卡上网要预存话费，一旦欠费自动停机，可他捡到的这张卡，一连用了几个月都没停，小伙子自以为这是电信公司的一个漏洞，便索性放开上网，用得不亦乐乎。不料，7个月后，他被警察“请到”了派出所，原来，他捡到的手机卡是一家公司的，这家公司交费时发现这张卡账户使用异常，一核查，才发现卡原来丢失了，随即报警。

小伙子如实交代了事情经过，面对丢卡公司坚持让他支付20多万元的上网费用及警方要追究的刑事责任，他欲哭无泪，后悔不迭。后来，虽然在律师据理力争下小伙子免除了刑事追究，并且根据电信公司相关条款、合同规定以及其工作上的失职失察之责，按照每月500元的标准进行了支付，让事情落下帷幕，但由此事带给他的不幸后果却依然蔓延。小伙子的老母亲因担惊受怕，胃病转化成了胃癌；小伙子也因此成为当地“喜欢占便宜”的名人，出去谈业务，别人总是委婉回绝；他所在的公司因人品问题和他解除了合约；以前和他准备合伙做生意的人，撤资悄然离去……

什么叫得不偿失？什么叫追悔莫及？什么叫“贪小便宜

吃大亏”？我想，怕是没有人比这个小伙子有更痛彻心扉的领悟吧！

但偏偏生活中爱占便宜的人随处可见，而且很多人大事小事不占点便宜心里就很不舒服。我二姨是个卖菜的，她的顾客中就有这么一个人，这人每次来买菜，走的时候，总是顺手要么拿几个蒜瓣，要么扯几根小葱。我看不惯，二姨却轻描淡写：“让他拿吧，没事。说他几句，不但会令他没面子，还说不定他以后不来我这儿买了。”我没好气：“不来拉倒，谁稀罕。”二姨笑了：“做生意图的是人气，别看他拿走了几颗蒜瓣几根葱，俗话说‘买的没有卖的精’，你当他在我这儿占了便宜？放心吧，我不吃亏。”说着，二姨朝我眨了眨眼睛。

我愣了愣，虽然不太明白二姨眨眼睛的含义，但她一定有她的“经营”手段。世上的事，讲究公平二字，你占了别人便宜，别人心里能舒服吗？况且谁的便宜也不是好占的，很多时候，你认为你占到了便宜，也只是因为你看到的是表象而非本质。

其实，细细想来，占便宜说到底也不是什么好事，顾盼四周，大概还没有人因为占便宜而发家致富、飞黄腾达吧！但因为占便宜身败名裂、得不偿失的人却是大有人在。可现实往往是，一旦有便宜可占，一个个趋之若鹜，眉开眼笑，从来不去想占到的便宜有可能是洪水猛兽，引火上身，这恐怕是人性固有的劣根吧！“吃一堑，长一智”这话被很多人奉为警世恒言，可要是放到“占便宜”这里，有多少人追悔莫及，就有多少人前仆后继，但凡之前没有过剜肉削骨般的重创，稍微遇到点儿诱惑，多半还是会重蹈覆辙。

如果有个人对我说“某一天，当幸运突然降临在你身上时，你先别高兴太早，首先要保持冷静、理智、克制”，我一定会对这个人心生好感并刮目相看。

载于《做人与处世》

一切恶果皆起于贪念。天下没有免费的午餐，上当受骗的都是企图不劳而获的人，但是你想，怎么可能有那么好的事呢？

我只能帮你到这儿了

文/学　学

真正的自由属于那些自食其力的人，并且在自己的工作中有所作为的人。

——罗·科林伍德

亚当斯是南美洲玻利维亚一名著名的房地产商，最近，他又在嗒里哈省开工了一个新项目。这个新项目建成后，将成为嗒里哈省最大的现代化商业城，里面有五星级酒店、度假村、住宅区等设施。

一天，亚当斯来到建筑工地检察工程的进展情况。亚当斯虽然是一个大企业家，但他每次外出，都轻车简从，自己开车，也从来不用什么专职司机和保镖，只有一个秘书跟着他。

他常说，我虽然是个大老板，但也要节约每一分钱，绝不能奢侈浪费。确实是这样的，他身边的人都知道，亚当斯生活很节俭，一顿饭常常简单的一盒快餐就行了，他手腕上的那块手表，也是才值20几块玻利维亚诺的电子表。

突然，一个妇人带着两个小姑娘来到他的面前，妇人向亚当斯泣诉道："我本来是住在这个地方的，后来土地征迁，我的家搬迁到达瓦尔地区了。我没有工作，孩子的父亲是一名卡车司机，工资又低，家里一点也照顾不了，您是一个大富翁，帮我在这找一份工作吧！”

亚当斯不仅是一名腰缠万贯的大富翁，也是一名慈善家，每年都要为慈善机构捐款达几亿美元，平时他看到需要救助的人，也总是慷慨解囊，人们都亲切地称他是大善人。听到眼前这位妇人的哭诉，亚当斯也同样动了恻隐之心，于是问道："请问你有什么文化和特长呢？”

妇人说道：“我没有什么文化，我只会做家务。”

亚当斯思考了一下，说道：“这样吧，你在工地食堂后勤帮忙干干活吧，每月 2000 玻利维亚诺。”

妇人听了，高兴地喜极而泣，不停地说道：“您真是个大善人啊！”

过了一段时间，亚当斯又来到这里检察工作，突然，一个妇人挡在了他面前，那妇人说道：“亚当斯先生，您还认识我吗？”

亚当斯看着眼前的妇人，努力地想了一下，还是摇了摇头。

妇人说道：“我就是上次在这带着两个孩子，求您帮助的那个妇人啊！”

亚当斯这才想了起来，问道：“你现在还好吧？”

妇人眼睛一下红了，她抹了一把眼泪，哽咽道：“我的男人开着大卡车，一直奔波在外，一直照顾不了家里，工资又低，我想求您让他到这里来开车好吗？”

亚当斯一愣，微微皱了一下眉头，沉吟了片刻，说道："好吧，那就让他到工地开车吧，每月 3000 玻利维亚诺。”

妇人听了，立刻喜极而泣，不停地说道：“您真是个大善人啊！”望着亚当斯进了小车，自己坐在驾驶室里，妇人脸上露出惊愕的神色。

商业城如期完工，嗒里哈省省长和许多来宾都来到现场表示祝贺。在竣工现场，亚当斯当场宣布，再次向慈善机构捐款2000万玻利维亚诺。亚当斯的举动，引起了现场一片喝彩声。

竣工典礼结束了，亚当斯走向自己的小车，正要打开车门，一个妇人来到了他的跟前，那妇人问道："亚当斯先生，您还记得我吗?"

亚当斯望了望那妇人，笑道："记得，你现在还好吗?"

妇人眼睛一红，抹起了眼泪，说道："我家男人在工地开车太辛苦了，让他来给您开小车好吗？这个工作既体面又轻松，和您在一起，他还能学到许多做生意的诀窍。说不定他将来也会像您一样，成为腰缠万贯的大富翁，那我就再也不用辛苦干活了。刚才我在现场看到了，您又捐了那么多善款，我真羡慕啊!"妇人脸上露出激动的红晕。

亚当斯身体摇晃了一下，他扶了一下车门才站稳了脚。亚当斯脸上露出一丝不快，他淡淡地说了句："对不起，我只能帮你到这儿了!"

说罢，坐进了驾驶室，他好像想起了什么，将车窗摇了下来，说道："我曾经也是一名卡车司机。"说罢，小车绝尘而去。

妇人望着远去的小车，一脸失望的神情，她将手中一样不知什么东西，狠狠地摔在了地上。

这一幕，被正在现场采访的记者迪亚斯看见了，随后，他在玻利维亚《拉美联合新闻报》发表了一篇文章，题目是——我只能帮你到这儿了。

记者在文章中写道：人性从最初的基本需求，最后发展到一种贪婪，这就有违人性最本质的善良，慈善不是无止境的索取。对慈善的需求，如果有违背最初的需求，那就是对人性的亵渎和践踏，那是任何人也帮不了你的。

载于《演讲与口才》

慈善是善良的，可是如果过了，便成了溺爱。人性是贪婪的，给予得越多，越觉得理所应当，便索取得越多，殊不知这些东西本就不是属于他的。

你必须跟我走

文/周月霞

爱之花开放的地方，生命便能欣欣向荣。

——梵高

这是最末一班车了。

夏天昼长夜短。都快六点了，太阳才不情愿地往西爬。算上那个气喘吁吁跑上来坐到我身边的女孩，正好满座。司机发动车子，满意地吆喝了一句：走着！

昏昏欲睡的我，给这一嗓子嚷得清醒了许多。一个戴红色旅游帽，身材高挑而瘦削的老年女售票员俐落地跳上车。她的眉眼和影星朱琳很相似，脸上挂着矜持而优雅的微笑，她的出现骤然使我回想起当年我做客车售票员的时光。

身边的女孩笑吟吟地把票钱递给售票员，她伸手接过，呆望着女孩，笑容猛地凝住。

女孩脆生生地说："阿姨，我去邢家屯，得在三里桥下车。您别忘了到站让司机师傅停车！"

"哦，三里桥。"女售票员诺诺地应声，却紧跟着问："这个时间没有去邢家屯的班车了，你怎么回家呀，步行?"

"那个路口有很多顺风车的，总有好心人让我搭……"女孩浓密的长睫毛自然上翘，她忽闪着大眼睛，不无得意地说。女售票员欲言又止，认真看了女孩一眼，叹口气，摇摇头。我分明看到她扭过脸的瞬间，眼里噙了泪。

她怎么啦？我心底陡然生出一股好奇。女售票员却再没回头，把直挺挺的脊背决然给了我。女孩掏出手机，表情温柔而生动，嗯哦着跟男友打起电话。大体意思是说，她有生日礼物送他，她马上就到了……

太阳变成个大红球，努力着做一天最后的跳跃。公路两旁的庄稼长势喜人，绿油油密匝匝的叶子在夕阳下闪着光。大巴车陆续丢下一个个旅人，挟着花香的晚风，飘进车窗，冲淡了越来越空的车厢里的汗渍味道。

太阳落山了，天空变成灰蓝色。女孩不时向窗外眺望，三里桥快到了。女孩低头开始整理身边的几个手提袋。

那桥越来越近，桥那头的路两旁是一人多高的夏玉米，一眼望不到边，桥栏边居然停着一辆黑色轿车。

女孩吐了吐舌头，偷偷笑了笑，她在窃喜那或许是一辆顺风车。

这时候，女售票员突然转过头看了女孩一眼，似乎想说什么，却张张嘴什么也没说。已经看见三里桥的红白栏杆了，她猛地一把扯下帽子，赫然露出满头白发。她几步来到司机身后，凑近他耳边低声说着什么。司机诧异地看看她，回头瞥了一眼，又顺她的手指望向窗外，若有所思，使劲点点头。

三里桥就嗖的一下被汽车甩到身后。

“停车！我在三里桥下！”女孩噌地站起来，喊了一句。

女售票员头也不回，好像没听见。

“哎！过站啦！我要下车！”女孩急了，大声叫起来。乘客们也帮着喊："怎么到站不给人家停车啊！听见没，啥工作态度……"

"停车，我要下车！"女孩在颠簸的车尾摇晃着，几步冲到女售票员面前。

女售票员伸出双手扶住女孩，她望着女孩，轻声说："孩子，你别急，你自己下车，我不放心，天都黑了……"

"关你啥事啊！我在哪儿下车是我的自由，我家人都在等我。停车，停车！"女孩咆哮起来。

"不行！今天，你必须跟我走！"女售票员脸一沉，声音提高了几度。毋庸置疑的语气突然使骚动的车厢安静下来，她长舒一口气，柔声央求女孩："孩子，我不要你车钱。阿姨真的是为了你好，我送你去邢家屯！"

车厢里有旅客恍然大悟，附和着说："是啊，闺女，晚到一会没事的……人家是好心，你就别生气了！"女孩也一下理解了女售票员的良苦用心，不再执拗，悄悄退回到座位上开始拨打手机。

女孩下车的时候，天已经完全黑了，她的男友早就在村口等候。

女售票员把脸紧贴在车门上，望着女孩远去的背影发呆。司机一边倒车，一边问："这是今年第几个了？"

"记不清了！不好意思，又害你多走了十来里路。可我控制不住！大眼睛、长睫毛，真的太像我女儿了，还有，庄稼地，顺风车……我的青青！十年了，妈啥时才能找到你啊……"女售票员有些语无伦次地喃喃着，她颤抖着双肩，泣不成声。

我也哭了，却没有勇气说出哭得一塌糊涂的原因。十年前，也曾有个女孩在夜幕降临时独自走出我的车门，后来就失踪了。我一直自责，当时为何不坚决地对她说："孩子，你必须跟我走！"

载于《做人与处世》

人生有好多遗憾，因为没能及时挽留，便再也见不到彼此了。世界就是这么大，走丢了，便再也寻不见。愿所有的父母都能看好自己的孩子，不要骨肉分离。

向死而生

文/凉月满天

作为一个人，要是不经历过人世上的悲欢离合，不跟生活打过交手仗，就不可能真正懂得人生的意义。

——杨朔

刚看了一本小书：《殡葬人手记》，作者托马斯·林奇，美国密歇根州一个小镇的殡仪馆的老板。

这个特殊的职业虽使他见惯死亡，却在心里保有鲜活的非职业化的感想，这一点殊属难得，就好比沙漠里开出鲜艳的潮润温软的大瓣花朵，那感觉很奇特。

生者营营，一个牧师打高尔夫球，穿爱尔兰亚麻布的法衣，开高级轿车，还想当红衣主教。就是这样一个家伙，居然放胆宣言："死的时候不要铜棺，不要鲜花，只要有一个简朴的葬礼和一个平民化的坟墓。"托马斯很客气地跟他讲，不用到死的那天才这么搞，你现在就可以做活着的圣徒：退出乡村俱乐部，不开豪华敞篷车，不穿高档毛衣和皮鞋，不吃上等肋条肉，不殚精竭虑地攒钱，你的钱我还可以帮你分给穷人——然后，他收获了这位高贵的牧师的诅咒的眼神。这样的人并不稀罕，他是世间虚伪的典范，表面光鲜闪耀，内里一团败草，只有死亡才能使他摆脱欲念的困扰。

相对这个牧师而言，托马斯的邻居米罗朴实善良，他开着洗衣店，不声不响地帮助刚刚离异，带着四个小孩艰难生活的托马斯，每天早晨来带走五大包脏衣服，中午再洗得干干净净，叠得整整齐齐地送回。“我”去交付欠账的时候，顺便向他致以谢意，他笑着说：“别放在心上，一只手洗另一只手，谁跟谁呢？”现在，米罗死了，双眼紧闭，目光熄灭。“我”郑重地对待他的遗体，先是让右手压在左手上，然后再左手压在右手上，后来，“我”不再折腾了，因为不管怎么放，都是一只手洗另一只手，有什么关系，又分什么彼此。

托马斯的父亲也是殡葬师，托马斯子承父业的同时，顺便也从父亲那里继承了对于死亡的恐惧，他们眼中看到的一切，包括疯狗和能传染疟疾的蚊子，以及冒充邮差与教师的歹徒，都有可能谋杀自己的孩子，就连蝴蝶都难逃嫌疑。见惯了死亡，也深刻理解死亡是怎么一回事的人，却仍旧对于孩子的死备感恐惧，是因为老人的死和孩子的死，实在是有着不同的意义。“当我们安葬老人时，我们埋葬的是已知的过去……记忆是压倒一切的主题，是最终的慰藉。但埋葬孩子就是埋葬未来，和被我们的梦想所拔高的美好前程。这样的悲伤无边无际、无始无终。”记忆的完满和梦想的永未实现，对于整个人类而言，永远都是前者可供欣慰，后者足资伤痛，古今一理，天下大同。

可是，无论怎样，有生便有死。刚生下来需要清水洗一洗，刚刚死亡也需要用清水洗一洗，这既是仪式，又是需要，就像托马斯充满幽默风趣的调侃，“在生命的此端，我们宣告：他活着呢，好大的味道，得赶紧洗洗。在生命的彼端，我们回应：他死了，好大的味道，得赶紧洗洗。”可是，无论洗与不洗，对于生者也许是必需，对于死者却已是毫无意义。

“意义的丧失正是重大事件即将发生的头一个明确迹象。”的确如此。

虚伪的人活着搜罗鲜花和尊敬，真诚的人死后收获怀念和哀悯；老人死后获得尊重，幼者死亡引发悲伤。可是无论什么样的人，一旦死亡来临，便铜棺和木棺平等，鲜花和荒草平等，地宫和土坟平等，老人和幼儿平等……生为物役，营营不休，逝随流水，一无所求。

偶翻纳兰性德的《饮水词》，看到一句“风絮飘残已化萍”，词意不过是援引古说，讲杨絮飘零，会入水化作浮萍；那么杨絮便是浮萍的前世，浮萍便是杨絮的今生。几天前，家人闲话，说起早已逝去的祖母。母亲说这么多年，谁都不肯给她上一次坟。我的父亲此时已七十余岁，平生胆小，一向怕打雷，怕坟地，现今正端坐如佛，乖乖看电视，却忽然大声抽泣。当时不以为然，我是无神论者，偏要讲往生，安慰他说不要哭，上不上坟都没关系的，人早转生，如絮化萍，我们所见，只是一座空坟；可是现在想起，却心里酸痛，因为它印证了这本书中的一句话：“我死了，是你们活着的人面对死亡。”

这是死者对于生者的最后宣言。是的，逝者早得解脱，面对死亡的，从来，一直，永远，都是生者。

载于《特别关注》

我们一直都在向死而生。所以重要的不是怎么死的问题，而是如何好好有意义地活着。所以，尽可能地让自己活得有意义吧。

舌尖上的大雁和槐花

文/林少华

忍一时风平浪静，退一步海阔天空。

——佚名

偶尔翻看小学三年级下学期用的江苏版语文课本。一篇题为《争论的故事》的课文引起了我的注意。故事说以打猎为生的兄弟俩为怎么吃大雁发生了争论。哥哥说煮着吃好吃，弟弟说烤着吃好吃。兄弟俩争论不休，谁也说服不了谁。

这时有个老人经过这里，兄弟俩就找他评理。老人觉得他俩说的都有一定的道理，就建议说："你们把大雁割开，煮一半，烤一半，不就两全其美了吗?"而当兄弟俩抬头看时，大雁早已飞得无影无踪。故事的主题是：不管做什么，关键是要先做起来，而不是争论不休。

出于慎重，我又看了一遍。课文主题没有什么不妥——尽管我的职业主要就是争论并且经常围绕什么争论不休——相比之下，引起我注意的明显是那位老人的话："你们把大雁剖开，煮一半，烤一半……"

眼前随即出现大雁惨遭屠戮的血淋淋的场面。剖、煮、烤，这是何等残忍的动作啊！须知不是剖树皮不是煮豌豆不是烤地瓜，而是对待一只大雁，一只可能领着小雁飞去南方过冬的大雁，一只作为国家保护动物的野生大雁！作为智者化身的老人怎么可以对年轻人这样说话呢？或者莫如说，这样的表达怎么可以出现在小学三年级语文课本中呢？

不由得，我想起自己念过的小学语文课本："秋天到了，天气凉了，一群大雁往南飞去，一会儿飞成个人字，一会儿飞成个一字……"也是因为当时乡下常有这样的雁群飞过，两相对照，使我对大雁自觉排成的队列、对它们飞往的南方产生了朦胧的敬意和向往。

尤其它们在一碧如洗的秋日晴空中高高飞翔的优美身姿，不由得让我产生一股冲动，恨不得自己也变成一只大雁，悄悄跟在它们后面飞去，飞出那个三面环山的穷山村，飞去山那边、天那边……

我这么一边想着回忆着一边继续翻动手中的课本。也巧，翻到了另一课《古诗两首》。一首是杜甫的绝句："两个黄鹂鸣翠柳，一行白鹭上青天"。看插图，白鹭也飞成个一字。白鹭和大雁应属同一家族，无论体形和颜色都很相近。

但同这本语文书上关于大雁的表述相比，古人对白鹭的描写多么富有诗情画意啊！按理，古人获取食物的渠道比现在困难得多，而古人目睹白鹭的反应是做了一首千古绝唱，今人编的故事却要"把大雁剖开，煮一半，烤一半……"——作为杜甫的嫡系文化后代，怎么会差这么远？

也就是说，这篇课文至少有两点值得思考和警觉。

一是美的教育的缺失。这点即使同半个世纪前我学过的那篇课文相比也高下立判。前者对大雁投以欣赏的目光，给人以纯粹的美感；后者则将大雁视为猎物，投以凶狠的视线，让人感受的是赤裸裸的贪欲和血淋淋的残酷。

二是爱的教育的缺失。在某种意义上，或许可以说懂得美、懂得审美、才懂得爱。审美让人对万物产生爱，产生悲悯情怀。故而古人有对失群或失偶的“孤鸿”、“哀鸿”的同情，有对“雁过拔毛”之人的痛恨，有对鸿雁传书的感激和对惊鸿照影的心动。

而在这篇课文中，全然看不到这些正面的美好的感情，看不到人与自然、人与动物和谐共生的理念，看不到爱。或许你说人家不过是要以此表达“关键是要先做起来”这个道理，何必大动肝火！

可问题是，这个主题难道非这样表达不可吗？记得已故毛泽东主席在说明实践出真知这个类似道理时是这样说的：要想知道梨子的滋味，就要亲口尝一尝。说得多好，干净、健康、浅显、“接地气”！至少，渴的时候都不觉渴了。

更令人担忧的是，在这本语文书中这并非孤例。如另一课《槐乡五月》，较之对槐花之美的赞赏和描绘，着墨更多的是对槐花的采摘和食用。只是，这回采取的食用手段不是“剖、煮、烤”，而变成了“拌、蒸、晒”。

关键词是槐花饭。“槐花饭是用大米拌槐花蒸的……槐乡的孩子还会送他一大包蒸过晒干的槐花”。这还不算，小男孩“衣裤的口袋里装的是槐花，手上拿的还是槐花……不时就朝嘴里塞上一把，甜丝丝、香喷喷的，可真有口福呢！”

总之，注重的仍是怎么吃这种舌尖上的感受——舌尖上的大雁、舌尖上的槐花……

也是因为住处附近山坡就有许多槐树，加之正是五月，看完这篇课文，我就上山了。四下看去，较之树上盛开的，更多的槐花是树下横七竖八折断的树枝甚至整个拉断的树冠上零零星星早已蔫巴的槐花，有的被人踩得一塌糊涂，看着令人心疼。

不用说，这是摘剩下的没有变成舌尖槐米饭的槐花……

载于《经典阅读》

冷静如同是灼烧烈火之后的一场大水，冷静的人，才能成就未来。

只有秃子，才能成为秃子的朋友

文/孔　超

世间最平和的快乐就是静观天地与人世，慢慢地品味出它的和谐。

——三毛

今天，我要给大家讲个有趣的故事。

在天津老街，有一条幽深幽深的小巷，青森森的石板，已磨得光亮。路两旁，是高大虬屈的法国梧桐。在这条小巷的东头，生活着一个秃子，姓李，在家排行老三，学名叫李三，但不少人都叫他李三秃子。他那颗脑袋，光溜溜的，寸草不生，上面还有一道难看的大伤疤。

这一天，他刚出门，就碰上了邻家的小男孩。这个小男孩六七岁，粉妆玉琢的样子，十分讨人喜爱。小男笑嘻嘻的，故意拉长着声音："秃——子叔。"李三眼睛一瞪，做出生气的样子："叔就叔，什么秃不秃的，不准叫！"小男孩也不怕，摇晃着小脑袋："我偏叫，偏叫！"

李三乐了，满脸的皱纹都舒展开来。他从兜里摸索出几颗水果糖，往小男孩子手里一塞："就数你最顽皮，哪凉快哪呆着去。"小男孩得了水果糖，活蹦乱跳地跑了。

走到巷子口，李三又遇见一个人。巷子西头的王大宝，二十来岁，在不远的修车铺里当学徒。“秃叔，这是要上哪去啊？”李三脸色一寒，不乐意了：“你叫你爹叫不叫秃？下回再这么没大没小，我甩你几个大耳刮子！”见李三真生气了，王大宝忙打躬赔礼：“叔，瞧我这嘴，你老别见怪，别见怪。”李三也不理他，重重哼了一声，就出了巷子。

不远处，有个花鸟市场。李三正逛着，忽然听见有人叫他：“李三秃子——”李三抬头一看，脱口而出：“张二秃子——”原来是隔壁巷子的张二，跟李三一样，张二那颗脑袋也是光溜溜的，寸草不生。

“走，喝一盅去。”

“走！”

这两人一见面就热乎，手挽着手肩搭着肩亲热得不得了。

喝完酒，李三趁着微熏的酒意，往家里摇晃。刚进巷子，迎面过来一个人，是马老板。这马老板打小是跟李三一块儿长大的，这几年做生意，算是发达了。“三秃子，从哪喝酒来？”

“你喊我什么？”李三站稳了身子，硬着脖子质问道。

“切！你不就是秃嘛，叫叫怎么啦？”

“你再叫一声试试！”

“三……哎哟！”马老板那个“秃”字还没叫出口，李三就一拳砸了过去，两人很快撕打在一起。

事后，马老板主动向李三道歉，但是李三，却再也不愿搭理马老板了。

故事说完了，下面我要说的是：为什么这四个人同样喊李三“秃子”，但李三却反应迥异呢？对邻家小男孩是喜爱，对王大宝是严厉，对张二秃子是亲近，而对马老板，已经是愤怒了。

其实，这里牵涉到一个心理学上的问题，我在这里估且称它为“秃子法则”：秃子可以原谅弱者的冒犯，却不能容忍强者的挑衅，因为，秃子觉得这牵涉到自己的尊严。追根究底，是秃子的自卑感在作祟，面对强者时，秃子会自然而然地产生一种隐秘而强烈的自卑。这种自卑的外在表现，就是过分地维护自尊。

所以我要说：只有秃子，才能成为秃子最亲密的朋友。

“秃子法则”告诫我们：不管是面对弱者还是强者，我们都要保持一份平和的心态，对于小事小节，不妨一笑而过。有时候，看似很有骨气地维护了自己的尊严，却恰恰暴露了自己内心深处的自卑。

载于《才智》

面对弱者，我们应该以谦虚的姿态应对，给人以尊重；面对强者，我们不妨微微一笑，不露锋芒。

最珍贵的不是画

文/凤　凰

夜把花悄悄地开放了，却让白日去领受谢词。

——泰戈尔

刘利民不是画家，却整天想着画画，整天就知道画画。虽然他画了不少画，却一直没有成名，命运好像一直在跟他开玩笑，现在他家徒四壁，不得不抱着画出去卖。

刘利民走出村子，走进了城里。一进城，他就走进了一家商店。他一走进商店，老板就赶紧上前笑脸相迎，连忙问他买什么。刘利民说："老板，我不买东西，我是来卖画的！"

老板看了刘利民一眼，说道："卖画？我不买，去去去！"老板说着就冲他挥手。看老板不耐烦的样子，刘利民打开了自己的画，说道："老板，你看看，我画得很好，你就买一幅吧，我只收你十块钱……"

老板再一次挥挥手说："去去去，就是一分钱，我也不买！什么破画，还想拿来卖钱！"说完，老板把脸转开，再也不看刘利民一眼。

刘利民心里那个气，没法说，眼泪差点都掉下来了。不买就不买吧，也用不着这么打击人啊！破画？这是破画吗？这些画，每一幅都是刘利民花了心血，精心画出的作品。刘利民抱着画，退出商店。然后他去了下一家商店，结果，他同样遭到了拒绝。一上午，刘利民走了十几家商店，不但一幅画没有卖出去，还遭到了一次又一次的嘲笑。

无精打采的刘利民准备回家了，这时，他看到前面一家商店的老板正看着他，他想，不如再去问问他吧。现在他太需要钱了，他得抓机会卖画。

刘利民走了过去，他说："老板，买幅画吧！虽然现在我不是画家，但将来我会成为画家的，我成了画家，画就很值钱了。现在我只卖十块钱，你就买一幅吧！"刘利民说着把手中的画递了过去。

老板接过了刘利民的画，打开看了看，然后笑着说："你画得很不错啊！十块钱，太少了，这样吧，我给你一百块钱，这画我要了！"老板真是爽快，把画收起来，然后就给了刘利民一百块钱。刘利民捏着钱，连忙对老板说道："谢谢，谢谢！"刘利民太激动了，太兴奋了，他的画居然卖出去了，而且还卖了一百块钱，这是对他的肯定啊！

卖出去的这幅画，给了刘利民帮助不说，还给了他巨大的信心，让他坚持了下来。十年后，他终于成为了一名著名的画家。这时的他，有了别墅，有了豪车，而且每一幅画都价值不菲。当然他不再轻易画画，也不再轻易出售。这时，与他交往的，都是达官贵人。而想得到他画的人，更是排起了长队，可是他却一概拒绝，重金也难求一幅画。

既然从刘利民手中得不到他的画，于是人们就从别的地方购买。有一天，刘利民听说有人手中有他早期的作品，而且是他卖出去的第一幅画，找那人买画的人络绎不绝，个个都出价很高，但全都被拒绝了。这时，他想起来了，他的第一幅画卖给了一个商店老板。他想，那是早期的作品，还是卖出去的第一幅画，太珍贵了，得把它买回来！

刘利民经过多方打听，终于找到了那位老板。此时，老板已经成了一个老人。刘利民告诉老人，自己就是当年的那个年轻人，当年，他帮了自己，现在，自己拿两幅画来换那幅画。老人说："换啥换？我把它给你就是了！"老人找出那幅画给了刘利民，刘利民见老人不肯收这两幅画，便问老人："大家出那么高的价，你为什么不卖啊？"

老人说："我卖它干啥？换钱吗？它可是你早期的作品，画得不怎么好，我要是卖出去了，一传开，大家就会笑话你。我可不能让人笑话你，你是名家啊！要是一笑话你，说不定你的画就不那么值钱了，那我不是毁了你吗？"刘利民不由吃了一惊，原来老人捂着这幅画不卖，并不是为了惜售，为了赚钱，而是为了他的名声，为了他的未来。

刘利民说："当初你买我的画，并不是为了留着赚钱？"老人笑着说："当然不是。那时，我看你连进十几家店都一无所获，我怕你经不起打击，才出高价买了你的画。现在，你成名成家了，我很高兴，我帮对人了！"刘利民感动地说："谢谢您！是您成就了我！"他决定改天登门送老人十幅画，因为，最珍贵的不是画，而是老人的善良。

载于《思维与智慧》

有些爱是无声的。感谢那些曾经默默支持过自己的人吧，如果没有当初那些无声的鼓励，恐怕就没有今天成功的自己。

老根叔

文/崔永照

一个宽宏大量的人，他的爱心往往多于怨恨，他乐观愉快、豁达、忍让而不悲伤、消沉、焦躁、恼怒。

——穆尼尔·纳素夫

老根叔在村里辈分大，才五十五六岁，大半个疃家中的人都是他的晚辈。他农活把式高人一筹，不到 20 岁就当生产队长，没两下子谁服哩？他养了个好儿子，大学毕业分到北京，混得人模人样儿，才三十郎当岁，听说当上和县太爷一般大的官儿，老刘家祖坟冒烟儿哩！疃家中的人一提起刘二爷，哪个不竖大拇指头？

但是，这两年人们说起老根叔，背地都骂他财迷，说他天生是打钱眼儿里钻出来的。人这一辈子，有啥都好，就是别有权、别有钱，一有这两个玩意儿，好人都变坏人哩！

无风不起浪，疃家中的人也不是生着法儿说老根叔的不是，这人实在是舍命不舍财，叫财迷了心窍哩！

三年前，儿子把他老两口接到北京，不说住洋楼，也不说茅坑（厕所）在炕头，更不说顿顿拎着小酒壶，单说那大伙儿心里景仰的天安门，就在他的眼皮子底下！你见天溜达一趟天安门，瞧瞧那共和国开天辟地放礼炮、升国旗的地界儿，那心里恣儿得要上天，一准得活到九十九哩！

老根叔是天生出大力的命，过不了城里人那舒服的日子，没挨到仨月就跑回村里来了。人们问他咋回来了？他说待不惯，见天闲得浑身不自在哩！人们笑，说别人做梦都巴望的好日子，你却有福不会享哩！

他诡谲地笑笑，骑着驴（背着手）叼着小旱烟袋去山上陂里转悠去了，好像他又是当年的生产队长。有时候，坐在那地头上，望着那满地野草，眉心儿里拧起一个大疙瘩。

那时候，村里的青壮劳力都天南地北地打工去了，家家承包的土地都撂了荒。土里抠钱难，没出息，没人做那营生，他却打起这些撂荒地的主意。果然，他东家进，西家出，和人家合计那撂荒地的事儿。条件十分简单：你家没人手，地俺种，村里上缴的粮食俺缴，所有花费俺担，你啥心甭操，等有了人手，地仍归你。

这里头的好处谁心里都是明镜儿，老街古邻，一疃一庄，谁好意思？个个都一个音儿说："老根叔，亏你的一片心哩！"他说："撂荒白丢白瞎，丢上种就打粮食，土能生金哩！"他又去找村长，说了自个儿打的谱儿。村长说："你舒服饭不愿吃哩？"他说："啥也没有和土坷垃打交道这碗饭吃着舒服哩！"村长笑说："村民自治，只要不少缴村里的粮食，有多大能耐你就可劲儿使哩！"

第二年一开春，儿子先回一趟家，陪着老爹在山上陂里转悠。儿子刚走不几天，两台 45 马力的大拖拉机就开进村里。又过了几天，他聘用的四五十号人也进了村，他们先是放火烧荒，接着就是深翻土地，再接着就是播种了。

疃家中的人冷不丁醒了腔，大眼儿瞪着小眼儿，老根叔这爷儿俩原来是要当大老板，怪不得当爹的打北京城先跑回来，打的是村里这一大片撂荒地的主意，要学当年村里的大地主李家大院那派头儿哩！街面儿上出动静了，都说画龙画虎难画骨，知人知面不知心，闹了半天老根叔爷儿俩是借船出海，借鸡下蛋哩！那些把地交给老根叔种的人家，心里总觉着有点儿上当受骗的滋味儿。

老根叔不言声儿，就像啥也没有听见。头一年粮食丰收，该给各家向村里上缴的粮食一粒不少，他自个儿赚多少，街面儿上传的不一样，有说三十万斤，有说五十万斤，不管多少万斤，反正老根叔发了。有些人家打不着鹿也不让鹿吃草，就撺掇一些人家把地收回来。

这当口，村长出头了，他说土地撂荒本身就违反政策，有人替你种地，有人替你缴粮，天上掉馅饼哩！人们盘算着，也是这么个理儿，收地的事儿就不了了之。

第二年，老根叔的买卖做大了，庄稼杆做饲料，养猪养鸡养奶牛。儿子从北京请来专家，建起肉联厂，肉类食品出口日本东南亚。瞳家中的人眼红了，特别是那些把地交给老根叔种的人家，非要收地不可，放着自个儿的财不发，为啥叫人家发哩？大伙一起哄，地就真的不给老根叔种了。

这年冬季天，风声传得不对劲儿，说钱紧了，不少买卖干不成了，打工的人都得回老家重操旧业，种地就是老本行。瞳家中的人就像葵花盘儿着了霜，一下子耷拉头了。

村长又出面安慰老少爷们，他说老根叔说，土能生金，他心疼那些撂荒地，叫儿子帮他的忙，两年的光景，除了所有花费，他一共攒了一百万斤粮食，价值约计五十万元，办起了禽畜养殖业和肉联厂，置下一部分农用机械。他个人没留一分钱，统统交给村里，有老根叔创下的这个基础垫底儿，大伙就不愁二次创业哩！瞳家中的人猛然醒了腔，脸上一阵红一阵白，都觉着错怪了老根叔。

过年的时候，疃家中的人成群结伙来老根叔家拜年，千错万错，一个悔字儿值钱，借着这正月，破解破解，你还是俺们大伙的老根叔哩！谁知，老根叔家大门锁着，人不见影儿了！有人吆喝，说老根叔一准生气了，上北京儿子那儿再也不回来哩！

这当口，正好村长走过来，立马接过那人的话茬儿，说老根叔才不是那号人哩！刚才俺打电话给他拜年，说起这事儿，叫他千万别往心里去，你猜他咋说？大伙大眼儿瞪着小眼儿，盼着村长的下文。村长笑着说，老根叔开春就回来，今年要建大棚，在经济作物上多下工夫哩！一疃一庄的，哪来那些讲究？俺从小偷李家爷爷的枣儿吃，叫他打了个腚瓜子；俺当兵那年，就是他送俺一程又一程，直到俺上了车，他还站在那儿朝俺招手哩！

人们的心里难过，个个眼圈儿都红了。

载于《中外读点》

我们总以为有些人有钱了就跟自己不一样了，总以为生活好了就忘本了，其实没有。有些人一直惦记着自己的本分，有些人却真的就变坏了。

第五辑

性格不决定人缘好坏

人际交往中，你话多话少没关系，性格内向外向也无关紧要，关键是看你品质如何，因此在我看来，一个人只要乐于助人，为人一副热心肠，不损人利己，懂得宽容与谅解，内心阳光正义，就能拥有好人缘。

为别人的黑夜留一盏灯

文/一枚芳心

一个人的力量是很难应付生活中无边的苦难的。所以，自己需要别人帮助，自己也要帮助别人。

——茨威格

楼道里的灯坏掉了，每天早晨或者晚上，我只好拿着手电筒接送上下学的女儿。那天碰到邻居，她说："这该死的灯咋说坏就坏了？昨天晚上我去上夜班，下楼时一脚踩空，摔倒了，你看，手都擦破了，还好没伤筋动骨。"我说："是啊，这灯坏了，还真是个麻烦事。"

许多天过去，楼道里的灯依旧黑着，我们抱怨着、牢骚着，却没有一个人去真正关心这个事。

那天买菜回来，李婶叫住我："家里电坏了，是不是得找物业的电工啊？"我说："电坏了当然得找电工了，怎么？您家里停电了吗？"

李婶笑笑："没有，我只是问问。"

第二天，看到李婶正和物业电工小王争吵，看到我，李婶不再争辩，敷衍着笑了一下，回家了。

去物业交水电费时，我又碰到李婶，她又在跟物业经理争吵。我过去劝她，她说："没事，你忙你的吧。"我很奇怪，李婶这是怎么了？住邻居这么多年，从没见她和谁大声说过话。

晚上八点，照旧拿着手电筒下楼去接女儿。关门的一瞬间，楼道里的灯忽然亮了起来。嘿，这灯终于亮了！我关掉手电筒，无比轻快地下了楼。

日子又回到平常，清早或者晚上，除了有力的脚步声，几乎听不到抱怨声了。邻居来串门，与她说起楼道灯重新亮起来的事，邻居说："多亏了李婶，李婶对我们这么好，她儿女不在身边，以后我们要常去她家陪她聊天唠嗑。"

"谢李婶？"

"嗯，楼道里的灯是李婶花钱请电工来修的。"

原来，李婶看到楼道灯坏了没人修，眼见着上楼下楼的人磕磕碰碰的，就想着这样下去也不是个事儿，就主动找物业来修。物业说维修可以，但必须要给务工费什么的，李婶说"业主每月都交物业费，这点小事，你们就不能帮帮忙吗？"

拗不过物业，李婶又怕是自己找的事，再去找住家们收钱不好意思，就自己掏钱给了物业。

我的心升腾起缕缕感动，李婶常年住在储藏室，她是最不需要楼道灯的人，而她却为这事忙前跑后，费心尽力。

想起了曾经读过的一个故事：18 世纪初期，本杰明·富兰克林在费城经营一份报纸。他在看稿的时候，发现抢劫等暴力犯罪大半都发生在晚上城里黑暗的街道上，很少有人光天化日之下还胆大包天地攻击别人。

为了让身处的城市更安全，富兰克林向费城政府陈情，要求在最繁忙的街道上装设煤气街灯。政府拒绝了，当时的城市装设街灯的街道寥寥无几，而且耗资不小。

富兰克林自掏腰包在报社前装设了一盏路灯，又去求助当地的商人，请他们在自己的商店前装设路灯，但每一个人都拒绝了，说这样的花费完全没有道理。

黑暗的夜晚，人们习惯到富兰克林那盏孤灯的光亮里聊天寒暄。后来，一名商店老板也在店门前装设了路灯，接着一个又一个的店家开始跟进。不久之后，路灯不再是可有可无的奢侈品，而是小区守望相助的必需品。最后，政府接管了这些路灯，并负责出资设置和维护。富兰克林望着报纸笑了，因为他报纸报道的犯罪案大大下降了。

富兰克林为费城的黑夜带来一盏路灯，他也得以住在安全的城里。

身处黑暗，最大的渴望就是一缕光明。为别人的黑夜点亮一盏灯，把别人的福祉看得跟自己的福祉一样重要，别人也会以同样的方式对待他人，光明便会在黑暗里散布、传播。

载于《妙笔·阅读经典》

伸出你善良的手，为别人点亮一盏关爱的灯。如果每个人都把别人装在心里，那这个世界就温暖了。

稻草与大树

文/李兴海

信念是鸟，它在黎明仍然黑暗之际，感觉到了光明，唱出了歌。

——泰戈尔

我与你一样，时刻在想，如何向后一辈的人阐述信念的重要性，以及信念为何物。当我在公共场合有意传达这类思想时，旁人经常会讪讪地问我："信念能吃吗？能填饱肚子吗？"

信念如梦想一般，纯属虚无之物，飘渺至极。没人能说出信念的形貌，体态，或者是年龄。它与我们不仅仅是天涯之隔，阴阳相离，甚至可以说，它从始至终就没有在人类历史的长河中显现过。

那么，我何以要推崇并且宣扬它呢？原因很简单，它对所有存活于世间的生物都有着不可言喻的功用。

很多人问过我，有什么功用？难不成能把所有的人都变成比尔·盖茨，变成爱因斯坦？当然不能，信念本身需要生命作为载体，而每一个生命所具有的天性都存有细微的差别。因此，注定会创造不同的历史，取得不同的成就。

很久以前，我手底下有过一个异常调皮，又极具文学天赋的孩子。我每日闲暇时必会催促他，专心攻于写作。可他不爱遵从我的吩咐，他说，文字是在心中，并非跃于纸上。可我知道，他仅仅只是懒于动手提笔。

他和很多人一样，而这类人什么年龄段的都有。自己本身心存希冀，尚有鸿鹄大志，却不甘脚踏实地，为此志就地挥汗。于是，时日一长，所见收效甚微，胸中大志便成了小志，最后，全然无志。无志不说，还好提“当年勇”。

大怒之时，我曾骂过他，心中毫无半点信念。他如旁人一般问我：“何为信念？你能指给我看吗？”

我领着他，穿过城市的车水马龙，来到秋日的田野上。

弯腰割稻的辛勤劳动者与金黄的果实构成了一幅绝美的画面。我步入田野之中，随手拣起一根稻草，放到他的手里，让他开怀抱住这根稻草，并做一个双脚离地的动作给我看。

他见我异常严肃，便一声不吭地抱住那根如筷子般粗细的稻草，试图双脚离地。可这样的事，终究是不会成功的。最后，他一脸委屈地说：“我做不到。”

路旁，一棵茂盛的大树正迎风招展。我指着壮实的树干对他说，你抱着它，并做一个双脚离地的动作给我看。

他欣喜地双手抱树，一跃而起，双脚离地蹬于树干之上，“噌噌”几下爬了上去。然后站在高高的树枝上冲着我笑，像是在炫耀他的技艺。

我问他，上面的景色美吗？他对着一望无垠的田野远眺几次后大声地告诉我，美！美极了！

我令他下树之后，拍拍他的肩膀道：“你刚才所抱的两种东西，就是我平日所说的信念。”他不解地看着我。

“信念虽是虚无之物，可你却能拥抱，或是依靠着它来行路。只有当某一日你心生绝望，或是豁然开朗时你才会明白，它就在你身旁。也许，它是刚才那根弱不禁风的稻草，任凭你如何努力，也无法与困境脱离。也许，它就是面前的这棵大树，既能让你无畏风雨，又能让你站得更高。”

刚说完这些话，田野上就起了秋风。那些杂乱的稻草再次被席卷得狼狈不堪。不远处，一棵大树正立于狂风中，“哗哗”地朝空中咆哮。

载于《中学生》

信念是黑暗中的光亮，信念让我们在极度痛苦中找到自我。无论在多么艰难、多么困苦的环境中，只要我们拥有坚定的信念，我们就可以迎难而上。

有间小屋

文/语中清荷

虽然我们走遍世界去寻找美，但是美这东西要不是存在于我们内心，就无从寻找。

——爱默生

一

笔记本里收藏着这样一幅画：绿荫浓密的森林深处，有间小屋，白墙壁，小木门，双层屋顶，底层是厚厚的干草，外层是深棕色的格子竹条状覆盖其上。门前的小池塘里漂浮着碧绿的睡莲，一条石板路铺在水面上，蜿蜒曲折，伸向小屋门前。

环绕整座小屋的，是苍翠欲滴的宽叶芭蕉，那颜色，轻轻一挤，就能挤出清凉的绿汁来，一点一点，从画里流出来，将心濡湿得柔软。多么清新脱俗的世外桃源，绝美得令人窒息。

画是好友相送，附上的文字尤为感动：送给简单纯净的你，知道你喜欢。原来，这世间的懂得，和时间无关，和距离无关，和名利无关。纯粹得犹如冬夜围炉里的根根柴火，只是轻轻一撩拨，温暖的焰火就逼走心底的道道忧伤。岁月清了清嗓子，在烟火生活里重新噼里啪啦地响作一片。

二

终究是世间的人，心不染尘，身惹烟火，虽是喜欢，却只能远远地赏。太绝美，太遥远的人或物，多半会伤得寸断肝肠。素色光阴里，还是守着身边的小小惊喜方为妥帖的安然。

客厅墙壁上挂着一幅画，说是画，其实是十字绣，是一个心灵手巧的亲戚相赠。深秋的森林深处，落英缤纷，地面像铺了一层五彩的地毯。一座玲珑精致的小木屋坐落在池塘边，烟囱里正冒着袅袅炊烟，墙壁的两头各生长着一棵粗壮的树木。

圆形的小池塘像是森林那只明亮的眼睛，四周深深浅浅的芦苇，恰似小池塘浓密的睫毛。紧邻着池塘的，是一座弯弯的小桥，好一幅天净沙。沐浴着夕阳的余晖，整个画面温暖而质朴。画前伫立，禁不住浮想联翩：何时才能拥有属于自己的小屋？

那天，和孩子各骑一车沿着环城河并肩慢行。车至半途，孩子惊喜地喊道："妈妈，看，那边有间小屋！"顺着他手指的方向看去，可不是，草木葳蕤的环城河公园里多了间崭新的小木屋，古色古香，静静地立在蜿蜒曲折的石板路一侧，简朴而不失新颖。

经不起好奇心驱使，我俩支上车架，绕着小屋前后左右地看，里面空无一物，外面也没有任何解释的文字。碧绿的草地环绕四周，像是给这座小小的木屋戴上了一串绿色的项链。一条水泥修建的小路曲折有致，由远及近，经过小屋的门前，又晃晃悠悠地伸向远方，一路向西，像微醺的红颜，莫非，路的那头有等待她的故人？

不得而知。只是，谁的心里不曾住过一个故人？谁的记忆里不曾有过一间小屋?

忆起那年，正值盛夏酷暑，结伴去万佛湖游玩。岛上绿树成荫，凉爽的湖风拂面而来。流连在人间仙境，全然忘却外面世界的烦忧和浮华。一座座别致的度假小木屋散落有致，有着异域风情的格调，在青山绿水掩映下，分外醒目。只是隐隐觉得，和一百多年前瓦尔登湖畔的那间小木屋相比，这里的小木屋似乎缺少点什么。

三

1845 年 3 月，春暖花开。28 岁的梭罗带着一柄借来的斧头，一头扎进瓦尔登湖的寂静森林里，自己动手，造了一间木屋，开始了他两年零两个月的湖畔生活。和他不离不弃的，是自然界的万物生灵。

他和鱼儿絮语，穿林听风，聆听鸟儿的啾啾欢唱，泛舟吹笛，湖边垂钓。每年他花上六周的时间用于劳作，以供日常生活所需，余下的 46 周专注于阅读、写作和思考，为世人留下了独一无二的心灵鸡汤《瓦尔登湖》。

一个人，一支笔，一片湖，一间屋，年轻的梭罗用孤独的智慧和从容的淡然来抵达内心的自省，从而完成了自我的升华。他留给我们的，是一个孤独者的幸福。他的小木屋，也定格在阅读者的脑海中。

无独有偶，19 世纪的巴黎乡下，也有间小木屋，住着的是福楼拜，他和爱人分隔两地，以信传讯。他在这间小屋里，拼命工作，天天洗澡，不接待来访，不看报纸，不穿外衣，不出寂静的书房半步。

毋庸置疑，他们一贫如洗，然而，他们又是最富有的，精神明亮，思想清澈。与自然融为一体，是抵达生命最简单、最简朴、最简洁的生活方式。

四

19世纪英国女作家伍尔芙说过：女人要有自己的房子。是的，纷扰红尘里的女子，每个人的内心深处都渴望拥有属于自己的小屋，当作心灵的栖息地，哪怕只有巴掌大小。如美国人谢弗那样，小的可能没有别人家的衣帽间大，但是喜爱之至。疲惫的时候，在小屋里休养生息；受伤的时候，在小屋里舔舐伤口；幸福的时候，在小屋里细品回味。

我向往的，是小屋的冬夜，屋外雪花纷飞，白茫茫一片。屋内围着火炉一边说着话儿，一边烹雪煮茶，用炉火和语言守住温暖，抵抗严寒。若是有友短信过来：天寒，多穿衣。抿嘴，暖心一笑。

载于《中学生》

我们该有这样一个心灵的栖息地，像是个安静隐秘的世界，超越平日白开水般枯燥庸碌的生活。可以在那里憩息、沉睡、思考；也可收放自如、激昂跳脱，甚至是什么也不做，却也是极好的体验。

碎片也可以拼出美好人生

文/莲叶深深

故不积跬步，无以至千里；不积小流，无以成江海。

——《荀子》

每天早晨起床我都信心百倍，告诉自己一定要抓紧时间完成各项工作，然后好好读书给自己充电，可工作和生活却并不能如我所愿。

作为教导处主任，每天来到学校就被各种事情纠缠。比如这一天的早晨，我刚刚安排完老师们当天的带班带课，校长的电话就把我叫过去要我写个爱生学校的汇报。结果回到办公室不到10分钟，有家长敲门进来，向我投诉某个班主任作业太多，我只能放下刚写了题目的汇报，耐心给她解决问题。

与此同时，各种QQ群交替闪烁，不敢不看，唯恐错过什么重要通知。结果十有八九都是无用的闲扯。身在教导处，办公室里人来人往，各种家长学生老师和外面来办事的人川流不息，就算忙完了工作，也无法静下心来读书。

下班到家脱下外衣就开始忙碌起来，等到米下锅、肉菜摘洗切完，我便拿起一本书看，一段还没看完，就听到儿子在屋里喊：妈妈，你来给我听写单词！只好放下书去给孩子听写。好容易听写完了，半个多小时的时间过去了，我忙去炒菜。

等吃完饭收拾完，我重新再拿起书，正看了一页的精彩处时，电话铃声响起，妈妈打来电话，问寒问暖、各种家事絮叨。等放下电话再看时间，半个小时后又要安排孩子睡觉了。想着这一天就又这么荒废过去了，便再也看不下去书，只坐在那里闹心发呆。

这只是平常的一天，没有这些事也会有类似差不多的事情纠缠着我，影响着我的情绪。衣服要洗，家要收拾，水电煤气电话费要交，孩子的情绪要关注，还有水管子漏水、孩子生病，朋友的邀请等等突如其来的意外，都让我疲于应付、心力交瘁。

上天作证，我不是不思进取的人，我也想给孩子做表率，努力读书工作，做最好的自己。

可是，我的工作和生活时间都被这些琐事割成了碎片，什么都干不了，让我无比郁闷。就算偶尔无人打扰，自己也时刻都在焦虑中，总是担心被打扰，还是看不下去书。

我无比苦恼，在 QQ 群中跟女友们抱怨，她们纷纷给我出主意：

一人说，在单位没办法，回到家可以选择关机啊，为什么不对自己好一点吗？又一人说，你要学会拒绝，给自己留更多的时间空间；还有人说，没时间就别为难自己，人到中年的女子，何必还要努力读书，平平淡淡也挺好的。

前两种说法我不能接受，我是妈妈、女儿、妻子、是教师，怎么忍心只顾自己，逃避放弃我的责任和义务呢？那么，我就只能像第三个人说的那样，放弃自己吗？

忽然，有一个姐姐用小窗对我说：小时候我家里不富裕，妈妈就用各种布头缝缀在一起做成坐垫，真是美丽啊！后来有了孩子，看他用一张张零碎的拼图拼出一张大画卷，居然和妈妈缝的坐垫一样漂亮。所以没有抽不出的时间，只有不想抽出的时间。就算是碎片，可那也是时间，把它们拼起来也一样可以让你有所收获。

她的话让我如醍醐灌顶，顿时明白了自己的误区。

从那一天开始，我将一本书一支笔放入包中随身携带，在完成工作家务之余，开始争分夺秒地读书写作。

于是，就在枕边、厕上，等车开会的间隙，我都在手不释卷地读书，同时也及时记下了偶然产生的灵思顿悟；在做家务的空闲，在午休时间，我一段又一段地写下了我的所思所想。我不再怕思路被打断，也不怕记下的内容支离破碎，我享受着读书写作的快乐。

我有了很多节约时间的“发明创造”。我把孩子叫到厨房，一边做饭一边听写孩子单词，检查孩子的朗读；我为年迈的妈妈读书，既让她开心也让自己有时间读书了；后来我又接受朋友的建议，用手机下载了专门的软件，常常在上下班路上听或者可以一边做家务一边“听书”……

日复一日，月复一月，年复一年。

就在这些碎片的时间中，我读完了一本又一本的书，文学、历史、教育，这些书籍让我的视野更宽广，内心更丰富安宁；我写下了几十万字的小说散文，发表在报纸杂志上，周围人都对我纷纷赞赏。

因为读书多，让我的知识更丰富，工作变得游刃有余。我的口才也随之提高，我成了学校的家庭教育指导教师，经常为家长做讲座，我内涵丰富、旁征博引的讲座受到了他们的欢迎。

因为经常在这些碎片时间内读书写作，我有了极强的抗干扰能力，内心越来越强大坚韧。同时也能分心二用，经常可以一边聊天一边写作，让别人大为惊叹。

耳濡目染，看我这么抓紧时间读书，原本不爱读书的儿子也爱上了读书，不仅学习再也不用我操心，读书的氤氲也让他更加明理懂事，顺利度过青春逆反期，我们始终互相尊重深爱。

光阴继续向前走，生活慢慢又有了新的变化。

读了初中的儿子对我说，妈妈你去读书写作吧，我已经自己抄写完了需要家长听写的单词，背诵好了古文。我向你保证，这些单词和古文我已经全会了！我不放心，抽查了几次，果然单词准确无误，古文倒背如流。

妈妈说，你那么忙，不用想着来看我，我有空去你家看你。于是妈妈经常来我家，不仅帮我做点力所能及的家务，节省了我的时间，也让我在家里就能享受合家欢乐的情景。

我的老师们对我说，郭主任我家里有事要请假，但我自己已经串好了课，安排好学生，肯定不会有问题的，不用你费心了。你那么忙，专心做你的事吧。

因为我始终不怕麻烦不怕辛苦地爱着我周围的亲人朋友同事，她们也真心为我着想，还给我更多安宁美好的光阴，我的时间竟然越变越多了。

把每一块碎片都珍惜收藏，把每一分钟都妥善利用，我成了好妈妈好女儿好教师，仰俯无愧，被我的孩子妈妈女友领导下属深爱着、体谅着、包容着、信任着。

当然，我也努力做着最好的自己。我用无数的碎片时间不仅拼出了一本本书一篇篇文章，更拼出了自己美好温暖的人生。

载于《初中生之友》

很多个碎片堆积，就堆起了自身的高度。而那些散落在日子里的碎片，就好比是整个岁月长河里的每一天。把握每一天，过好每一天，好多个日子聚集起来，就成就了你的一生。

你不必追

文/倪西赟

天生我材必有用，千金散尽还复来。

——李白

你不必追，天空的鸟儿。

在宁静的清晨，你只需慵懒地躺在床上，就可以听到鸟儿在你的窗台上天籁般地清唱；你也可以光着脚丫，走在挂满露珠的草尖上，看鸟儿轻盈地在霞光里扇动翅膀，低低飞，低低飞……

你不必追，调皮的春风。

在云朵低垂的田野上，你只需带上一只风筝，它便会调皮地带着风筝去远方流浪；你也可以站在嫩草青青的山坡上，它会悄悄回到你的身旁，轻轻揉乱你的秀发，让你很美，很美……

你不必追，流淌的溪水。

在一个温暖的黄昏，你只需坐在河边的大石块上，伸出脚丫，撩拨那清冽的水，便可浸入骨髓；你也可以采一朵一朵的桃花，一瓣一瓣地轻轻撒入溪水，让桃花追随，让桃花追随……

你不必追，天上的月亮。

选一个月明星稀的晚上，你只需站在一棵古老的大树下，仰起脸，微闭双眼，让月光慢慢吻上你的唇；你也可以去村口看看那口池塘，那里有一位穿白裙子的姑娘，微醉，微醉……

你不必追，恋人的身影。

你伤心的泪水载得起船，却留不住他决绝离去的身影；你只需重新拾掇心情，给自己一个笑脸，给自己一个晴天；你也可以把他冰封在记忆里，爱情的路上不需要眼泪，不需要眼泪……

你不必追，父母的脚步。

他们的脚步履蹒跚，或许会在哪一天，在哪一个拐角，就会突然不见。你只需常常回到他们身边，听听他们的唠叨，听听他们的抱怨；你也可以多吃几次他们做的饭，尽心了就不后悔……

你不必追，在这个世界，你如果拥有一颗花儿般的心，就会看得到美，等得到美；你不必追，在这个世界，你如果拥有一颗感恩的心，醒悟的心，你就会领悟到，逝去的美……

载于《作文与考试》

每一朵花都有自己盛开的方式，每一只鸟都有自己飞翔的方式，每个人都有属于自己的方式。你不必羡慕，亦不用去追！

快乐幸福的中年

文/清　翔

当我们为一去不复返的青春叹息时，我们应该考虑将来的衰老，不要到那时再为没有珍惜壮年而悔恨。

——拉布吕耶尔

你的心中不再觉得有俗事庸事的纷扰，而是一种坦荡洒脱磊落自然。你日日置身于繁华闹市，却又能兀自独立于喧嚣。名利是非，自当一扫浮云的匆匆，那么，你就进入你人生的中年了。至少，你的心灵已在中年的原野流连徜徉了。

中年是一种熟稔是一种贮存。相对于少年的稚嫩，青年的华丽，老年的静穆，中年是洞察世态炎凉之时，又还未曾呈现蹒跚步履之态。中年者脚下不再是力的拱动，眼前不再是色的迷离，耳边不再是声的轰鸣，他已经被岁月积攒下了丰盈的内涵。尽管他的前方只是一围沉静默立的囤，但也是开敞的、高耸的、厚重的、踏实的。是的，中年是一种丰收，那是以汗水浇灌滋润出的金灿灿的稻谷红通通的高粱还有那黄橙橙的梨……

中年不仅仅是物质上的丰收，它还是一种心绪的廓落，一种精神上的升华。梦里空花已醒，风雨暗晦已过，心中一烛明灯，驱散了所有积聚的夜色。中年者或伫立或端坐于山岗高坡，静心凝思，超逸如禅。万山逶迤足下，观天地匆匆过客就宛然看身边的云起云涌花开花落。他埋葬并穿越了青春年华特有的晦涩哲学的泥泞之路，他趟过了勃发盛年溪沟河流暴涨的浑浊之水。那脸孔上岁月的风尘怎么也掩盖不住由他内心的智慧滋养出来的坦然的光辉，怎么也遮蔽不了他心湖的澄澈与明净。

中年，从某种意义上说，是人生另一种生命抑或人生另一种生活的重新开始。中年是从沸腾喧哗炎热炽烈的大道拐向一个略显悄然、和风丽日的弯角路上。曾经满地的落红，已化作脚下黑黑的土地；曾经头顶的一天暑热，已剔除遮蔽过多的虚浮的繁荫。秋草有情，径自苍劲；黄花无意，引领南山远眺，天边那如绸似缎的蓝色托起中年蓝色的畅想。天高，云淡，鹊飞、雁鸣，天籁拨动你的心灵，好景涤荡你的肺腑。那是中年书写不尽的诗情，那是中年挥洒不尽的画意。

中年是一种博大。蓝天是大地的眼睛，睿智、恬淡是中年的眼睛。人长有一双眼睛，是观瞻世间万事万物的，是接纳世间万事万物的。水、山、树、云，投映其间，那水、山、树、云，也会反观辉映着你。中年当是一种天人合一，地人合一，物人合一，人人合一。

中年是一种智慧与恒定。如果说中年尚是绚烂与凋敝并存，热烈与淡漠同在，敏觉与木讷共处，此算不得是一种真正意义上的中年。中年的太阳已携着灿烂滑过山顶，黄昏在前方依然可以把你照亮，那更多的却是你的襟怀你的智慧你的阅历在为你秉烛。中年是矗立岿然，是意象悠远。它穿越的只是穹窿和浮云，走过的只是历史和光阴，那不曾改变的是自己的一颗既执着又坦荡的灵魂。他从不曾在光中衰老，他只曾在光中死去。

你、我、他，无不皆会走进这样的中年，而我们都应该也都可能一直拥有这样的中年。由此，快乐和幸福也就永远会伴随着自己。

载于《智慧背囊》

很大程度上，决定幸福感的，不是年龄，而是心态。

九句真话和一句谎言

文/孙道荣

有些精灵奉承你，诱哄你，其实它们也只想咬人，而且都是火辣辣的。

——罗曼·罗兰

被朋友拉去听一个关于养生的讲座。主讲人有一串很大的名头，在圈内有不小的影响力。

说实话，我是带着抵触情绪来听的。对类似的讲座，我一向没有好感，认为不过是一种推销术，讲来讲去，其最终目的，无非要推销某个理念，或者某种产品。

这次，听着听着，却入了迷。不得不承认，主讲人讲的都是养生常识，以及容易让人混淆的误区。比如，一段时间十分流行的一个养生之道，每天喝八杯水保健康。主讲人言辞恳切而尖锐地指出，每个人所需要的水分其实并不一样，喝多了不但无益健康，还会造成肾脏的负担。

对诸如此类的养生误区，主讲人一一剖析，言之凿凿，发自肺腑，听讲的众生，不时发出感叹之声。看得出大家显然都被错误的养生之道贻害已久，所幸今天遇到了真正的养生大师，讲的句句是实话，字字乃真言，没有虚夸，没有谎言，坦诚而真切。大家报以热烈的掌声。

主讲人忽然话锋一转，拿出了讲台下的某个产品，开始介绍起特殊的功能。

我猛然惊醒，这才是她要讲的正题啊。而前面所讲的所有的真话、实话，只是一个又一个铺垫。

那场讲座的尾声，是很多人甘愿掏腰包，纷纷抢购其带来的某养生产品。

和朋友探讨主讲人的手腕，很简单，前面讲了九句真话，就为了最后一句谎言。而因为有了九句真话的铺垫，使最后一句谎言，看起来像真话一样诚恳可信。于是，众人被迷惑了，一切水到渠成。

一个谎话连篇的人，很容易就被人识破，戳穿。换句话说，没人会信任一个满口谎言的人。但如果九句真话后，只附了一句谎言呢？情形恐怕就完全不同，人们很容易在前面真话的诱导下放松警惕，而将那句谎言也奉为真话。

看过很多科幻电影，为什么明知是科幻片，很多人看着看着，却信以为真？道理很简单，科幻片的基底，是建立在众多早被验证了的科普知识之上的。前不久看过一部科幻大片《盗梦空间》，故事惊心动魄，引人入胜。我们知道梦是虚幻的，那么，梦境可以被入侵窃取吗？常识告诉我们，这是不可能的。但是，这部电影里面，告诉了我们很多“科学知识”，比如它明确地告诉你，梦是非现实存在的；梦里的 5 分钟，相当于现实中的一个小时；心理学上的研究表明，催眠师很难让被催眠者做出违反他们自身意愿的举动，基于这个科学依据，电影中将思想植入设定为最困难的境界，使人相信它的科学合理性，而不是胡编乱造的无厘头……在合理的“知识”的掩护下，盗梦变得似乎不再是遥不可及，而成为一种可能，使现实和虚幻相互交融。

有个同事，自诩从来不讲假话，在我们平素与他的交往中，也确实感受到了这一点，他的实诚，为他赢得了信任和尊重。一次几个人聚在一起打牌，他的妻子忽然打来电话，问他在做什么，他平静地回答，在和领导谈工作。他的妻子相信了。我们都错愕不已，这本是一个无伤大雅的谎言，但这句小小的谎言，却让我们对他开始重新审视，他真的如他所言，从没有对我们说过谎吗？还是我们根本没有识破？

我宁愿相信这个世界上，真的有从来不说谎的人，但更大的可能性是，他说了九句真话，后面却有一句假话。一种可能是，他无意间不慎冒出了一句谎言；还有一种可能是，他讲了九句真话，目的就只为了让你相信最后那句谎言。被九句真话层层包裹的那句谎言，往往具有更大的欺骗性，听起来比真话更像真话。我们要小心谎言，尤其要警惕真话掩盖下的那句谎言。

载于《微型小说月报》

我们经常会陷入这样的误区，认为一个人不讲谎话，那他就永不会骗人。一个人老是做正确的事，那他就不会犯错。最可怕的不是处心积虑的人，而是冷不防被你最信任的人重伤。

藏在心底的那一抹柔软

文/晓　蕊

因为爱过，所以慈悲；因为懂得，所以宽容。

——张爱玲

一

初秋的一天，我们公司组织去画眉谷旅游。开车的是司机张师傅，他为人忠厚，平时沉言少语，大家都亲切地称呼他“张哥”。

车开了两个小时后进入山区，行到拐弯处时，遇到了一件意想不到的事。就在前方不远处，几只灰褐色的山鸡在路上悠闲地溜达着。张哥想刹车已来不及了，他放慢车速，鸣起喇叭，想把山鸡惊飞。

只见一只老山鸡扇动翅膀，“扑棱棱”地向前奔去，把吓得惊慌失措的小山鸡赶往路边。他急忙调转方向盘，让车从它们的空隙间穿过，但还是隐约听到异样的声响。

当车停下来时，他跳下车向车尾处跑去。老山鸡身后溅出一道血花，小山鸡们伸着脑袋啾啾地哀鸣着。以老山鸡的健壮体魄，原本可以逃过一劫，想到此他不由心里一颤，双手托起它放进草丛里。

上车后，他难过地说："咳！撞死一只山鸡。"那声音像一阵轻风，被大家的说笑声淹没。到达景区后，我们穿行在山林间，尽赏秋色斑斓。看到张哥挎着相机，不时有人冲他喊："来，给我拍一张。"

到家后，我点开张哥的QQ空间，看他拍的照片，却意外地读到一篇短文。他记录了路上发生的事情，在结尾处不无伤感地写着："面对如此伟大的母爱，我的心好痛。唉！"

我的心，跌落在这云朵般柔软的叹息里。忽然明白为什么晕车的我，那天感到格外地踏实，一个对自然界弱小生命充满敬意的人，心中自会多一分责任与担当。

二

有一天，母亲买菜时突然昏倒，被送往医院。经过一番检查后，医生说是心跳过缓引起的，建议安装心脏起搏器。

我跟医生沟通确定了手术方案，手术时间定在次日下午，负责手术的是该院心血管内科的梁主任，听说是位颇有盛名的医学专家。

我正犹豫要不要给他送红包，抬头见母亲苍白的脸上显露出忧虑的神情，额头上渗满细密的汗珠。经过一番考虑，我还是揣着钱来到主任办公室。

起初，主任客气地回绝，后来经过几番推让，还是收下了红包。我长嘘了一口气，回病房把情况跟母亲讲了，她心里这才稍稍安定下来。

手术进行得很顺利，母亲的身体日渐好转，主任多次到病房巡视，嘱托按时服药及保养事宜。母亲说："医生还是挺负责的。"我低声附和道："那是！收了红包态度就是不一样。"

过了几天，母亲要出院了。我去收费处办理出院手续，发现押金多了些，细问之下才知是主任转来的，正是我付的红包钱。

原来他是怕病人心理负担过重，用一种委婉的方式，悄悄地回绝了患者家属的好意。我想去跟梁主任道个别，顺便表示感谢，谁知办公室的门敞开着，但他人却不在。只见桌子上的玻璃下压着个纸条，上面写着一行小楷："吾厚吾德。"

那字迹刚劲而飘逸，透着古朴与禅意，看上去严谨刻板的医生，也有温软柔和的另一面。这让我既感动又惭愧，怔怔地默立片刻，眼角泛起一阵潮意。

三

下面这个故事是听邻居刘姨讲的：

那天，她正在屋里做家务，听到一阵急促的敲门声。打开门，是一位陌生的邮递员，他从邮包里掏出一张贺卡，一脸着急地说："你快看看，是不是出啥事了？"

刘姨疑惑地接过来一看，刹那间泪如雨下，她顾不上跟邮递员多说，转身回屋给女儿打电话。

事情的起因是这样的，她的女儿在网上认识了一位年轻男子，深深地陷入这场恋情中，却遭到父母的极力反对，她和家人大吵了一架后离开了家。

交往一年后她才发现那男人是一只多情的蝶，并不肯为某一朵花停驻。正值春节临近，羞愤交织的她含泪在贺卡上写道：妈妈，请原谅这个不听话的女儿，这是我最后一次跟您道声祝福了……

邮递员送信时发现地址有误，原来女孩的父母因旧房拆迁搬了家。他看到贺卡上的内容，意识到可能是一位女孩跟家人的最后道别。他不由得心急如焚，忙向周边的居民打听，终于问到新的地址。

彼时天色已晚，又下着大雪，可他觉得一刻都不能再等了。在雪地上蹒跚行走了近一个小时，他终于找到收信人刘姨。于是，就出现了开头的那一幕。

这封及时送达的贺卡，拯救了一颗濒临绝望的心。在母亲的苦苦相劝下，女孩踏上了回家的路。然而，让刘姨感到遗憾的是，至今不知道那位邮递员的名字。

林清玄曾说："柔软心是莲花，因慈悲为水、智慧做泥而开放。"纵观尘世，确如他所言，心中蕴藏着柔软的人，更具仁爱悲悯之情。亦唯其如此，人生的荷塘里才能开满清净的莲花，微风吹来，花香盈怀。

载于《正能量·美文馆》

慈悲是大爱，是内心的柔软。一颗慈悲的心，可以像花香那样令人沉醉。

性格不决定人缘好坏

文/金　珠

勿以恶小而为之，勿以善小而不为。惟贤惟德，能服于人。

——刘备

前些日子，接到一位学生鼓足勇气打来的电话，他向我诉说了他的苦恼。他说："我自己性格内向，不善言辞，与人交往不得方法，都说人缘的好坏能决定一个人成就的大小。我真担心工作后不能拥有良好的人际关系，成为一个不受大家欢迎的人。我想，他的苦恼，很多性格内向的人都有。确实，性格外向的人在人际交往中显得很有优势，但这并不意味着性格内向的人就没有好人缘了。

我孩子所在的工厂有个焊工周师傅，他性格内向，不爱讲话，手艺却是一级棒。下班时，经常有人推着自行车来请周师傅焊接缺损断裂的零部件。他也曾经帮我焊接过东西，周师傅从来不急不火，一丝不苟，让每个人满意离开，并没有因为自己急着下班而马虎、懈怠。虽然焊工是配合工种，可周师傅年年获选先进。我孩子跟着周师傅学技术，进步很慢。有人说周师傅不想把真本事传人，周师傅也不辩解。后来，在他的细心调教下，孩子荣获厂里"金牌"焊工，很多人要拜周师傅为师，他翻来覆去就一句话：“只要自己肯下功夫，各个能成才。”

去年，周师傅生病住院，看望的人络绎不绝，不仅是厂里的人，还有像我这样的职工家属。

周师傅性格内向，可他默默无闻，一副热心肠，面对误解不与人争，坚持事实说话，他沉默却不冷漠，寡言却不寡情，一举一动彰显着高贵的品质，吟唱着无声的赞歌，像他这样的人，怎么可能不会赢得别人的敬重和爱戴呢？

和周师傅一样，在我们小区当了十几年门卫的李大爷，居民无人不记得他的好，接收快递、帮忙看东西……每一次，李大爷都是一个字“行”，不多说一句话。他性格很内向，进小区，我们常跟他打招呼，他也多是点头致意，惜字如金。平时，自己捧本书，戴上老花镜阅读，很少与人交谈。一次，我半夜醉醺醺地回来栽倒在大门口，李大爷把我背回了家。第二天，我又回来晚了，喊开门连自己都觉得不好意思，李大爷看到了，默默地给我开门，就简单三个字“回来了”，便再也没说什么。上个月，看车棚的师傅辞职回家了，以前他和李大爷搭伙做饭，他一走，李大爷吃饭就成了问题。一天中午，我家包饺子，便想到给李大爷送一碗，等我到了传达室，嗬，桌上摆着十几个碗。李大爷告诉我，这些都是大家送来的！

大家为什么会记着李大爷，是因为平时麻烦他的事实在太多了。像李大爷这样沉默寡言、性格内向，但天性善良、乐于助人的人有很多。这样的人谁不喜欢，谁不愿意结交？做好事当好人，坚持默默付出远胜于偶尔大张旗鼓，没有人会对别人的帮助无动于衷，而人缘就是在这样一点一滴付出中积累起来的。像周师傅、李大爷这样的人在我们身边很多，普普通通，但却让人感到亲切，值得信赖。

热心肠是赢得好人缘的前提，一个人的素养也很重要。我们单位以前有个叫黄华的人，性格内向，领导主动牵线，让他追求同事李丽。可李丽觉得不合适就拒绝了。黄华觉得没面子在单位待下去，便辞职下海了。几年后，赚了不少钱的黄华娶了一个年轻貌美的妻子。前不久，黄华开着豪车、带上美丽的妻子来到我们单位，特意在李丽办公室转了一圈，明眼人都看出他是有意来显摆，要找回自己当初丢失的面子。我和几位同事当初和黄华接触不多，但印象中他至少还算是谦谦君子。然而，经此一事，完全颠覆了我们对他的那点好感，受到大家的一致唾弃和鄙夷。

人际交往中，你话多话少没关系，性格内向外向也无关紧要，关键是看你品质如何，因此在我看来，一个人只要乐于助人，为人一副热心肠，不损人利己，懂得宽容与谅解，内心阳光正义，就能拥有好人缘。

载于《演讲与口才》

不是善于交际的人就有很多朋友，也不是沉默寡言的人就缺乏朋友。其中的关键在于你的性格是否成为你的闪光点，并以此聚集一批朋友跟随。

淬炼过的金子才发光

文/唐　仔

烈火试真金，逆境试强者。

——塞内加

去浙江遂昌的金矿国家矿山公园游览，恰逢一队参观的学生团。领队的老师，拿起两块矿石，问同学们，哪个是金矿石？

老师手里的两块矿石，在灯光下，呈现出两种截然不同的形态。一块矿石里面，像撒了金粉一样，每一个角度，都发出耀眼的光芒；而另一块矿石，则像被墨涂过的一样，周身是黑色的，几乎没有什么光泽，与我们平时见到的石头，似乎并无二样。孩子们叽叽喳喳地争论开了。很快，一个声音占了上风，那块闪闪发光的，肯定是金矿石，没看到里面全是金粉吗？但也有人小声地质疑，如果答案是明摆着的，老师为什么还拿来考大家？

见同学们各自表达了看法，老师揭晓了答案，那块黑色的矿石，才是真正的金矿石。而闪闪发光的那块，则是普通的硫铁石，里面没有任何黄金的成分。它就是人们常说的“愚人金”。

同学们炸了锅。很显然，大部分学生，都被那块硫铁石的闪闪亮光给迷惑了。

有人提出了自己的疑惑，不是说是金子总是会发光的吗？为什么金矿石里的金子却黯淡无光，没有呈现出金子应有的光芒？

老师赞许地看了一眼那名学生，这个问题问得非常好，这也正是今天我想和大家探讨的。老师挥挥手中那块黯淡的金矿石，环视一遍大家，这块石头里面的金子，需要粉碎、淘洗、提炼，才能从石头中分离出来，成为我们平常所见的熠熠生辉的金子。而淹没在石头和其他矿物质中的金子，是看不出它的光泽的。也就是说，真正金光灿灿的金子，是经过了一遍遍淬炼之后才最终呈现出金子的本色的。

我一直默默地站在旁边，好奇地注视着他们。听到这儿，我对老师的良苦用心恍然大悟，这真是一个聪明的老师，他不仅要告诉他的学生科普知识，还潜移默化地向孩子们传授做人的道理呢。

果然，老师话锋一转，对围在他身边的学生们说，在老师的眼中，你们每个人都是这样的一块金矿石，但是，必须经过一道道的淬炼，你们才会成为一块金子，散发出你们青春应有的光彩。

老师的话，引来一阵阵掌声。我留意到，孩子们稚气未脱的脸上，都流露出兴奋的神采。

忽然，有个学生，高高地举起了手。

老师示意他说话。迟疑了一下，那名学生似乎是鼓足了勇气，大声地说，老师，我在上海的一家黄金博物馆看到过一种"狗头金"，它通身都是金黄的，耀眼的，据说，这就是它本来的面目。我觉得真正的金子，就应该是这样的，天生的气质，"腹有诗书气自华"嘛。学生越说越流利，也越说越兴奋，语气中充满了自信。看得出，这是一个很聪明、也很自负的孩子。

老师不停地点着头。学生说完了，老师赞许地说，你的课外知识很丰富，很好。你说的“狗头金”，确实是一块完整的金疙瘩，它是黄金家族里面的瑰宝。不过，它并非天生一块金砖，事实上，它是天上富含黄金成分的陨石，在坠落地球的过程中，因为与大气层发生剧烈摩擦、燃烧，其他的物质都燃烧掉了，只剩下来黄金，才凝集成完整的金块的。也就是说，它不但经过了淬炼，而且是更加严酷的淬炼。如果没有经过大气层严酷地淬炼、燃烧，那块金子，就会一直黯淡无光地散布在矿石之中。

老师再次环顾大家，动情地说，我刚刚说过，在老师的眼中，你们都是金矿石，你们都具备金子一样的潜质。但是，如果不经过千锤百炼，你可能一辈子都无法发现自己的潜能，也一辈子都不会发出金子的光芒。

老师喝了一口矿泉水，继续说，其实，我们每个人，都是一块金矿石，只是太多的人，没有被开采出来，或者没有经过淬炼，而错失了自己本该灿烂的人生。因此，我想告诉大家，别以为自己是块金子，就一定会闪闪发光，发光的金子，都是经过一遍遍淬炼的。

沉默。忽然，同学们都鼓起掌。

我也鼓掌，为这位循循善诱的老师，也为了我们本该熠熠生辉的金子般的人生。

载于《少年儿童研究》

时常思考的问题是，从前孱弱不堪的自己，终于在时光的磨炼中变得强大起来。社会本就是残酷的，只有经历过摔打的人，才能有更强的抗击能力。正所谓物竞天择，适者生存！

第一次出门远行

文/邢占双

在不幸中所表现出来的勇气，通常总是使卑怯的心灵恼怒，而使高尚的心灵喜悦的。

——卢梭

第一次出门远行时我 18 岁，那年寒假只在家待了两天，因为实在受不了父亲，他顿顿喝酒，日夜牢骚，我无法静心读书写作。于是，在一个寒风刺骨的早上，母亲眼泪汪汪地送我到村头，“要不就别去了。”“路上注意安全啊。”“过年，早些回来啊。”我不忍回望，踏着积雪，踩着小道，奔向镇里，来到县城，踏上北去的火车，去山里舅舅家。我要在毕业之前完成一篇小说。

旅途上遇到了一个邻城大学生，他比我高比我帅，戴着眼镜，是师专的，我们很谈得来，谈论最多的是文学，我知道的他也知道，他知道的我也知道。旅途不再寂寞，他说他喜欢写诗，他赠我一本杂志，我赠他一本小说集。我们互留地址，握手告别，有事写信。

火车继续向北行进，车里真冷，光板的座椅又硬又凉，坐一会儿便得站起来活动活动手脚，否则冻木了。旅客稀稀拉拉，坐车的都是一站地两站地就下车，有时整节车厢就剩我一人。火车慢慢悠悠有个小站就停一下，车窗上了一层霜，看不见外面的景色，我吹口气哈出一个猫眼，只见火车穿行在两山之间，没有什么新鲜的景色，很快就倦怠了。

穿过两个山洞之后，我的心便紧张起来，要到地方了，真怕过站。年轻女列车员特意来告诉我，下一站就是乌尔奇了。火车在一个小村旁顿了一下，我刚跳下车，它便呜的一声，不屑一顾地走了。

舅舅家的茅草小屋位于河岸的一个高岗上。白天，舅舅上山伐木。我只身一人盘坐在石头炕上，写一篇青春小说。累了，就到外面走走，天空瓦蓝瓦蓝，像水洗过似的。踏雪到密林深处吼几嗓子，向树林深处走走，可惜我来得不是时候，欣赏不到美景，采不到山珍野味。

晚上，独坐昏黄灯下，读我带去的十几本书，反复听那几盘磁带。舅舅到邻家串门，总是很晚才回来。舅妈带着两个孩子回娘家了，年后才能回来。

火车开过，石头炕也跟着抖动，令我追想它连接的那个世界，那个世界很精彩，要想走得更远，我就要努力。

几天后，我要去看姥爷，好些年没见他了。他在市里一家医院烧锅炉。舅舅领我坐火车来到市里，将我送到地方。那是一所军队的医院，一所空荡荡的大房子，在房子的一角，是姥爷的房间，里面摆放着一张床和一张地桌。姥爷见到我，很高兴。晚上为我做了炒羊肉，羊肉是附近一家给的，那家死了只羊，不会剥羊皮，姥爷帮忙剥的，得到了两条大腿和一些羊排。姥爷看我吃得很香，老眼里闪着欢乐的光。

晚上，我常常熬夜写小说，地桌下的凉风嗖嗖地钻进裤管，没办法，只好将裤管扎起来。姥爷一觉醒来总会劝我：“时间有的是，你要注意身体，你这样不睡觉，到老时病就找你了。”我对姥爷的劝告不以为然，觉得他说得很可笑，睡觉嘛，想睡时就睡，困时再睡也不迟。现在才懂得，姥爷说得有理。

姥爷领钱了，他用枯黄的手指数着角票，两个月的工钱，160 元。他数来数去，拿出 30 元给了我，告诉我省点花。他这一生，从来没有积蓄，贫穷像影子一样伴随他。他一次给了我这么多钱，让我深感意外，感动得嗓子眼发堵。等到我挣钱时，一定好好孝敬他老人家。

第二天，我拿着姥爷的钱，逛了新华书店，买了几本诺贝尔文学奖获奖作品。在城里逛了一圈，到城外登了回山。

除夕之夜，我回到舅舅家。我走出很远，去铁路边上看《春节联欢晚会》。李春波的《一封家书》使我忍不住落泪，我怀念家中满桌的菜肴，怀念与伙伴在一起甩扑克的快乐，怀念家乡过年的温馨气氛。我和舅舅在一起度过了冷冷清清的一个年。

临近开学，我穿着舅舅送我的一套崭新铁路服，回家，回学校，将小说投给了一家杂志社。

不久后，我收到那位大学生的来信，他说我是值得交的知己，同时也收到了退稿信，我默默地将稿子压在了箱底。

但我至今忘不了第一次出门远行的日子，那是我寻梦旅途的开始，虽然距离成功遥遥无期，但苦涩中有宁静，自由中有幸福。那座茅屋，那座城市，那些日子我将永远铭记。

载于《阅读经典》

每个人都有成长中的第一次，第一次出行，第一次独自坐火车去很远的地方，第一次谈恋爱，第一次尝试做一件事……你还记得你最勇敢的第一次吗？

我长大反正不买宝马

文/张素燕

成功，是内心的造就。

——拉尔夫·M. 福特

一位青少年心理专家应邀来给我们学校师生做讲座。在谈到理想这个话题时，专家说，每个人都要有理想。从小就要树立远大的理想，就像你们现在就要树立考清华、北大的理想一样。如果你连想都不敢想，那你这一辈子肯定与清华、北大无缘。如果一个十几岁的男孩子没有自己长大了要买宝马的理想，那他以后也不会有什么出息的。你首先得敢想。有了理想之后，就朝着既定的目标去奋斗、去拼搏、去争取，即使最后没有达到目标，也无怨无悔，总比没有理想，平平庸庸，碌碌无为地过一生要强上百倍。

突然想到我9岁的儿子前两天曾问过我一个问题。“妈，你为什么而读书?”我知道儿子是想拿周恩来为中华之崛起而读书来考我，我故意说：“我读书是为了更好地生活，为了用知识丰富头脑，让我更加充实地、有意义地度过每一天。”“哼，胸无大志!”儿子嗤之以鼻地说。我趁机反问他：“那你为什么而读书?”“我为了振兴中国而读书，让中国走到世界前列，看谁还敢看不起中国!”儿子气宇轩昂地说。我顺势问道："那你怎么样才能振兴中国呢?""我有远大的理想!"儿子自豪地说。"那你的理想是什么呢?""嗯，多了，想当地理学家、历史学家、歌唱家和作家。噢，对了，还有考古学家。嗯，考古学家、地理学家还有历史学家是一回事吧，妈?"儿子充满憧憬地认真地说。没想到儿子竟一连串说出这么多理想。我不以为然地淡然一笑，"行，那你就朝着你的梦想努力学习吧!"

现在想想儿子的远大理想也不是那么凭空一说，信口胡诌，虚无缥缈的。儿子很喜欢地理和历史，超乎一般的喜欢。他闲暇时间经常抱着大大的世界地图和中国地图认真研究。有时还像发现新大陆似的向我报告，"妈，你知道吗?……"随便问他一个国外的什么地方，他都能说出大体位置来，对于世界各国的位置及首都更是对答如流。儿子对历史的痴迷程度更是到了无以复加的地步。光历史书籍都看了好多本。每天中午科教频道的《百家讲坛》更是潜心观看。他对历史事件了如指掌，有很多我不知道的历史他都知道。为此我还得向他请教。一些历史人物，何朝人也；什么年代，发生了什么历史事件；对这个人物的评价，以及跟这个人物有关系的其他人物，等等，他都能娓娓道来，讲得津津有味。这不得不让我汗颜，同时也佩服他小小的脑瓜里竟然装了那么多的知识。儿子的记忆力真好，很久以前，我无心说过的话，他都记忆犹新。

至于儿子说歌唱家，我只能说是他喜欢听歌和唱歌罢了，他并没有这方面的天赋。儿子说当作家，我想是因为他对自己写的作文比较满意吧。儿子读的课外书多，每次作文都得满分，而且还有好几篇被刊登到了报纸上，这对他是很大的鼓励。到现在儿子每天晚上睡觉前都要背一篇国学经典文章。但我深知，文学这条路是任重道远的，我小小的儿子还无法体会到其中的艰辛。

听完讲座回到家，我认真地问儿子："你的理想是什么?""我不是告诉过你吗？地理学家、历史学家、歌唱家和作家。"天哪，一点儿都没变，还是上次的口气。我又问了一句："那要从中选一个呢?""那就历史学家吧!"

"你长大了要买什么车?"我想用专家的问题考考儿子。"嗯，我想买一种非常环保，又非常省电，又不费油的车。车上装有平板电脑、电视、多功能键盘、可视电话、遥控手机还有自动导航系统。"儿子闪烁着透黑的大眼睛，叽里咕噜说了一大堆。"你不想买宝马吗?""宝马算什么？像宝马呀、法拉利呀、奔驰呀，都太污染环境了，又费油。""那你说的车是什么牌子啊?""不知道，以后肯定有。要是没有，我就发明呗!"儿子天真地笑着说。

中国梦，我们的梦，孩子的梦。

原来儿子的理想是这样子的。我长舒了一口气。

载于《莫愁·家教与成才》

当下的这个时代，似乎都习惯把一些物质来作为衡量是否成功的标准。认为只有有了钱，有了豪车，有了好房子，这样才算是成功的。但这都是片面的。真正的成功是什么？是做你理想中的自己，真正的成功是，内心世界高度自由和充实。

知识改变气质

文/林振宇

知识是产生对人类自由的热爱和原则的唯一源泉。

——韦伯斯特

人与人之间性格差异在于气质。每个人都有自己的气质特征，就像树的叶子，没有一片是相同的。

气质并不神秘，就是指一个人的个性特点和风格气度，是个体长期形成的相对稳定的一种心理特征。一个人的气质可以从他的思维方式，言谈举止，行为习惯等几个方面表现出来。

气质虽然没有优劣之分，但有高雅与低俗之别。大凡气质高贵的人，或是见识卓尔不群，或是言谈口吐珠玑或是举止优雅得体，给人一种彬彬有礼、有教养的感觉。而气质低俗的人，即便她有西施的美，或是他有潘安的貌，亦或是高官、大款，倘若胸无点墨，也会俗不可耐，面目可憎。

那么，气质究竟能不能改变呢?

对于一个人来说，气质虽然相对稳定，但是通过后天的学习是可以改变的。高尔基说，“学问改变气质”，这句话是有一定的道理的。

所谓学问，即泛指知识。气质的形成，与知识有着非常密切的关系，知识塑造性格，知识改变气质。如果把一个人比作自然生长的花木，那么，只有经过知识的修剪才能成为一种有形的景致。

书籍是知识的载体，思想和智慧的宝库。一个人长久地浸淫在优秀健康的书籍里，内心就会变得丰盈，心胸也博大了。视野更加开阔，思想会深刻，智慧随之增长，性情也得到陶冶，气质在潜移默化中改变了。宛如深谷幽兰，散发馨香。

有这样一个例子，三国时期的吕蒙，本是行伍出身，没有文化，打仗很勇敢，粗俗但有机智。有一次，孙权开导他，应当多读书，使自己不断进步。打那以后，吕蒙开始勤奋学习。鲁肃掌管吴军，上任途中路过吕蒙驻地，受到他的款待。但鲁肃还以老眼光看人，觉得他有勇无谋。在酒宴上，俩人纵论天下事，吕蒙的真知灼见使鲁肃很受震惊。于是，才有了“士别三日，刮目相看”这句成语。

吕蒙前后气质的变化，说明了知识是变化气质的根本。如果说气质是潜藏内心而又表现于外的一种“相”，那么，“相由心生”，一个人的内心若被知识美化而改变，他的相也在无形中变化了，所呈现出来的气质就会和从前大不一样，或者说，气质变得高雅了。

载于《才智》

一个有学问的人，就像一片宽广的大海，接纳、包容、洞悉万物；一个匮乏的人，就像贫瘠的土地，干涸、粗暴、一无所有。

要的就是“过”

文/张云广

乐观主义者总是想象自己实现了目标的情景。

——西加尼

去一所陌生中学听课，讲课内容是“诗歌鉴赏之虚实结合”。

我并不认识授课教师，正如授课教师并不认识受课学生，又如受课学生并不认识我一样。

执教的是一位男青年，衣衫整齐，一脸严肃，给人一种很正统的感觉，但很快他的表现就轻而易举地颠覆了我的第一判断。为了融洽师生关系，上课伊始，这位老师就引吭高歌了几句何晟铭的《佛说》，颇具磁力的歌声很快就赢得了一阵掌声，气氛一下子轻松了许多。

掌声过后，老师顿了顿，然后进入了他的开场白，“佛说，前世的五百次回眸换来今生的一次擦肩而过；佛又说，前世的五千次回眸换来今生的一泓秋波；佛还说，前世的五万次回眸只为今天的这一节语文课！”

出人意料的第三个分句话音刚落，掌声笑声便同时响彻教室，显然学生们对眼前的这位陌生老师已经产生了极大的好感，这种好感又把刚才由于后面听课者云集所带来的无形压力冲淡了许多。

师生之间的配合就这样驶入了“无间道”，老师讲得顺畅无比，学生听得带劲儿“异常”。不时有学生主动站起来提问或回答问题，每一次老师都让他们自报家门然后再坐下。评语也结合学生的姓名临时确定，如“王佳宁就是佳!”“宋长新的见解实在新!”……低烈度的笑声持续不断。

中间有一个环节是让学生把练习题的答案书写到黑板上，本来只有两个人的答题空间硬是上去了六个人在上面争地盘。你不让我，我不让你，气氛经过一再的积累发酵近乎火爆，就差肢体冲突了。

这次同样要在下讲台前把答题者的名字亮出来，其中有一个叫“白焱”的同学的署名引起了他的注意。待大家都答完题撤回座位后，只见老师含笑步入讲台，用红笔圈起了一个“焱”字，然后就地取材故作严肃地说，“给这六名同学一个总体评价——焱，如果一定要用一句歌词来表达的话，我想应该是——“我的热情就像这三把火，燃烧了整个语文课堂。”随后自顾自地唱着改编自费翔的《冬天里的一把火》，台下高烈度的笑声也紧随而至。

课近结束，老师又哼起了这节课刚开始时的那首《佛说》，然后继续推介他的新版《佛说》，“佛说，握紧拳头，你会一无所有，因为世间万物皆空；佛又说，伸开手掌，你将拥有全世界，因为唯有空才能包容万物；佛最后说，万条真理一句话，虚实结合就是好!”

一个个大拇指竖起来，一次次叫好声经久不断。

老师抱拳致谢，对眼前的学生做了如下的评价：“反应过度，配合过好，热情过火，战力过牛，表现过疯，让人实在印象过于深刻！简称‘六过’。”

持久的掌声中，老师挥手告别，全体同学追出了教室……

这是我平生听到的最给力的一堂课，受教之余不禁想到，国人喜欢奉行中庸之道，凡事求和求稳，力求不偏不颇，不冷不热，不远不近，不悲不喜。这固然是一种做人与处世的智慧，但凡事皆如此势必会让思想趋于保守，行动滑向拘谨。长此以往，难免会忘记其实在不违背大原则的前提下，人生许多精彩风景都要由一个“过”字来实现启动和维持的。让一次次展示自我的好机会空自擦肩而逝，想来这将是多么遗憾的事情呀。

天地不限人，而人自限之。难怪“佛说，过，过，过！”

载于《中国校园文学》

生活不必拘谨，不必一成不变，不必循规蹈矩。适时地放“过”，生活将变得更加精彩。

第六辑

后退不一定失败

当我把实习锻炼当成人生积累，摒弃单纯追求利益得失时，我突然发现我的人生变了，变得开朗了，豁达了，也变得沉稳了，我也在这段时间里学到了职场里的很多东西，也学到了生命中的很多东西。

开卷并非皆有益

文/飞龙在天

尽信书，不如无书。

——孟子

关于开卷是否有益这个问题，常引起人们的争议。有人说有益，认为只要打开书本读书，总会有好处的；有人说无益，认为书有好有坏，读了坏书就没什么好处。

那么，开卷到底有没有益呢？这个问题要辩证来看。

我们知道，“开卷有益”是一成语，来源于《渑水燕谈录》。当时，宋太宗赵光义每天坚持阅读《太平御览》三卷，有时因国事忙耽搁了，他也抽空补上，并常对左右的人说：“只要打开书本总会有好处的。”

后来，“开卷有益”这句话便作为成语，常用以勉励人们勤奋好学，多读书就会得到益处。于是，有的人以为凡书皆可读，既不问书籍的内容，也不加以甄选，信手拈来，认为读了就有好处，事实难道真的是这样吗？

《庄子·列御寇》篇有则故事：一个叫朱泙漫的年轻人什么都想学，为了学会一门特殊的本领，他变卖了家产，带了一千两黄金到一个叫支离益的地方，拜师学杀龙的技术。三年后，他学成回家，兴奋地向人们吹起杀龙的技术，怎样按住龙头，踩住龙尾，怎样从龙颈上开刀。大家听完以后笑着问他："什么地方有龙可杀呢？"朱泙漫这才恍然大悟，原来，世界上根本没有龙这种东西，他的屠龙之技算是白学了。

有些人读书不就像朱泙漫学屠龙一样吗？盲目地学习而不作选择，结果误入歧路，不仅浪费了时间和精力，还学无所用，这便是读书无益的表现。

有时候，读书不仅无益，还会有害。我曾看过一篇报道：有个年轻人因为犯强奸罪而锒铛入狱。此前，警方在抓捕他时，在他家的卧室里翻出大量的淫秽书籍。事后，年轻人向警方如实地交代说，只因为长期看这种淫秽书籍而不能自拔，最终才走上了犯罪的道路，现在他后悔莫及，是坏书害了他。

由此看来，单纯地说开卷有益或无益都是片面的，但可以肯定地说，在一定条件下，开卷并非有益。

臧克家说："读过一本好书，就像交了一个益友。"那么，读过一本坏书，不就像交了一个损友吗？益友会带给我们很多好处，对我们有所帮助；损友恰恰与此相反，可能会把你戕害。

交友要慎重，读书也要慎重。所谓"近朱者赤，近墨者黑。"交友要有眼光才能交到好友，读书要有鉴别才能选到好书。屠格涅夫告诉我们："不要阅读信手拈来的书，而要严格地加以挑选。"好书是营养品，有益身心健康；坏书是毒草，不但无益，还会害人！所以说，开卷并非有益。

载于《阅读》

读书的过程，是去除糟粕留下精华的过程，尽信书则不如无书，理论跟实际有时候是相悖的。

被重视的忽视

文/唐　仔

时间，让深的东西越来越深，让浅的东西越来越浅。

——佚名

在大家看来，他一向是被忽视了的。

而他理应获得足够的重视。他是单位里的业务骨干，很多业务问题，非他莫能解决。他的许多见解，成为业内的标杆。他的论文和成果，是单位里最多的。可是，他却是典型的墙内开花墙外香，外面很红很吃香，在单位里，却不大受待见，没有得到应有的尊重和重视。至少，在大家看来，领导就不怎么重视他。

有例为证。

他既没有得到提拔，也没有得到重用。以他的业务能力，早就该提拔了，即使不能提拔到领导岗位，也至少应放在一个重要的岗位。但是，没有，一直没有。他还是守在他那个听起来蛮重要实则几乎可有可无的部门。

很多时候，领导差不多把他给忘了。很多会议，不记得请他参加，虽然那些会议，大多是让人昏昏欲睡的无聊会议，但是有时候，能参加某些会议，那就是规格，就是待遇。这些，他没有。

各种应酬，也没有他。上头来人，不会请他做陪，因为他既不善喝酒，说话又很无趣，有时候还会很不合时宜地放一些空炮，弄得领导很尴尬；领导常和身边的人聚一聚，乐一乐，关系由此更融洽了，这都没他的份儿。

出外考察、调研、学习，更没他什么事了，说是考察、调研、学习，往往是借机游山玩水。说穿了，就是领导带着一帮心腹，用公款出去走一走，散散心，见见世面，加深感情。他从来就不是哪个领导圈子里的人，有好事的时候，自然谁也不会想到他。

这不是被忽视，是什么？

很多人为他愤愤不平，没想到他自己却并不这么认为。

他说，恰恰相反，他很享受这种不被重视，或者说是被忽视了的状态。

被忽视了，也就不用钻营，不用溜须拍马，也不用看谁的脸色，反而可以一心一意做自己喜欢的事情。

被忽视了，才能跳出圈外，逃离了应酬，才有时间静下心来，钻研业务，有所成就；被忽视了，固然在有的场合，没有了存在感，但在自己的天地里，你反而可以自由驰骋。

他说，其实，如果真想做事情，真想做成事情的话，不被重视，甚至是被忽视，反而是好事。少了羁绊，多了自由；少了束缚，多了空间。换句话说，有时候，被忽视了，恰恰是被重视了。虽然这个重视，有点尴尬，或有点无奈。

每个单位，都会有这样几个人，他从没有坐过主席台，各种先进也与他无关，他总是默默地偏守一隅，他经常被忽视或遗忘……但是，他依然默默地坚守，无怨无悔地付出。没错，他被忽视了，但他乐在其中，并因为执着的坚守而最终总能有所斩获。

对有所追求的人来说，被世俗所忽视，恰可以在自己的世界里，获得莫大的自由及应有的尊重和重视。

载于《做人与处世》

是啊，我们时刻保持内心清醒，学会避开那些所谓的“重视”。能够在世俗中始终保持自己本真的心真的很不容易，人应该时刻清楚自己应该干什么，不该干什么。

做个稻草人

文/张珠容

山气日夕佳，飞鸟相与还。

——陶渊明

贾米·福克斯前不久毕业于英国班戈大学，在大学修的是音乐专业，毕业之后他四处找工作，可几个月过去了却一无所获。一天，福克斯去应聘又失败了，他万分沮丧，干脆坐上一辆计程车到郊外散散心。

计程车经过一片嫩绿的菜地时，福克斯突然喊“停”。这段时间以来他为了找工作一直奔波，此刻，他迫不及待想要徜徉在那片绿色的油菜花田当中，尽情呼吸新鲜的空气。

福克斯在油菜花田待了一个多小时，心情非常愉悦。就在他想离开的时候，突然被一个声音叫住：“年轻人，请等等！”

福克斯回头一看，身后站着一个满面红光的老农夫。他向福克斯自我介绍：“你好，我叫威廉·扬斯，是这片油菜花田的主人。”

福克斯不好意思地说：“你好！刚才我没看见您在花田里，所以冒昧地在此处游玩了很久。”

“哦，年轻人，我叫住你并不是要责备你，而是想请你帮一个忙。不知你是否愿意以后每天帮我看护这片油菜花？当然是有薪酬的。”扬斯解释说，自己去年承包了这片土地，种植各类蔬菜。近来地里种植的油菜花结籽了，很多鹧鸪日复一日地飞来啄食，为此给扬斯造成了巨大损失。刚才，扬斯看见穿着亮橙色外套的福克斯一站到油菜田，偷食的鹧鸪就吓得赶紧飞走了，所以他希望福克斯帮他看护这片油菜花田。

福克斯听了一口答应：“反正我现在也没有工作，我就暂时在这里干吧。只是不知道，我能否在菜地里弹奏我的乐器？”扬斯乐呵呵地说：“当然，在田间，除了帮我赶跑鹧鸪以外，你可以做任何事情！”

就这样，福克斯当起了“稻草人”。他每天都穿着亮橙色的外套在扬斯的菜田里穿梭，鹧鸪看到他那身晃动的亮橙色根本不敢靠近。福克斯闲余的时间很多，他就看书或者弹琴。如果看到有鹧鸪飞来，福克斯就会立即跳起来，用手风琴或牛铃弄出一些噪音，将飞鸟吓跑。对此，扬斯非常满意，他每周都支付给福克斯 300 英镑。

朋友们看到福克斯在田间悠闲地看书弹琴散步，都羡慕地说：“我们的工资比你高不了多少，但是我们要比你忙碌百倍。你真幸运！”

载于《故事林》

什么样的生活才是好的呢，没有定论，只要适合你，就是好的。你找到适合自己的生活方式了吗？

等

文/高宗飘逸

真正的幸运在等待着有资格享受的。

——忒俄克里托斯

人生处处都在等，等待春光明媚，等待鸟语花香，等待风调雨顺，等待人寿年丰，等待佳人有约，等待子成龙女成凤……一切的等都充满希望，充满未知，也充满变数，充满斑斓的色彩。

漫漫长夜，一只猫守在洞口，目不转睛，心无旁骛，静等老鼠出来觅食；丛林中，猎豹蹲伏于猎物附近，凝神屏息，寻找突破，只要发现猎物稍许懈怠，便会迅速出击；老虎、狮子等兽中王者捕食之时，无不是安静等待，等待时机成熟，最后捕获一份丰盛的美餐。它们的等是一种本能，需要足够的耐心。

生活在热带森林中的印度土著人，以捕蟒为生，有经验的捕猎者发现猎物后并不急于下手，而是跟在蟒蛇附近慢慢等，有时要等上几天几夜，他们要等蟒蛇完成一次捕食后再出手。因为这个时候，蟒蛇正处于心满意足的松弛状态，完全没有了捕食之前的警惕和好斗之心，这样，土著人仅凭两人之力就可以把蟒蛇轻松搞定。这种等是一种策略，需要足够的智慧。

想当年，司马相如以一曲《凤求凰》赢得了卓文君的芳心，在司马相如家徒四壁的境况下，卓文君毅然返回老家临邛与司马相如一起当垆卖酒，患难与共。后来司马相如被举荐做官，久居京城，卓文君独守寂寞，日复一日在家等待并思念着夫婿。忽闻司马相如“将聘茂陵人女为妾”，卓文君写了一首《白头吟》：“……闻君有二意，故来相决绝。愿得一人心，终老不相负。……”相如看后，“乃止”。卓文君继续忍受着寂寞，在家痴痴等待。不想司马相如花心复起，派人送来的一封信函再次打破了卓文君孤独而艰难的等待，信中只有十三字：“一二三四五六七八九十百千万。”卓文君看出丈夫的无意（无亿），提笔写了一首《怨郎诗》：“一别之后，二地相悬。只说是三四月，又谁知五六年。七弦琴无心弹，八行书无可传，九连环从中拆断，十里长亭望眼欲穿。百思想，千系念，万般无奈把郎怨。万语千言道不完，百无聊赖十凭栏。重九登高看孤雁，八月仲秋月圆人不圆。七月半烧香秉烛问苍天，六月伏天人人摇扇我心寒。五月石榴如火，偏遇阵阵冷雨浇花端。四月枇杷未黄，我欲对镜心意乱。忽匆匆，三月桃花随水转，飘零零，二月风筝线儿断。噫，郎呀郎，巴不得下一世，你为女来我做男。”司马相如读完这首回文诗，既感慨妻子的痴情与哀怨，又赞叹妻子的才华，这分明在向夫君暗示她一直等着自己“回心转意”，司马相如不禁羞愧万分，彻底打消了休妻纳妾的念头，他们千回百转的爱情故事从此被后人传为佳话。这里卓文君对司马相如的等，无疑是一种承担与考验，需要宽广的心胸，过人的定力和颇深的才情。

始于明代晚期的拔步床（又名八步床），分内外两层，外面回廊，内部床榻，整张床全部为榫卯结构，做工考究，纯手工打造，镂空祥云鸟兽及各种图案，雕刻精美，镏金描彩，古朴典雅，雍容华贵。有的经二三百年历史变迁，依旧完好如初，牢固如新。就是这样一张床，据说要选上等木料，采伐回家，放置四年，待水汽自然蒸发后，把木料锯开，再放四年，任其自然变形，然后请能工巧匠花上万千工时慢慢斧凿打磨。所谓“千工拔步床”或者“万工拔步床”。在制床工艺里的这种等是一种文化，需要丰富的经验与精湛的技能。

牛郎织女分隔银河两岸，一年三百六十五日，年年在等，只为等待七夕鹊桥相会，这一等，等来了千古佳句，等来了人们对完美爱情的祝愿和打破清规戒律的期盼，等来了尘世间人们的缕缕情思。白素贞和许仙的等待更是磨难重重，白蛇的千年修行只为等这一世轮回，然而法海的介入，使得水漫金山，以致白娘子被镇压于雷锋塔下。

“千年等一回”，等出了一种悲戚的浪漫，等出了人们对忠贞爱情的向往，等出了众生平等的爱的理念。后来人们不忍他们的故事如此凄惨，便把结尾改为小青数十载深山练功，终把法海逼进螃蟹腹中，救出白娘子，合家团圆，从而实现完美结局。这里的等成为一种信仰，需要自由博爱的精神。

孙悟空大闹天宫，被如来佛祖压于五行山下，整整五百年的等待，风吹雨淋，霜掩雪埋，终于等得唐僧来，为其摘下符帖，一路降妖除魔，历经九九八十一难，塑得金身，终成正果。这种等是一种机缘，需要些许佛心。

智慧超人的诸葛亮，因错用马谡痛失街亭，司马懿率领大军乘势大举进攻西城。当时孔明身边既无大将，又少士兵，只见他传令“偃旗息鼓”，洞开城门，派二十名士卒扮成百姓洒水扫街。而孔明身披鹤氅，头扎纶巾，领两个小书童，怀抱一琴，到城楼凭栏而坐，燃起香，慢慢弹起琴来。诸葛亮笑容可掬，镇定自若，一串串音符从他指间悠然飘出。凭他对司马懿的了解，等不了几曲弹完，司马懿必退兵。果然，乐曲未了，司马懿怀疑设有埋伏，引兵退去。孔明这种运筹帷幄的等是一种大气魄，大境界，它需要勇气，需要胆识，需要在等待中守候一颗宁静淡然且胸怀韬略的心。

等是生命的必然过程，许多事我们不得不等。投一篇小稿，烹一份美食，闲坐河边垂钓，赶赴公司求职，静候日出蒸蒸，期待春雨浓浓，掰着手指细数伊人归期……没有一件事情不需要等，任谁也逃脱不开。

但是等绝不意味着消极无为，等闲视之，我们需要在等中储备力量，在等中感悟哲理，在等中调整自己的坐标方向。只有这样，我们才能在等待中不断丰富自己的内心情感，感知自己的生活状态，让自己变得更加淡定自若。

其实等是一种人生态度，经不起等待的人生就像是等不及成熟的果实喷洒了催熟剂，虽外表光鲜，却生涩难咽。

载于《思维与智慧》

等待是生活的智慧。该到来的自然会来，机遇、成功、爱人，这些都需要你去等。等的过程，是蛰伏的过程，是积蓄能量的过程。有些东西是肯定会来的，你只需要等。

后退不一定失败

文/荒　沙

对于每一个人，他所能选择的奋斗方向是宽广的。

——爱因斯坦

大学毕业后，我应聘到了一家大公司，需要经过三个月的考察期才能转为正式员工。其实我还是蛮有自信的，我相信通过我的实力可以得到这个岗位。可我不得不面对一个残酷的现实，我所在的部门只缺一个编制员额，我必须和一同进入公司的李明竞争这一个岗位。

令我没想到的是，李明的素质和能力非常高，可想而知我们之间的竞争是多么激烈。那段时间里，几乎是我成一件事，李明也会成一件事，我获得公司的表扬，李明也会获得公司的表扬……可有时竞争并不是良性的，比如，有时我加班到深夜，李明为了让领导看见，他也加班；有时我病了，根本无法上班，可李明会趁这个时候再干成一件事……就这样，我们之间越来越不信任，虽然表面上没有过结，但心里却都在较着劲。

终于有一天，我们之间的矛盾瞬间爆发，发生激烈的争吵，从此，我们再无交流和沟通。那一天，经理和主管突然找我谈话，说为了更好地锻炼我，公司准备调我去分公司那边，我一听，脑袋嗡地一下。我知道和李明的争吵造成了很坏的影响，我有责任，但其实我挺委屈的，这件事包括同事们都说责任在李明那一方。现在把我调到了分公司去实习，明显是在惩罚我。可我能怎么样呢？经理和主管一起找我谈话，说明这是公司已经决定的事情了，不服从只有走人……

那一天，我一个人孤独地坐在广场上，回忆我来到公司这两个月来的点点滴滴，我哭了，突然感觉自己很累，每天都在一种高强度竞争和压力中度过的，没有一天快乐的日子。我也突然感到，在这种恶性的竞争中，我的人生不会有很好的作为，也不会提高和进步，我决定离开这里。那一夜，我无眠，打电话给我敬重的高中老师，诉说我心中的苦闷，老师的一个提问让我彻底开朗，我决定服从安排，到分公司再去锻炼一个月，然后另谋出路。

在分公司的这段时间里，我注重总结教训，虽然这里和公司总部没法比，无论是人员，还是工作都非常简单，但我还是谦虚地和同事们学职场交际，学管理，学技术，我快乐地全身心地投入到工作中，为我的未来积攒财富。当我把实习锻炼当成人生积累，摒弃单纯追求利益得失时，我突然发现我的人生变了，变得开朗了，豁达了，也变得沉稳了，我也在这段时间里学到了职场里的很多东西，也学到了生命中的很多东西。

转眼间，实习期结束了，我和同事们快乐地告别，奔向了另一家公司。这家公司虽然没有实习的公司好，但我很快地适应了这里，打开了局面，半年后我便当上了主管。一天，我到南方参加一个企业管理培训，正好遇上了将我下调到分公司实习的主管。他说起把我下调到分公司的事，一脸的遗憾，说那时没有掌握实情，可他还是不解地问我，当初为啥服从分配。我把老师开导我的问题转述给了主管，对主管说：“两个人拔河，是后退者胜还是前进者胜。”主管一愣，随后笑了，对我说：“当然是后退者胜。”我笑着对主管说：“当初我就是想到了后退者胜，才会后退一步到分公司锻炼的。”主管听后笑了。

那天，我和主管聊了很长时间，得知李明还在公司当员工，他好像也没有了刚来时的激情……可我却对我的工作前景充满期待，我一直在庆幸我的人生后退了一步，正是这后退的一步退出了我人生的成功。

载于《时代青年》

后退不是为了妥协，只是为了积蓄力量，寻找机会。愿我们能学会做一个敢于后退敢于转弯的人。

做一株柔韧的小草

文/高小宝

生活就像海洋，只有意志坚强的人，才能到达彼岸。

——卡尔·马克思

曾经挪开过一块已搁置了有些年月的大石头，发现石头底下竟压着一丛枝干弯曲颜色嫩黄的野草，看不出有多少株，只是互相之间纠缠着，攀附着。当即暗自惊心，想，这么重的一块石头，竟然没有将这丛娇嫩的草挤碎压扁，她匍匐在地上，终年不见天日，枯荣自知，不轻易屈从上天的不公，自顾自地顽强生长，悲喜着自己的悲喜，真是令人又怜又敬！如果没有这块石头的压覆，她也该是郁郁葱葱，有花开，有果收，朝迎晨露，暮送夕阳，顺着自己的生长轨迹，生命轮回里，尽情绽放着精彩和美丽，该是何等的快意一生。

石头挪开没几日，接受了阳光的沐浴和雨露的滋润，那丛野草颜色渐绿，竟也改变了她原来趴着的生长姿态，她的枝干一天天立起来，翘首向上，在风中摇曳，欣欣然，似有一股充满喜悦厚积薄发的势头。压覆时不自弃，顺境时顺势生，生命是何等的顽强和辉煌。我思忖，换作是人，在经受长期的磨难和不堪重压后，也不会这么快就恢复这样的心态，振作力量吧！

也见过这样一株草。是在陕北和内蒙古的交界处，当地土壤严重沙化，寸草不生，偏偏就在一处土沙丘后遇见孤零零一株草。是一种叫不上名字的野草，细窄的叶子如五指乍开紧贴着绵软的土沙，她的根系很浅但很庞大，枝干摸上去硬硬的，有一种生命的质感。对于她的生长和存活，我亦是心惊。这里的白天，热浪滚滚，烈日如炙，夜晚风沙肆虐，温差高低起伏，她抵抗过了恶劣自然气候的侵蚀，又是如何躲过了野兽的践踏和啃噬，我回答不出来，只是久久凝视着她，敬重之情油然而生。

没有花的浓郁芬芳和艳丽色彩，没有树的高大挺拔和壮伟丰姿，有韧性，不屈服，不抱怨，不叫屈，该是小草天生的品质和基因条件吧！

当遭遇生活的苦难、艰辛、坎坷、酸涩以及种种不公时，不妨学一学隐忍而卑微的小草吧。身处荒凉但心不荒芜，没有低迷荒芜、自暴自弃，而是选择默默继续，无声面对，自开自的花，尽管那花开的清雅需有人用心品味才能体会到；自结自的果，尽管那果结的个小如沙粒，也是对生命的一种完成和交付，但只要生长和存在，就是对自然法则不折不扣的躬行。

外表柔弱如小草，内心丰盈充实、喜悦坦然亦如小草。拥有了这些，再卑微的生命也能焕发出动人的光彩。

载于《语文报》

学会做一株小草，以最谦卑的姿态，无论生活有多艰难，依然顽强向上生长。

顾玉麟和张居正的育人观

文/顺　江

要记住，你不仅是教课的教师，也是学生的教育者，生活的导师和道德的引路人。

——苏霍姆林斯基

挫折教育，无论对家长育儿或是领导育才，都可以说是必需的措施。但如何掌握适度，却是一门高深的学问。运用得好，对人才是一种锤炼；运用不好，就容易使人才变成废材。

张居正从小聪慧过人，12 岁就参加荆州府的应试，并以立地交卷、文采横溢的文章，博得考官一致好评，被传为当地的神童。13 岁时，张居正赴武昌参加乡试，湖北按察院陈束读了他的试卷，拍案叫绝，当场决定录为举人。而当时正在武昌巡游的顾玉麟却要求将此事搁置了下来。顾玉麟并不是觉得张居正有问题，而恰恰相反，他认为张居正是个将相之才，如果过早让他发达，就容易使他自满，从而丧失了上进心，让他落第受点挫折，可以激励他发奋图强，而且他相信只要张居正真的是块材料，他就不会一蹶不振。

就这样，张居正落第了，他周身傲气受到沉重打击，垂头丧气地回家闷了好几天。沮丧的情绪过后，他果然更加发奋，埋头攻读。三年后又以更加优异的成绩夺得了头魁。被录用后，他逐渐成为明代重臣和杰出的政治家。

由此看来，顾玉麟的决策是正确的。虽然那个年代中国还没有教育心理学这一名词，但是不能不说顾玉麟在培养人才上的确有远见卓识。

相比之下，作为挫折教育成功受益者的张居正，在育人方面就没有那么成功，后来他作为太傅，对万历皇帝的培养甚至可以说是再烂不过的惨败。

万历皇帝九岁登基，从师于满腹经纶、德高望重的张居正。可是这位张太傅忘记了皇帝只是个孩子，他对万历皇帝施行的是摧残心智的挫折教育。

有一次，十多岁的万历童心大发，光着脚丫爬上了后花园的假山，弄得衣服又脏又湿。这事立即被张居正禀报给了太后，结果被罚跪半天，而且向其作书面检讨；万历从小写得一手好书法，这本是对他进行鼓励、树立他自信心的最好时机，但是张居正却以“不务正业，恐重蹈宋徽宗的覆辙”为理由大加训斥。

就这样，张居正满腔热忱、呕心沥血，利用自己的“大智慧”，却培养出了一个昏庸得不能再昏庸的万历皇帝。张居正死后，万历皇帝开始身居大内终日玩耍，不理朝政，成为史上绝无仅有的二十年不上朝的皇帝。

载于《学生家长社会》

十年树木，百年树人。教育是人之根本，容不得半点偏差，方式方法上的不得当，犹如小树缺乏肥料一样，注定是没什么前途的！

“腊肠”胜过“刀枪”

文/张艳君

没有任何东西比人类的爱更富有智慧、更复杂。它是花丛中最娇嫩的而又最质朴、最美丽和最平凡的花朵，这个花丛的名字叫道德。

——苏霍姆林斯基

文人遇事总爱把道理讲一个透彻，可许多时候，却是“秀才遇见兵，有理说不清”，一些尚武的军人，动不动就以武力相向。19 世纪德国科学家维碴就遇到了这样的事。

一天，正在潜心进行细菌研究的维碴突然接到了一份决斗邀请，这让他大吃一惊，因为维碴长年累月埋首于实验室中，从没接触过任何武器，连武器都不会拿，如何去决斗！发出邀请的是杰出的决斗家、“铁血宰相”俾斯麦，不仅决斗经验丰富，而且从来都是以决斗解决事情，因为对于他来说，每次决斗都是胜券在握。维碴十分后悔，不该为了一份道理惹恼俾斯麦。但世上没有后悔药可吃，按当时的习俗，决斗邀请不能不接受。

约定的时间到了，这天，俾斯麦掂量对手后，显得更加从容与大方，他让维碴优先选择决斗武器。接下来，倒是俾斯麦吃惊了！因为维碴既不挑选刀剑，也不选择手枪，而是拿出他事先准备好的两根腊肠，这时维磋对俾斯麦解释说："因为我是一个科学家，对其他的武器一窍不通，所以选择腊肠作为决斗武器。这腊肠一根十分可口，一根却灌满了致命的细菌。"他看了俾斯麦一眼说："来吧，亲爱的朋友，你选择你的'武器'，我们一起吃吧！"

在决斗场上从来都是信心满满的俾斯麦这一下如同被刺穿了的气袋，顿时瘪了下去，只见俾斯麦涨红着脸，愕然半晌，然后转身离去。第一次让人们认识了"铁血宰相"还有"不敢""不铁血"的一面，也让世上出现了腊肠胜过刀枪的奇迹。

《道德经》第七十三章云："勇于敢则杀，勇于不敢则活。"意思是：一个人遇事不顾客观条件，只知一味坚强，则充满凶险；知己知彼，不强便弱，则往往能化险为夷。

两兵相遇，勇者胜，勇于敢是必需的，人们不看好的只是匹夫的逞一时之勇；不敢是必要的柔弱，并非胆小怯懦。由此看来，敢与不敢都是基于深谋远虑、审时度势的智慧。因此，不能说"腊肠"战胜了"刀枪"，应该是智慧战胜了死亡，凡是失去智慧的"敢"与"不敢"皆会是耻辱与死亡。

维磋的以腊肠为"武器"，俾斯麦果敢地退出决斗，皆是一种智慧，正是凭着这种智慧的敢与不敢，使得他们"双赢"，写下了一曲智慧的胜利之歌。

载于《哲思》

一个智慧的人，胜过一支军队。诸葛亮运筹帷幄，决胜千里之外。每一个智慧的人，都是可以洞悉万物的人。

舍我不舍“手枪”

文/梅若雪

技能强于力量。

——托·富勒

舍我即成舍我，我国近现代著名报人。

他有一句在报界广为流传的名言：“一张报纸犹如一把手枪，如果社长或总编辑自己不看大样，就好比把自己的手枪交与他人，万一他乱枪扫射，责任都是自己的。”

“按龙泉血泪洒征袍”，许多名言背后都会有一则流泪的逸事，甚或是一则染血的故事。如著名之语“人但知强盗可怕，不知无法无天的官吏比强盗更可怕”，就是被誉为“铁肩辣手，快笔如刀”“飘萍一支笔，抵过千万军”的《京报》社长邵飘萍所言，他却被奉系军阀残忍杀害。

又如撰写盛传一时的对联“今日幸西苑，明日幸颐和，何日再幸圆明园，四百兆骨髓全枯，只剩一人何有幸；五十失琉球，六十失台海，七十又失东三省，五万里版图弥蹙，每逢万寿必无疆”的《社会日报》主编林白水，在邵飘萍被害不到百日，于1926年8月6日，又遭军阀张宗昌屠戮。

京城两位报界名流的相继喋血，让一些报人战战兢兢，如临深渊，如履薄冰。一次，《世界晚报》一篇报道字号“效坤”的张宗昌的文章，因按当时的习惯，文章中称张宗昌应为“效帅”，然而当大样出来时，社长成舍我看了一遍，排版人员将“效”字排成了“妓”字，竟然成了“妓帅”，这可要犯张宗昌的大忌，由于成舍我的一次细心，避免了一次不测之祸。

接下来的一次排版错误，让成舍我没有这么幸运。当时，北平城是直系军阀曹锟的天下，而奉系军阀张作霖一直虎视眈眈，终于在1934年酿成“直奉大战”。战况紧急，曹锟任命吴佩孚为统帅，防堵奉军入关。张作霖气势汹汹，当时北平城人心惶惶。

吴佩孚清末秀才出身，也许是《推背图》等书读得太多，他迷信地认为一个拥有好名字的人就可逆转战事，能够“逢凶化吉”。于是他突然想到手下一位名叫“张福来”的大将，让他喜不自胜：有了“福来”，一定能打胜仗了。于是，吴佩孚特地将张福来从河南开封调去，任命他为“前敌总指挥”。

成舍我得到这条独家消息后，就以“前敌总指挥张福来今早出发”为通栏标题发当天的头版头条。按惯例，报纸在下午两点钟以前就必须印刷出来。不巧那天他中午有事，不得不破例没看大样，成舍我再三叮嘱同仁，千万不可有错字。

办完事后，成舍我匆匆忙忙往报馆赶，途中报童已在叫卖《世界晚报》了。不太放心的成舍我似乎有预感地买了一张自家的报纸，一看，让他不禁惊魂。原来头版头条的通栏标题竟然把张福来的“福”错成了“祸”，张祸来，一字之差，天地玄黄，宇宙洪荒。此时已经是下午三点，还能做什么？三十六计，走为上计，成舍我打了一个电话，让报务主编把重要的物什收拾一下，赶紧关门，他则跑到了东交民巷的“六国饭店”避难去了。

晚上七点，报馆被封。

然而，军阀混战，此消彼长，竟然让成舍我因“祸”得福。就在《世界晚报》被查封的第三天，冯玉祥临阵倒戈，堡垒就这样从内部攻破了。曹锟遭软禁，吴佩孚仓惶逃到洛阳。那天的《世界晚报》成了直系的“祸殃”，却给奉系张作霖带来“福音”。三天后，《世界晚报》重新开业，据说张作霖暗中给了成舍我一大笔资助。复刊的当天，《世界晚报》销量大增，此后，好长时间都稳居京城报纸第一名。

其实，此举并没有让成舍我有多少欣喜，而更是让他坚信“不可放弃自己的手枪”。因为他明白，这种侥幸是极其靠不住的，它能够让你“因祸得福”，但一旦祸事上身，轻则让你永世不得翻身，重则丢掉身家性命。

“不可放弃自己的手枪”，告诉人们，只有兢兢业业做最过细的工作，才是一个人的安身立命之本。

载于《才智》

“手枪”即是技能，是立身之本。每个人都应把自己的事情做好，切不可好高骛远，不可贪图不属于自己的东西。

生活真是门艺术。我们从中学习到很多有利于自己和家庭的策略。适时地变通和妥协，有利于跟别人达成和谐。不论是爱人，还是朋友。

悬在空中的疤痕

文/麦 父

与人不求备，检身若不及。

——《尚书·伊训》

早晨走到阳台，惊讶地发现，阳台上的一块钢化玻璃竟然碎裂了，像一大朵裂开的花瓣一样。

幸亏是夹层的，碎裂的玻璃才没有“哗啦啦”坠落一地。细瞅，在玻璃的右下角，找到了一个着力点，原来是被人用石块砸的。竟然是被人为砸碎的！一股怒火，腾空而起。

谁会砸我们家阳台玻璃？自忖搬到这个小区住了六七年，从没和任何人红过脸，更没与谁结下过冤仇，那么，这个人为什么要砸我家的阳台玻璃？立即向小区物业报案。工作人员来查看之后，确认是人为砸的，但是，是谁砸的，为什么砸，却一直没查出来。我家住二楼，虽然楼层不高，不过，要用石块砸碎这种强度很大的钢化玻璃，还是需要不小的力量的，孩子基本可以排除，最大的可能，是成人砸的。

突然，“汪，汪汪”，花花莫名地狂吠起来。花花是我养的一条狗。恍然明白，也许是花花在阳台上狂吠，从楼下散步或路过的人，听了心烦，顺手从地上拣了一个石块，砸了过来，将玻璃砸碎了。

阳台上一排整齐的蓝玻璃，唯这块碎玻璃特别显眼。从楼下稍稍抬头往上看，一眼就能看到它，像个疤痕一样。我们这是幢高层，物管比较严格，当初各家在装修时，楼房的外立面，丝毫不准改变，所以，楼房的外墙，一直很整齐、美观。现在，因了这块碎玻璃，而有了伤痕，很不协调。

找来维修工，师傅看了看，摇摇头说，这种颜色、款式的钢化玻璃，已经没有了，而且，这种弧形的钢化玻璃，很难配，需要从外地调货，很费周折。不过，师傅安慰说，因为是夹层钢化玻璃，因此虽然一面碎裂了，但一时半会儿，是不会坠落的。也就是说，暂时不更换也可以，只是难看一点。

那块碎裂的钢化玻璃，就一直悬在那儿。

它就像一道疤痕一样，每次看到它，我的心都会隐隐地作痛，又气愤，又无奈。有时家中来了客人，看到那块碎玻璃，还得一遍遍跟客人解释，它可能是因为什么被人砸碎的，为什么又一直没有更换云云。不胜其烦。不过，每次花花无故吠叫时，我就会立即制止。倒不是怕别人再砸了玻璃，而是意识到它的吠声惊扰了别人。这是那块碎玻璃，无声地提醒着我。

慢慢地，我适应了阳台上那块碎玻璃，有时候，我甚至觉得穿过那块碎玻璃的裂纹看出去，有一种别样的美。

我差不多已经忘记了阳台上那块被人砸碎的玻璃了。

“咚，咚咚”，有人敲门。

打开门，是个陌生的面孔，但似乎又在哪儿见过。

他自我介绍，他也住这个小区，某幢某号。难怪有些面熟，原来是一个小区的。

问他何事？他瞄了一眼阳台，说，你家阳台那块玻璃是我砸的。

我一时错愕，没缓过神儿来。他又重复了一句，你家阳台那块玻璃，是我砸碎的。

终于明白过来了，但我又有点糊涂，这事都过去好久了，连我都差不多已经忘记这碴儿了，他怎么会突然自己找上门来“认罪”？

他自顾自地说，那天晚上我散步，从你家楼下经过时，你家的狗在阳台上狂叫不止，我听着心烦意乱，就从地上捡了一块石子，随手砸了过去。我只是想吓唬吓唬它，让它别叫了。只听到“啪嗒”一声。狗好像受了惊吓，还真的就不叫了。第二天散步时，我才发现你家阳台上的一块玻璃碎了，从楼下看上去，那块碎玻璃的裂纹特别刺眼。我也想过，来向你们解释一下，道个歉，赔偿你们，但又想想，反正当时也没人看到，我为什么要自投罗网，自找麻烦呢。

他咽了口唾液，继续说，我以为你们会很快将碎玻璃更换掉的，没想到，一天过去了，又一天过去了，那块碎玻璃一直没换。每天早晚，我都会在小区散散步，每次路过你家楼下，我都忍不住抬头看看，那块碎玻璃有没有换掉。没有，一直没有。我都不敢抬头了，我都不敢从你家楼下经过了。他重重地叹了口气，你不知道，那块碎玻璃，就像一个伤疤一样，一直悬在那儿，刺伤我，折磨我。我内心一直没有平静过，安宁过。

我今天来，就是想向你们道个歉，我愿意做出赔偿，同时，请你尽快将那块碎玻璃换掉。说完，他丢下几张百元钞票，转身走了。

等我回过神来，追出去，他已经走远了。

这是我完全没有想到的结局。那块被砸碎的玻璃，甚至已经激不起我丝毫的怨气和愤怒，我差不多已经将它彻底淡忘了，有个人，却一直为此不安。

我拨通了维修师傅的电话，请他想办法，无论如何将那块碎玻璃立即更换掉，让疤痕消失。

载于《疯狂作文》

如果每一个人都有这样犯错以后勇于改正的自觉，那我们的社会将会和谐很多。很多时候，这是修养支撑的。

人生如蝉

文/陈凤珍

人类的一切智慧是包含在这四个字里面的：“等待”和“希望”。

——大仲马

2013年5月，在美国东海岸出现了一种罕见的景象：数以亿万计的蝉的幼虫，似乎听从了号令一般从地下破土而出，迅速地攀附上垂直的物体，蜕去外皮，长出翅膀。整个森林一下子沸腾了，这里成了蝉的天下，这些扇动翅膀的精灵铺天盖地，每英亩地面蝉的数量达150万只，壮观的场面令人咂舌。

这不是普通的蝉，每隔十七年它就会再次来到地面，由于呈周期性出现，所以也叫“周期蝉”。其繁殖的速度极快，会在一个晚上的时间一下子就孵化出亿万子孙后代，它们凭借着数量上的优势保证着自身种群的生存。“周期蝉”在打凿通道时松软了泥土，使泥土通风。在鼹鼠、老鼠、蛇和燕雀等许多动物的眼里，它们是营养丰富的食物。

在回到地面的时间里，雄蝉为了找到自己的伴侣会发出十分响亮的鸣声，这些声音高达94分贝，大到你听不到头顶上飞机的声音，大到能令你抓狂，甚至连一场摇滚演唱会也不是它的对手。

它们在地下经历了漫长的十七年的等待，终于迎来了光明，迎来了繁衍子孙后代的机会。然而这样的场面却不会持续太久，几周后，一切都会归于沉寂。雄蝉交配后立即死亡，雌蝉也会在产卵后结束它们既漫长又短暂的生命。

那是一个何等悲壮的场面！地上铺上了厚厚的一层蝉的尸体。产下的幼虫则会继续潜进地底下，接下来又是一个十七年的轮回，又是一次漫长的等待。

从科学的角度来说，它们所做的一切皆源于本能，是一种无意识行为。可它们这种为爱蛰伏的耐心和毅力却让你不得不佩服。十七年！一个呱呱坠地的新生儿，也已成长为翩翩少年。它们在地下蛰伏十七年，在无边黑暗中等待的仅仅是几天的光明。光明的来临，也意味着死亡的迫近。

在这个人心浮躁的社会中，总是有人在慨叹：生活在身边，理想在天边。可又有多少人能为了实现自己的目标而进行十七年的等待和努力呢？理想的实现就犹如“周期蝉”的人生，是一个在黑暗中寂寞等待的过程，也是一个砺心的过程。它需要你付出时间、付出汗水，静等花开。即使刹那芳华，也终无怨无悔。

载于《语文报》

等待和蛰伏真的是人具备的非常优秀的品质，不急不躁、不温不火、暗自努力，静待那些重要时刻的到来。

倒木是森林的另一种姿势

文/凌　云

落红不是无情物，化作春泥更护花。

——龚自珍

去往长白山地下森林的游步道两旁，在参天的丛林之中，横七竖八地散布着一棵棵倒下的大树。这些曾经挺拔高大的树木，此刻安静地将它们的身躯横卧在大地之上，全身长满绿苔，有的已经枯烂，露出黄褐色的木心。

这是一个寂寞的世界，听不到鸟鸣，鸟儿栖落在高高的树枝上；见不到阳光，森林太茂密了，那些依然屹立的大树，尽可能地伸展枝桠，将所有能采集到的阳光都收入囊中；这里甚至听不到一丝风声，丛林里的风，都是从一个树尖，跃到另一个树尖，从一片叶子，跳到另一片叶子，发出迷幻般的哨音。

它们叫倒木——倒下的树木。

这些大树，大都是大风刮过森林时倒下的，还有的是垂垂老矣的大树，已经活了几百年，甚至更久的时间。巨大的树干差不多被时间掏空了。大风起时，它们摇摇晃晃地一头栽倒，停止了呼吸。

它身边的大树，差不多都是它的子孙和后辈，它们想搀扶住它，可是它的躯干太沉了，而且也许它自己也觉得活得够久了。它已经以一种姿势站了几百年，累了。事实上也可以理解为它是顺势倒下的。

也有正值壮年、生命旺盛的大树，骤然被大风连根拔起的。它们本是森林中的王者，树干比别的大树更加粗壮，树冠比别的大树更加繁茂，它们的根，也一定比别的大树扎得更深更密更牢固。但是，大风起兮，它们却轰然倒塌。

巨大的响声，令整个森林颤抖。在众多的倒木中，那些倔强地以倾斜的姿势不肯完全倒下的，就是这样的大树。它们像四五十岁的壮汉一样，还有很多未竟的人生，怎么甘心就此倒下呢。

不管它们当初是怎么倒下的，当我们遇到它们时，它们就已经倒下了，死了，枯烂了。我们没有见过它们挺拔站立的姿势，仿佛它们生来就是这样倒卧似的。从它们身边走过时，我听到了很多议论，大多是惋惜、唏嘘：这么粗壮的大树，怎么就倒了呢?

还有人不解地问："这么粗大的树木，为什么任凭它在森林中枯烂，而不将它们运出去，制成木材，让它继续发挥作用?"有人甚至当场计算，这样一棵倒木，如果开成木板的话，可以打出多少个柜子、多少只箱子、多少张桌子、多少把椅子……可都是绝对的实木哦。

景区的工作人员却告诉我们，千万别小看了这些倒木，它们是森林的温床。可以说，没有了它们，就没有茂盛的原始森林。

森林中超过八成的树木幼苗，是从倒木上繁育起来的，故有倒木是森林的温床之说；倒木又是微生物的栖息地，小树苗成长过程中，所需的大量的营养成分，如倒木自身所含的C、N、P等微量元素，就是靠这些微生物分解提供的。因而倒木，又是森林的奶娘，无私地把一棵棵小树苗拉扯大。

没错，看起来有点煞风景的倒木，事实上恰是森林不可分割的重要部分。一棵大树倒下了，成了倒木，它的叶子脱落了，枝杆枯萎了，躯干腐烂了，但它并没有死亡，也没有荒废。它只是换了一种姿势，像一位母亲一样敞开了怀抱，是一棵树之于森林的另一种姿态。

对于一棵倒木来说，重新站起来，或许并不是它的愿望，让更多的小树发芽、生长，站成森林，这才是它最大的梦想吧。而被打造成一只实用的实木家具，这恐怕是所有的倒木最不愿意做的事情。因此，一棵倒木一定是极不情愿走出森林的。

在森林之中，总有一些树木，会因为这样那样的原因倒下。不过，纵然倒下了、枯萎了、腐烂了，它们也还是丛林的一部分。如果你肯放下成见，蹲下身，从另一个角度去看它，你就会发现，它只是在丛林中换了一个姿势，它依然是挺拔的，高大的，令人尊敬并值得仰视的。

倒木，是大树的另一个境界。这与那些多舛而又不羁的人生是多么相似啊。

载于《做人与处世》

想起一句诗：落红不是无情物，化作春泥更护花。那些看似垂败的生命，却用另一种方式让其他生命能够更加茁壮地成长。

因为无知，所以有力

文/刘诚龙

冒险是历史富有生命力的元素，无论是对个人还是社会。

——威谦·博利多

小时候我们读过一首诗，是唐代诗人卢纶写的：林暗草惊风，将军夜引弓，平明寻白羽，没在石棱中。这诗写的是汉代名将李广的事迹，李广是史上大将，纵使放到两千年前去排名，也是武将英雄榜里名次很靠前的。

那时，他任职右北平郡太守，这地方常有老虎出没，为除虎患，他常常上山打老虎。"李广出猎，见草中石"，夜风劲吹，乱草摆拂，李广以为草丛里藏着一只猛虎，一箭射去，"中石没镞"。次日一早起来看，其箭所中者，并非老虎，而是一块坚硬如铁的石头，何止入木三分？入石三寸而不止。

李广的猛力出人意料，也出己意料。李广问自己："我有那么大的力量吗？"他再次站在原地，重放箭镞，箭却触石而落，"因复更射之，终不能复入石矣。"李广很费解："我不晓得这是石头的时候，我为何有那么大的力量？现在知道那是石头了，为何又乏力了呢？"

佛门有位罗什大师，在他七岁那年，在自家院子里玩。院子里摆着一件大铁钵。他好玩，双手抓起铁钵，一举举过头顶。站在旁边的人十分骇异，连连惊呼："这铁钵有两三百斤重呢!"一个毛孩子，哪来那大力气？小罗什也惊住了："这铁钵有这么重？那再看我的，我再举它几次。"罗什重复他刚才抓举的动作，却再也举不动了。

李广将军不知道草中物是石头而以为是老虎，力穿石头，那是因为感觉是遇上老虎，生死一瞬，产生强烈爆发力吧？因为知道那是石头了，没甚危险了，身骨有劲，也攒不到一处来了；罗什大师不知道那铁钵轻与重，气力盖世，那是因为初生牛犊，无所畏惧，心力不曾分散；因为知道那铁钵已有千钧，再去举时，心已胆怯，失去了自信，自然也就举不起来了。佛教解释罗什大师的这种现象，属于"事事挂碍"——有了心事，就碍着干事业了。

誉为线性规划之父的丹齐格，是美国科学院、美国工程院、美国人文与科学院三院院士。1939 年，他在加州大学伯克利分校读书，平时他爱睡懒觉，那天他又睡过了头，匆匆忙忙赶到教室里去才发现教授走了，同学走了，只看到黑板上有三个数学题目。

这是教授布置的作业吧？丹齐格把题目都抄了下来，拿回家去作，做啊做啊，他做了几天，终于把这三个题目解出来了，交给教授去检查。

第二天，教授派人来喊他，他吓了一跳。教授严肃着脸问他："丹齐格，这三个题目，你是怎么做的？"丹齐格小心翼翼地答道："教授，您布置的前两个题目，还比较好做，后面那个难度太大啊。"教授脸色放晴了："丹齐格，你知道吗？那是一个世界级难题，爱因斯坦都没解出的，你解出来了。"

这把丹齐格惊得不行，他若知道这是顶尖的数学难题，他哪会去做啊？智力不会输给这难题，心劲早输了，题都不敢问津，哪解得出？

我想起我小时候一件事，我娘打发我去舅舅家，舅舅离我家十多里路，中间隔着一条河、两座山。河水汤汤，山木森森，我娘叫我傍晚去，没走上一二里路，天黑了。走到河山之间，已是黑咕隆咚，我一直走一直走，没心没肺地走，走到舅舅家，已是月沉人睡。我舅舅吓了一跳：“你真勇敢，那里经常闹鬼的呢，你是如何走过来的？”

若知道那山里有着那样毛骨悚然的传说，我哪里还敢走夜路呢？此后，即使大白天去舅舅家，若一个人，我便坚决不去。

因为我无知，所以我无畏；因为我已知，所以我胆怯。

我在一本书里，看到一位明史专家撂过一句狠话：“你若没有经过 10 年的明史科班研究，你就不要就明史放一句厥词。”

教授这话，肯定吓到了好多人。以前不曾读过明史，那谁敢弄明史题材？读了多年明史，更不敢下笔了。这话可能不对，但那话说得也不准确，缩脚缩手，张嘴嗫嚅，生怕贻笑大方，连口都不敢开了。然而笔名为当年明月的石悦，却并非研究明史的专家，不是文学专业毕业，也并非历史科班出身，他一口气写了六卷本的《明朝那些事儿》，据说销售量已过千万册了。敢问那些皓首穷经的明史学家、专家、大家，谁有这么牛？

最近几年崭露头角的张宏杰先生，也在弄明史，他最初与历史都不搭界的，大学就读的是东北财经大学，学的是投资经济管理，他写作《大明王朝的七张脸孔》那会儿，在东北葫芦岛那疙瘩做一名银行的客户经理，但他现在写历史，风头正健。

不懂的，或许会输与懂者的知识，但懂者或许会输与不懂者的见识，你的见识也许可以去破坏掉知识的光环；缺学问的或许会输与学问家的功力，但学问家也会输与浅学者的才力，你的才力也许会破了功力的迷局。

有很多年轻人总是很自卑，看到人家博学，他便认输了；看到人家老成，他便气馁了；看到人家名大，他便胆怯了；看到人家强大，他便缴械了。

其实大可不必。

你羡慕别人的家学渊博，别人可能更羡慕你的懵懂勇气；你羡慕别人的世故老成，别人可能更羡慕你的天真未凿；你羡慕别人的全副武装，别人更可能羡慕你的赤手空拳呢。

别怕自己无知识，怕的是自己没勇气；别怕自己没功绩，怕的是自己没精神气。

载于《做人与处世》

无知者无畏，无畏就没有思想包袱。一个什么都不想的人，内心充满了力量，没有失败的概念，往往可以轻松上路，所以就成功了。所以，不要害怕自己一无所有，怕的是自己没有勇气。